IMAGES
of America

CONOVER

On the Cover: Holler Service Station and Taxi Service, located at the intersection of five points, was built in the early 1930s by owner and operator Henry C. Holler. He was prominently identified with the business life of Conover. This business would also serve as the local tavern. Played inside was the game of pitching coins into a knothole in the corner flooring. When the business closed, over $30 in coins was found beneath the floor. This business was once leased to Lester Sigmon and Ray Lindsay. Henry Holler was a lifelong member of Bethel Lutheran Church. He died in October 1951. The building still stands in downtown Conover. (Photography by Elmer McRee.)

IMAGES
of America

CONOVER

Donald Barker

ARCADIA
PUBLISHING

ISBN 978-0-7385-8576-5

Published by Arcadia Publishing
Charleston, South Carolina

Printed in the United States of America

Library of Congress Control Number: 2009940225

For all general information, please contact Arcadia Publishing:
Telephone 843-853-2070
Fax 843-853-0044
E-mail sales@arcadiapublishing.com
For customer service and orders:
Toll-Free 1-888-313-2665

Visit us on the Internet at www.arcadiapublishing.com

This book is dedicated to my parents, Bill and Lula Barker, who lovingly brought me out of darkness and put me on track for my life's journey.

"A wise man travels light on the road trip of life. Wisdom is his map, wonder is his fuel. A good story is his favorite souvenir."

Contents

ACKNOWLEDGMENTS

My sincere thanks go to the following people for submitting additional prints and material to the Donald Barker collection: Jim Isenhower, Stine Isenhower, Robert Holland, Nancy Moser, Olin Winters family, Joe Power, Larry Boston, Jack Gantt, Nancy Killian, Harvey Brady family, the 381st Bomb Group USAAF, the 490th Bomb Group USAAF, John Thomas Deveney, Adrian Hefner, Otto Lambert, Johnny Brown and the Brown Oil Company, H and W Drug Company, Mary Catherine Long (Eula Yount collection), Sally (Drum) Black, Jack Bolick family, Colonial Theaters, Bowman Drug Company, Southern Furniture Company, Conover Chair Company, City of Conover (Broyhill collection), City of Conover Police Department, Margaret Sparkman, Mabel Lawing, Joyce Curlee, Joan Rowe, Sgt. David Sigmon NPD, Sgt. Harry Williams (North Carolina State Patrol, retired), Martin Pannell, and to the many others who searched out their albums and shoeboxes to make public these historic and memorable photographs. Without them, this book would never have been completed. All images appear courtesy of this collection.

Appreciation is given to Alex Floyd, of the Rhodes Room at the Catawba County Main Library in Newton, for direction and use of the vertical and microfilm files, and Debbie Hovis, of the Conover Branch Library, for her assistance on this project. Very special thanks to Lindsay Carter, my advisor at Arcadia Publishing, for her professionalism, patience, advice, and encouragement during this project.

INTRODUCTION

In January 1877, the general assembly enacted corporate limits for the town of Conover:

> And so stated, under such name, Conover, a body Corporate, is hereby invested with all privileges and franchises, property and all rights pertaining to the Town of Conover. The Board of Commissioners of the Town of Conover, may expedite, acquire and hold property for the use of the town as necessary and that the corporate limits of the town of Conover shall be in part as follows. Beginning north eighty five degrees, east two hundred and twenty six and one forth poles from the depot of the Western North Carolina Railroad, at a stake, of J. [sic] Hunsucker's land and runs north fifty degrees.

The town of Conover had its early beginning as a railroad town with a boardinghouse specifically for railroad workers. Conover is located along the mainline of the Norfolk-Southern Railroad. The city is located at the headwaters of McLin Creek, which is a tributary of Lyle Creek on its journey to the Catawba River.

The town of Conover, North Carolina, began as German and Scotch-Irish settlers, mainly farmers and merchants, put down roots in the area because of its abundance of water and available land. There were only a few homes and farms in the surrounding area in the late 1860s when the Western North Carolina Railroad began laying its tracks from the Catawba River 10 miles east of town on its route to the larger town of Hickory. The Carolina Northwestern Railroad would use narrow gauge rails from Chester, South Carolina, to Lenoir. The Richmond & Danville Railroad also served the area. Later, the Southern Railway System established the new standard gauge for rail travel. This route later became the Norfolk-Southern Railway System. The railroad was the perfect ingredient for commerce and growth. With the railroad, Conover began to emerge into the city it is today.

With the rail trackage, Conover would make productive progress. When the railroads were built, the general pattern of sparse settlement concentrated within the rolling foothills of northern Catawba County was drastically changed. Wherever the tracks were laid, soon afterwards, the density of rural settlement and number of towns increased. The powerful influence of the railroads would be a sign that some settlements would die when the railroads missed them. This would be a negative forerunner of future growth and development.

During the years of 1851–1880, the railroads further intensified their influence across the state. The rail system also played an important role during the Civil War. War materials of all types were shipped to various front lines and to battlefields deep in the South and to points in the North. During the war, North Carolina would boast that it had the longest continual railroad in the United States, one that the North would continually destroy in the vicinity of present-day Goldsboro. In North Carolina, the military would transport prisoners to prisons at Thomasville and Salisbury. These prisons were the objective of the famous Stoneman's raid that began in the western part of the state. These raids would continue into the Catawba Valley to include Newton and Conover.

The origin of Conover's name is uncertain. Some say it was a name given by the railway officials. Others say it was named by Belle Seitz and Mattie Miller, two ladies of the town who had a fondness for the works of Antonio Canova, an Italian sculptor. They were pleased by the beauty and simplicity of his artwork. Others say that a Mrs. Wheisigner, of Morganton, named it "after the name of a family residing somewhere in the North." Or was it from a minister from the North, named in an early census of Conover? The word *Conover* is traced back to early Dutch settlers in New York, specifically to a Jacob van Kouwenhoven.

In the book *Hope is Remembering with Praise*, a history of Concordia Evangelical Lutheran Church in Conover, this context is given:

> Conover was born as a trade center with the opening in 1871 of an eating-place and boarding house for railroad men, by Francis and Ellen Miller Smyre. The Smyre's had purchased a small tract of land from a Confederate veteran John Pinkney Spencer and his wife, Diana Herman. The Hotel-Tavern residence was located in downtown Conover, across from city hall. This was Conover's first business. In the basement of the small hotel was a shoe shop.

Near the uptown was the wye junction. (A point from which the train can change direction.) Later, the railroad ran a branch line three miles south and backed the train into Newton. It was noted in a local newspaper that more corn, flour, and cotton bales were shipped from the Conover wye than from any other station in the county.

The city of Conover was chartered in 1876 and incorporated in 1877. It covers about nine and a half square miles in area. At the time of the city's founding, the need for education became apparent. Concordia High School was founded in early 1881 by a group of ministers and townsfolk at St. John's Lutheran Church. The school opened in Conover, and in 1887, it became Concordia College, a Lutheran institution that produced ministers in that faith. It continued until 1935 when the administration building was destroyed by fire.

Conover had two known depots. Early on, town officials could not decide where to lay the rails. One such trackage started near the rear of the Central Service Station (now the Texaco along First Street West), running in front of what is now Conover City Hall, to a point just past the Conover Medical Clinic. This was the location of Conover's first railroad station around 1875. The station stop was named Canova. The entire Conover rail configuration was later changed because officials in the city of Newton objected to the trains having to back into the new county seat. They felt slighted because they were the county seat and wanted the tracks east of Conover to be relocated so that the tracks would come through Newton. It was then that all of Conover's tracks were again moved across town and a new depot built. This is shown on an 1886 map drawn by R.A. Yoder.

The railroads brought food, farm tractors, tools, mercantile goods, mail, and lumber for the growing furniture and wood products industry. And yes, Railway Express even brought in fireworks to celebrate the Fourth of July. With the invention of refrigerated railcars came fresh fruits and vegetables to local stores and markets. The railroads served to send cotton, milled grain, and local manufactured products to cities across the country. The rail service also brought in new settlers, students, doctors, businessmen, and workers for farms and industry.

Along the tracks came new businesses, such as the Piedmont Wagon Company in Hickory, the Hickory Flour Mill, Hickory Packing Company, Martin Furniture Company, Elliott Mills, Shuford Cordage, and Spinning Mill. In Conover came the Conover Chair Company, Conover Furniture Company, Warlong Glove Company, J.A. Yount Cotton Mill, and the Jerome Bolick and Sons Buggy Shops. It was the upholstery of the buggy seats that would later begin the Southern Furniture Company. For a time, the Bolick Bus Works business would produce school buses for the state of North Carolina. Today, the Southern Furniture Company main plant remains along the tracks in the southeastern part of town.

One

In the Beginning

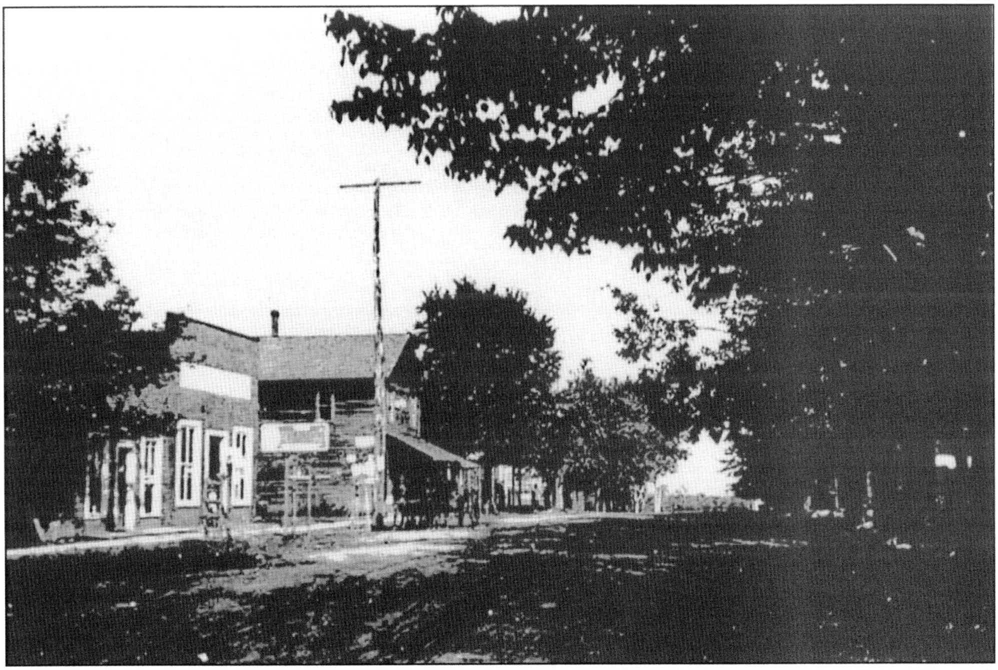

In the beginning, the stores in Conover were just wooden shacks. This is Main Street (First Avenue) looking north. Conover was just being founded in the early 1800s. The city of Conover was chartered in 1876 and incorporated in 1877. The name *Conover* is traced back to Dutch traders who settled a colony in New York around 1641. Jacob van Kouwenhoven was one of the settlers.

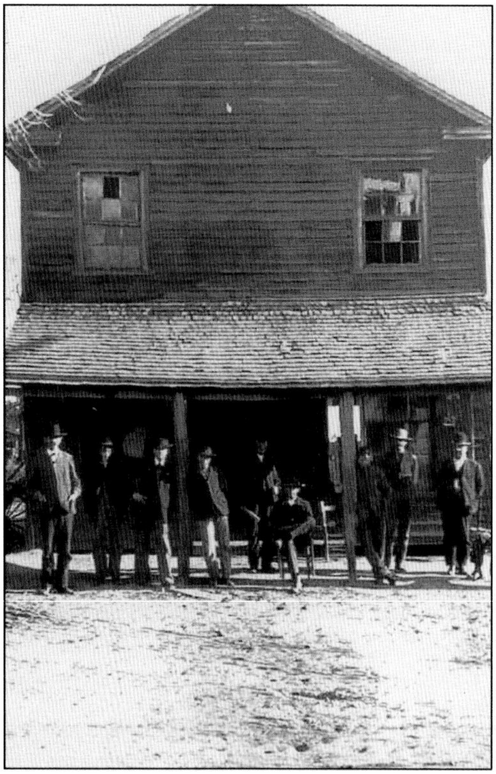

This photograph shows a gathering around 1911 of the early founders of Conover. At the time of the photograph, it was the Ed Herman Sr. building. Shown from left to right are Sam Jordan, Sylvanas Schell, Philo Isenhower, J. Able Isenhower, Pete Smith, George Brady, Clyde Hayden Herman, J. Pinkney Spencer, and Squire Jonas Hunsucker. Conover had its early beginning in the 1850s at a railroad junction, having a boardinghouse specifically for railroad workers. The town is located on the main east-west line of the Norfolk-Southern Railroad, constructed on a ridgeline at the headwaters of McLin Creek five miles east of the Catawba River.

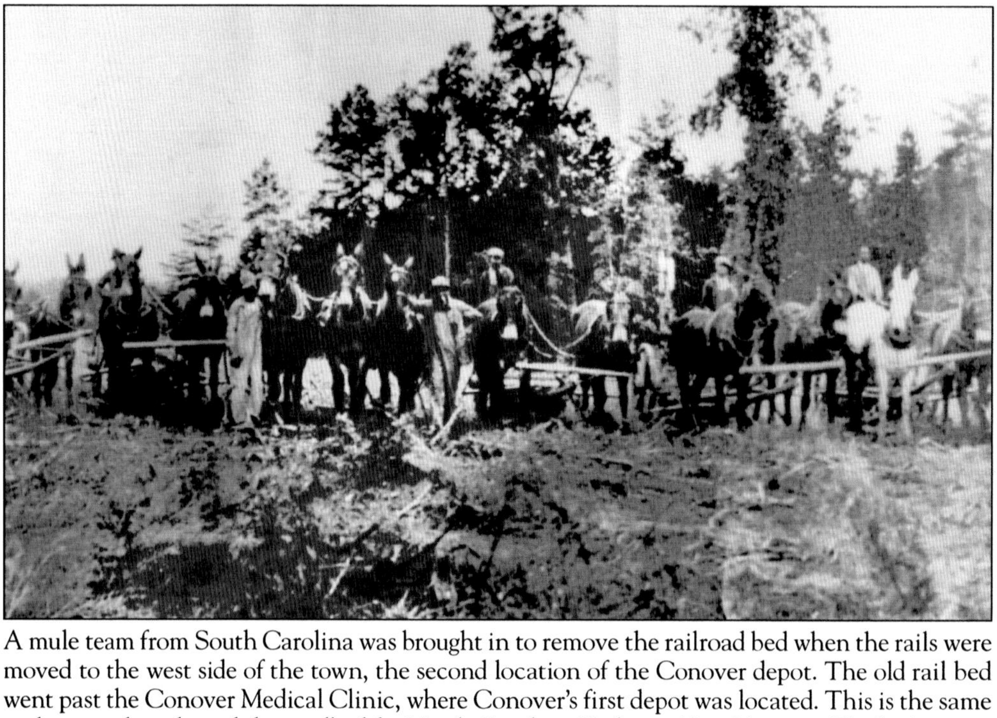

A mule team from South Carolina was brought in to remove the railroad bed when the rails were moved to the west side of the town, the second location of the Conover depot. The old rail bed went past the Conover Medical Clinic, where Conover's first depot was located. This is the same mule team that cleared the roadbed for North Carolina Highway 10 in Newton. The highway in front of the medical clinic was NC10A and NC70.

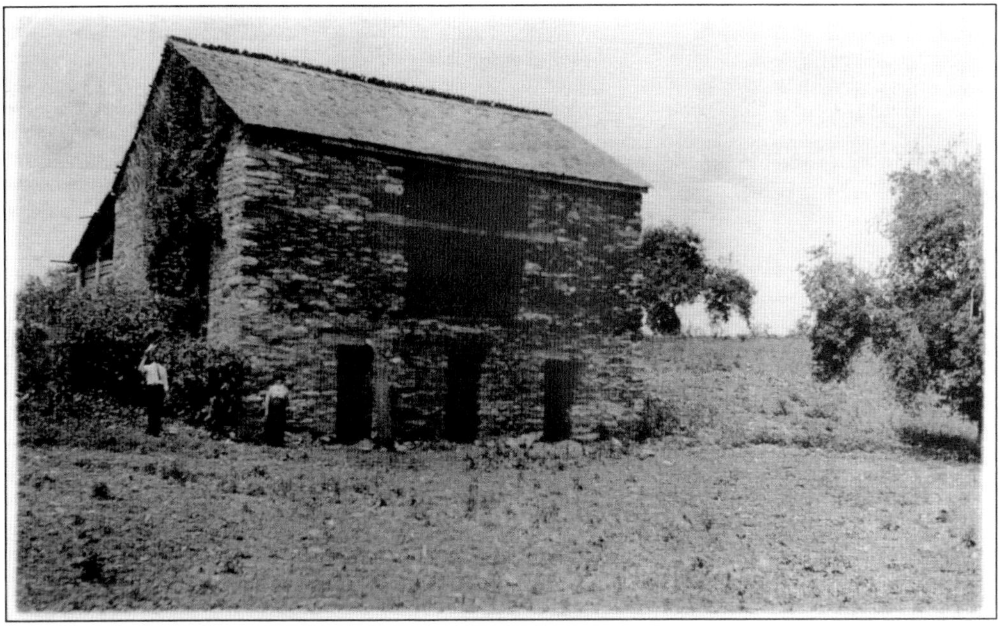

Frederick Hoke built the Rock Barn in Conover in 1822. It was built at a cost of only $75 using rock from nearby creeks and fields. In 1902, Dr. McDuffy Yount would give his daughter Eula a new camera for her 18th birthday. This print is from her original negatives. A good number of her photographs are displayed in Conover City Hall.

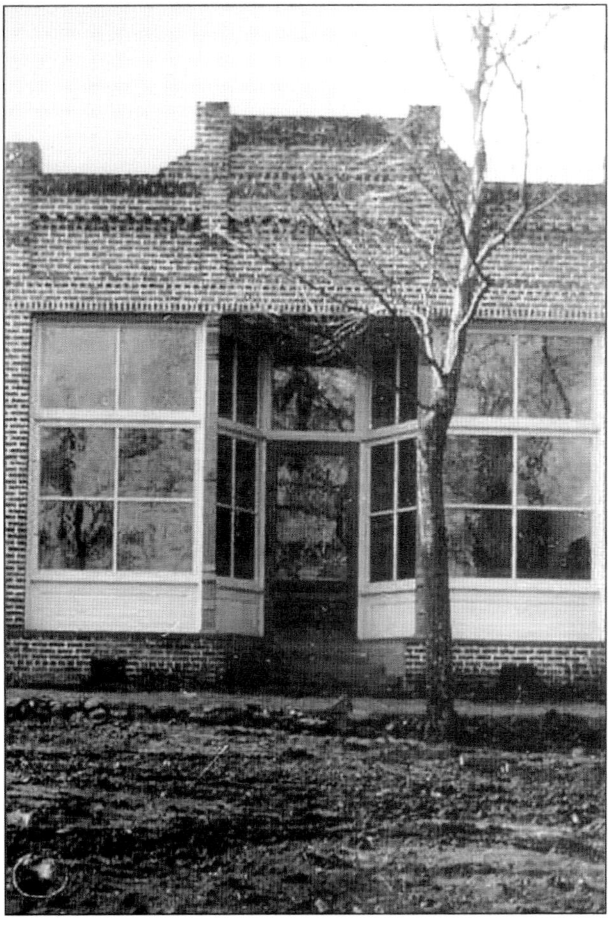

The Citizens Bank was Conover's first bank and stood on Main Street. The first president of the bank was J.A. Isenhower from 1911 until 1941. Jonas (Squire) Hunsucker was the vice president. The first depositor was Adrian Shuford Sr. These were the days of buggies and horses, with no automobiles yet.

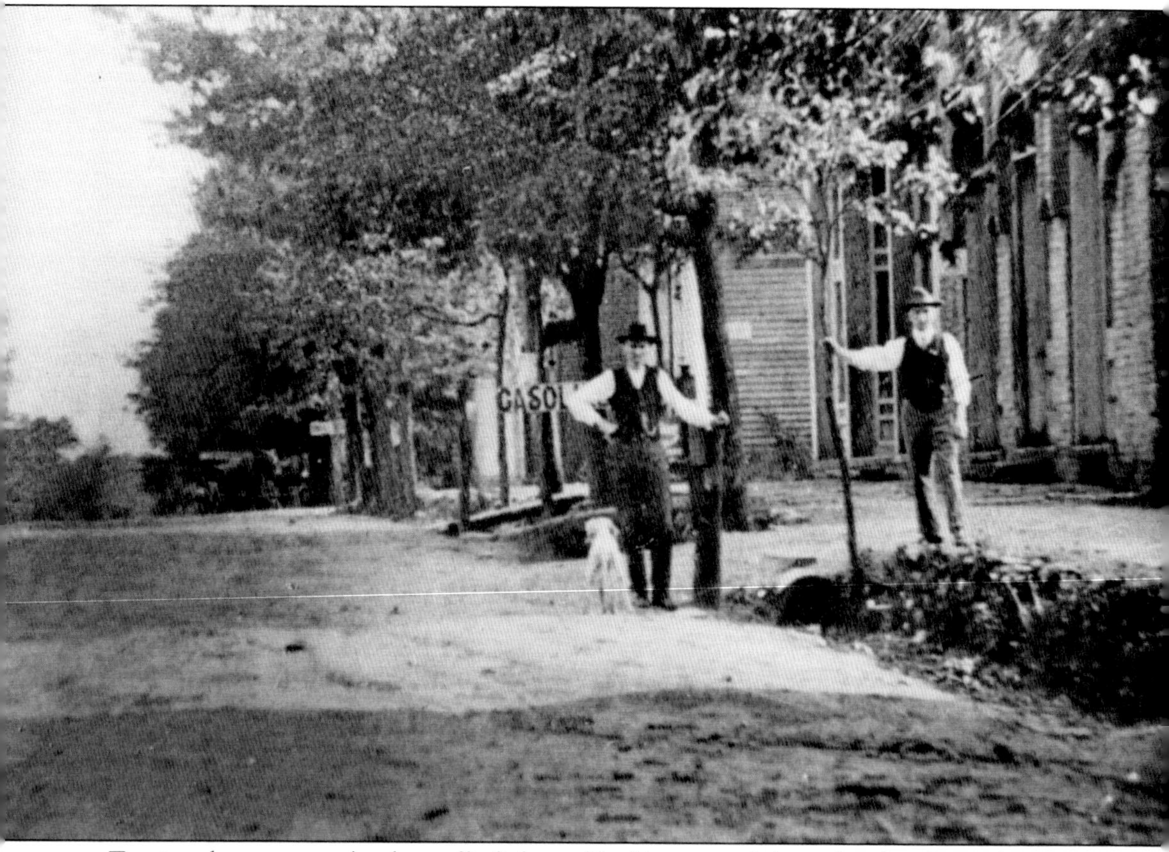

Turning the corner under the traffic light and looking toward the railroad is this wide view of the early Main Street in Conover. The two men are Sam Jordan (left) with Bob, his bird dog, and Robert Herman. In back of them is the Philo Isenhower store. The garage on the left belonged to Clayton Isenhower and Albert Deal. The area of the water well and tubs beyond was the noon-time gathering place for wagons, steeds, and their drivers. Such water tubs were on every corner of Main Street.

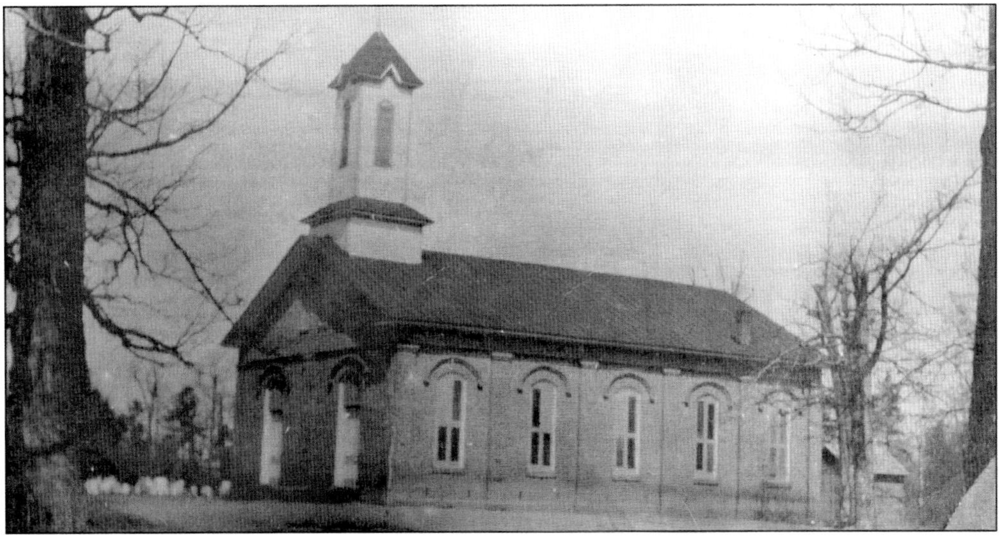

Just outside Conover is the historic, rural St. John's Lutheran Church that was founded in 1798. The first church was made of logs. In 1883, it was replaced with a brick structure. It was at a meeting in this church in 1877 that Concordia College was formed. Concordia Lutheran Church was formed here, as was Trinity Reformed Church. St. John's Lutheran Church has survived three devastating fires. The congregation always rebuilt, and today, they worship in a beautiful, well-designed structure.

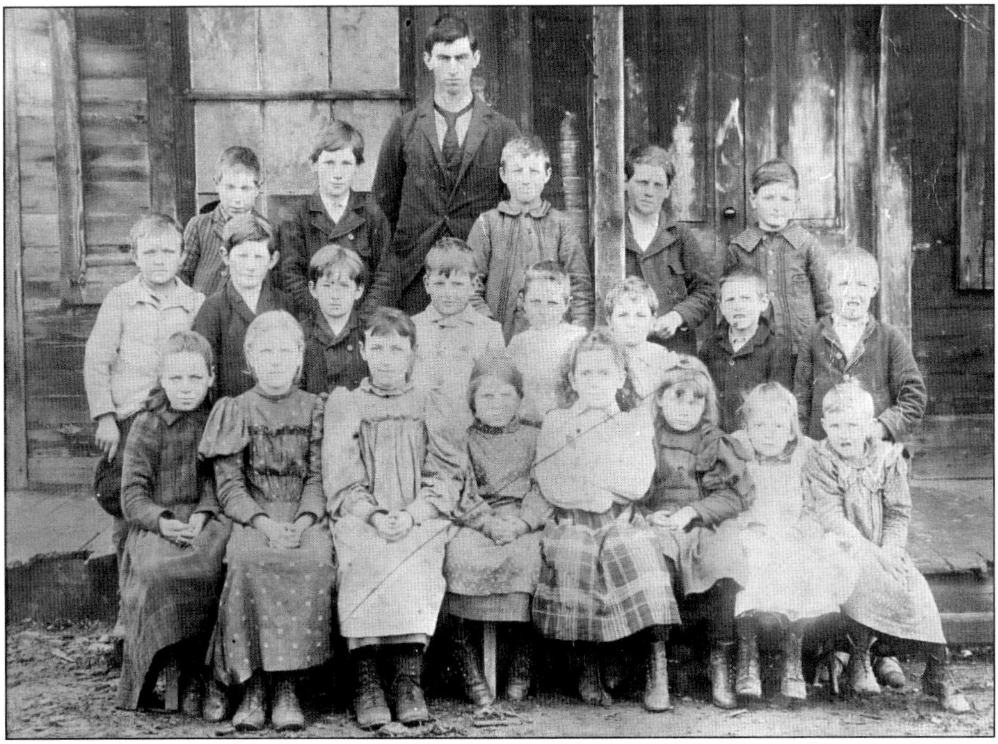

This rare 1898 photograph shows a class at the first public schoolhouse in Conover. It is believed to have been located across the street from the Concordia Day School soccer field. The students' names are not on record. The print was given to the Barker Collection by the Mrs. J.A. (Susie) Isenhower family of Conover.

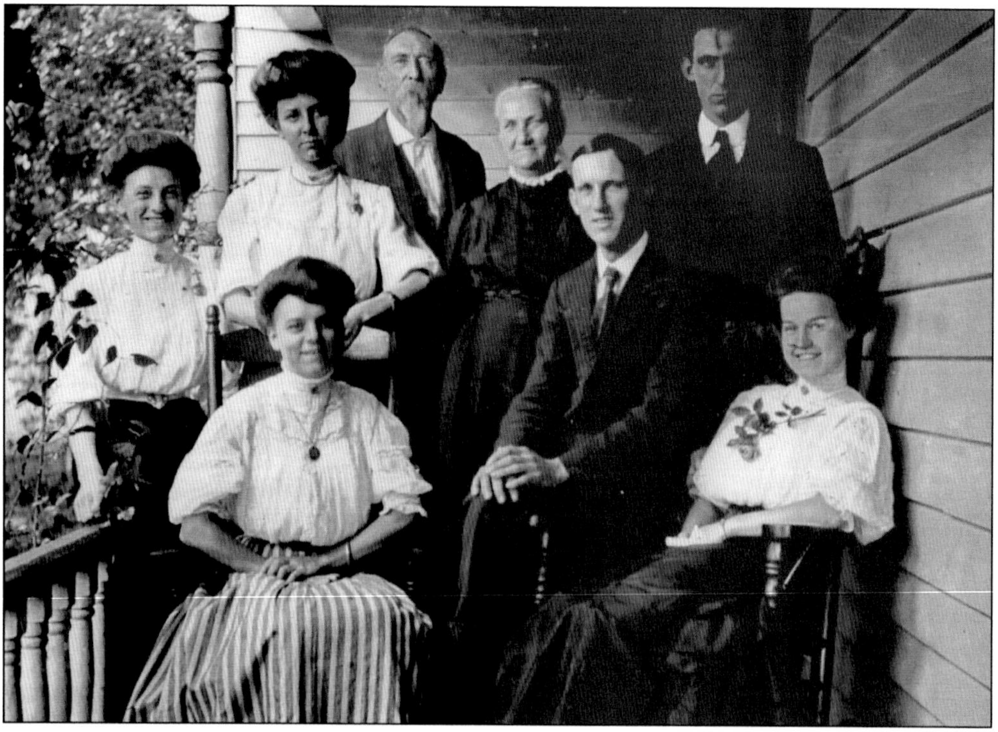

In the late 1800s, Dr. Daniel McDuffy Yount was Conover's first resident doctor. Pictured on their porch are, from left to right, (first row, seated) Miriam Estelle Yount, Gerhardt Long, and Lois Long; (second row) Cora Yount (on rail), Eula Virginia Yount, Dr. Yount, Eugenia Desdamona Yount, and John Yount. In the 1880s, other doctors in Conover were Dr. Albert Fox, Dr. Greenwade, Dr. Mashburn, and Dr. Marion Moser, who married Anna Yount, daughter of Dr. Yount.

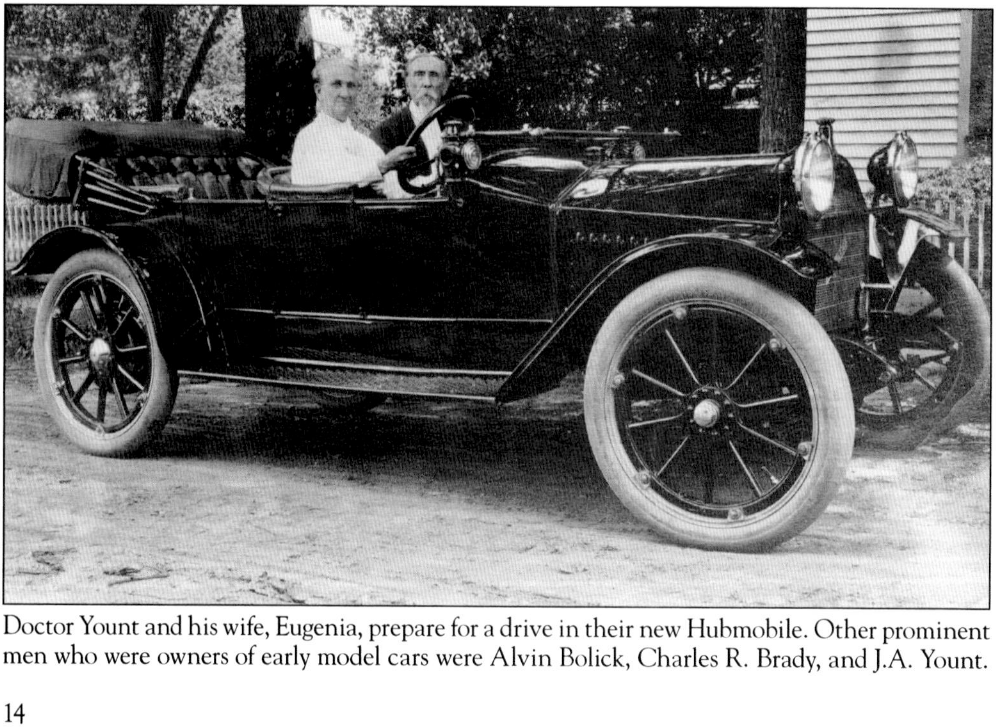

Doctor Yount and his wife, Eugenia, prepare for a drive in their new Hubmobile. Other prominent men who were owners of early model cars were Alvin Bolick, Charles R. Brady, and J.A. Yount.

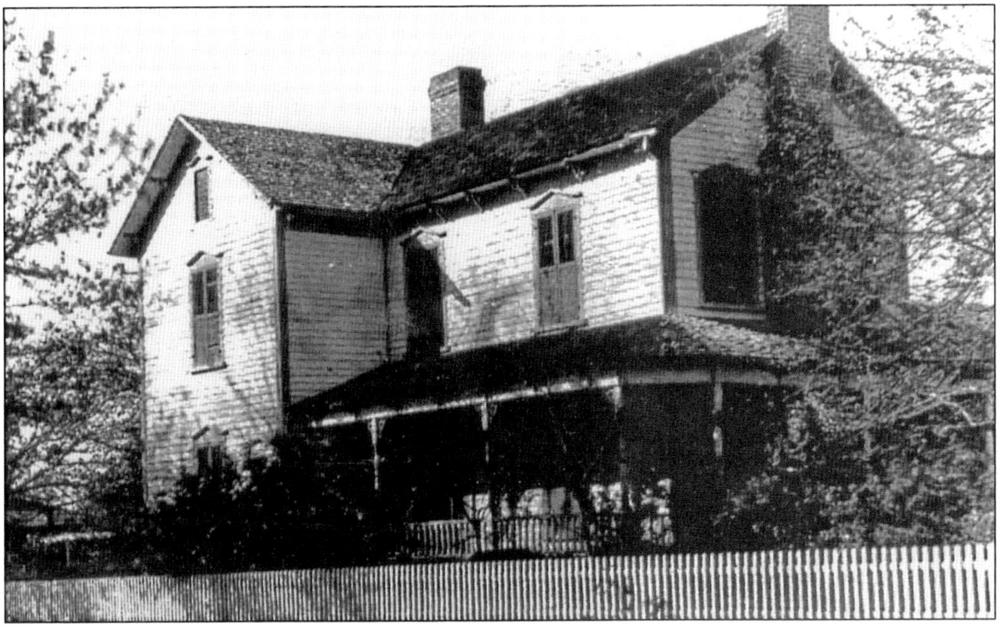

This early photograph shows the home place of Dr. Yount. He enlisted in 1861 in the Confederate army as a lieutenant serving with the Catawba Wild Cats division. After the deaths of the Younts, the contents were sold, and the home would be burned by the city of Conover. The Wachovia Bank drive-up window would replace it.

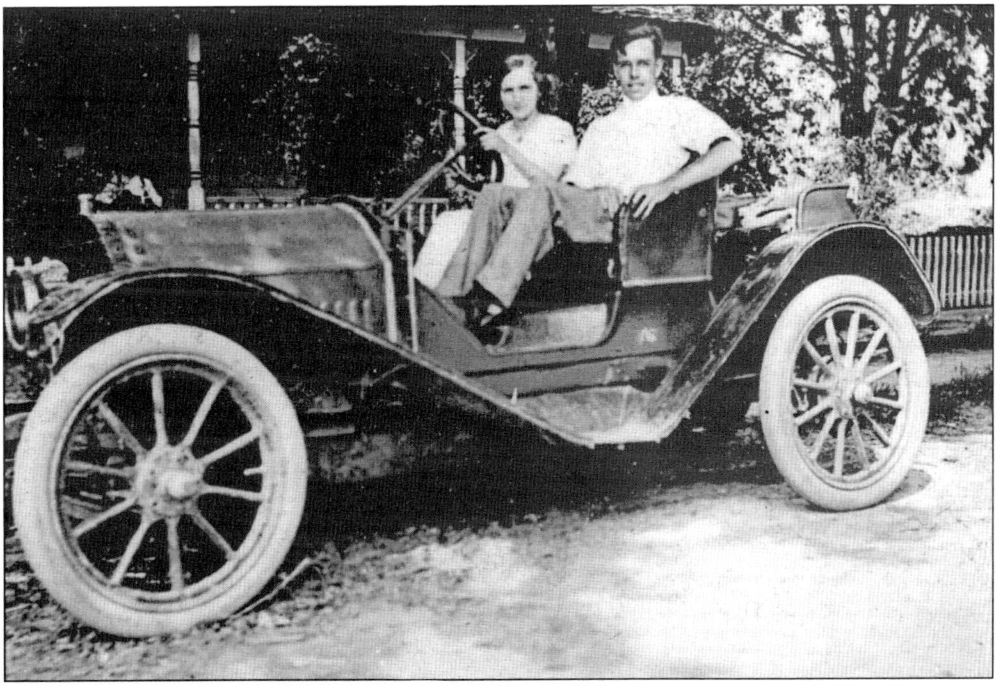

Eula Yount and Hubert Coyner are ready for a drive in Dr. Yount's new Buick. Eula Yount was an accomplished photographer and is recognized for her pictures of the early families of Conover and of the original Rock Barn just outside the city limits of Conover. This print is on display at the new city hall in Conover.

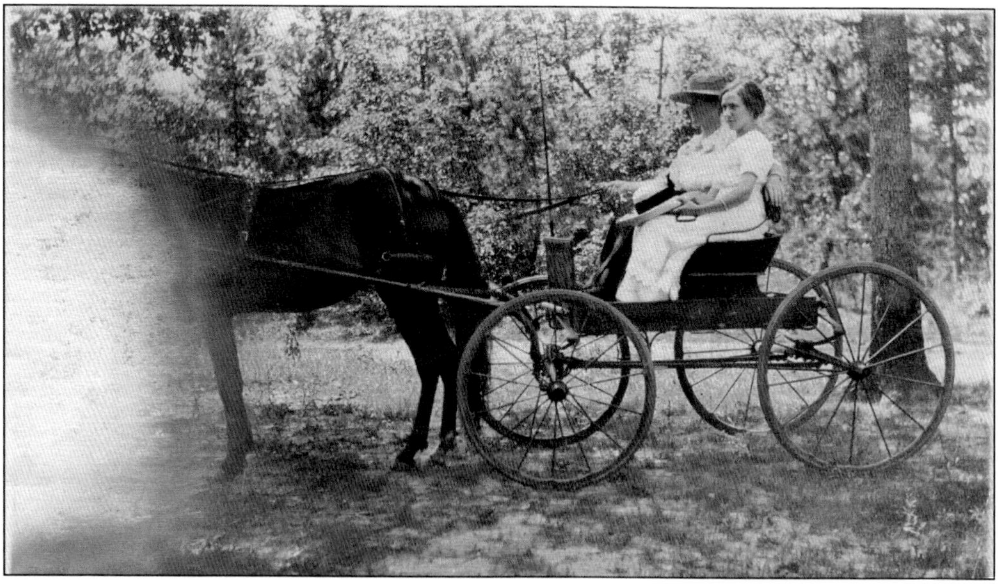

Lois and Miriam Yount prepare for a buggy ride in Conover. According to the sales catalog, this is a Marshall Pony buggy built by the Jerome Bolick Buggy Company of Conover. Jerome W. Bolick Sr. invented the new steel spoke for buggy wheels.

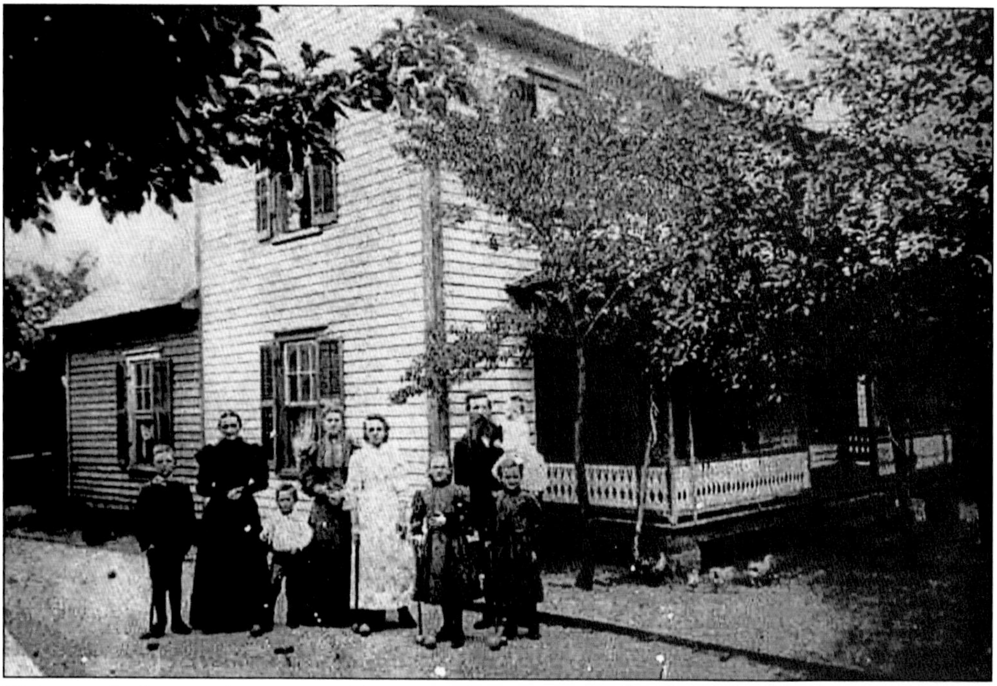

This was the home of prominent Conover businessman Philo Elmore Isenhower. Pictured from left to right are Isenhower family members John Abel, Margaret (mother), Clinton, Anna, Sarah, Mattie, Vertie, and Philo (father) holding Berman. The location of the home place is Second Avenue Southeast in Conover.

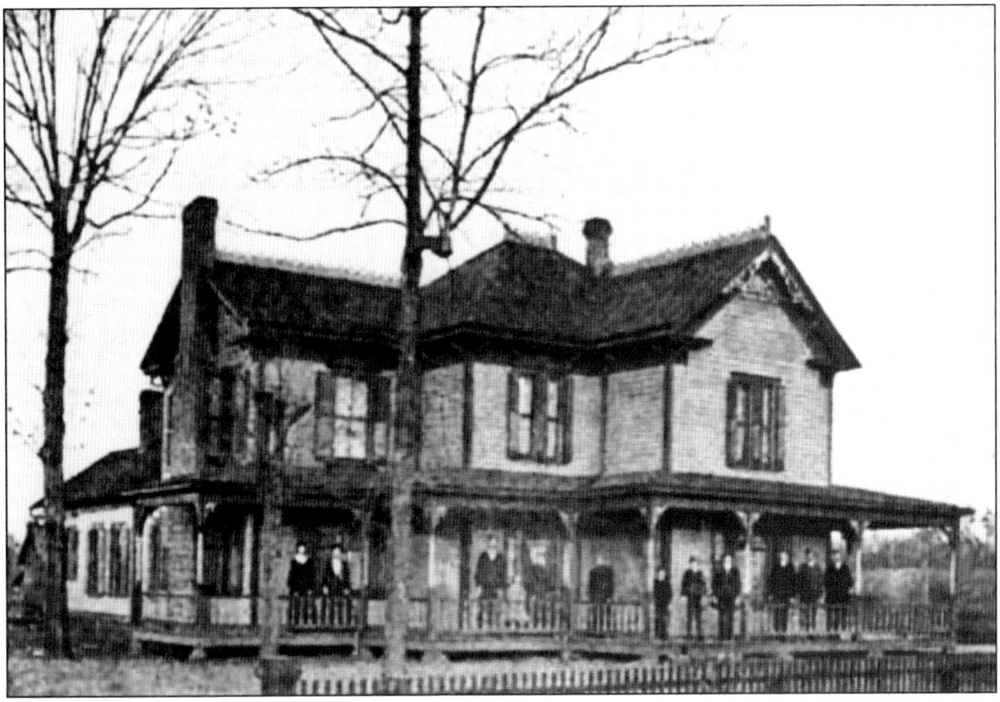

This is the Squire (Jonas) Hunsucker home. This home still stands in Conover. Hunsucker held a position at the Hickory Handle Manufacturing Co. Another man, also named Jonas Hunsucker, would operate a Sinclair Service Station at five points in uptown Conover. This building would later house Pappy's Restaurant. John Cline is now renovating the restaurant for multiuse.

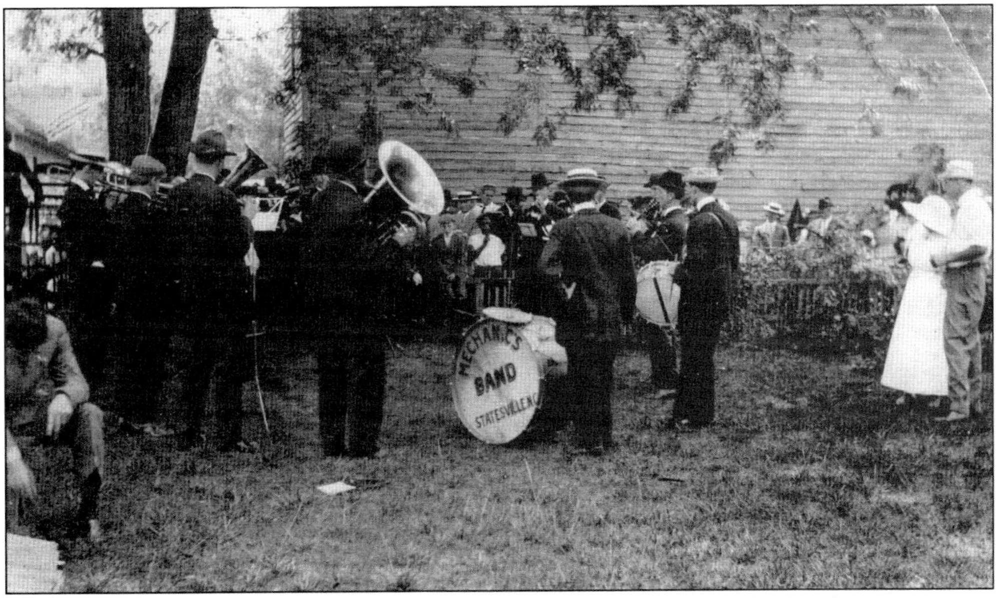

On a Fourth of July in the early 1900s, the Mechanics Band of Statesville played patriotic music on the lawn of the McDuffy Yount home. The event was attended by many townspeople, and food and beverages were served throughout the day.

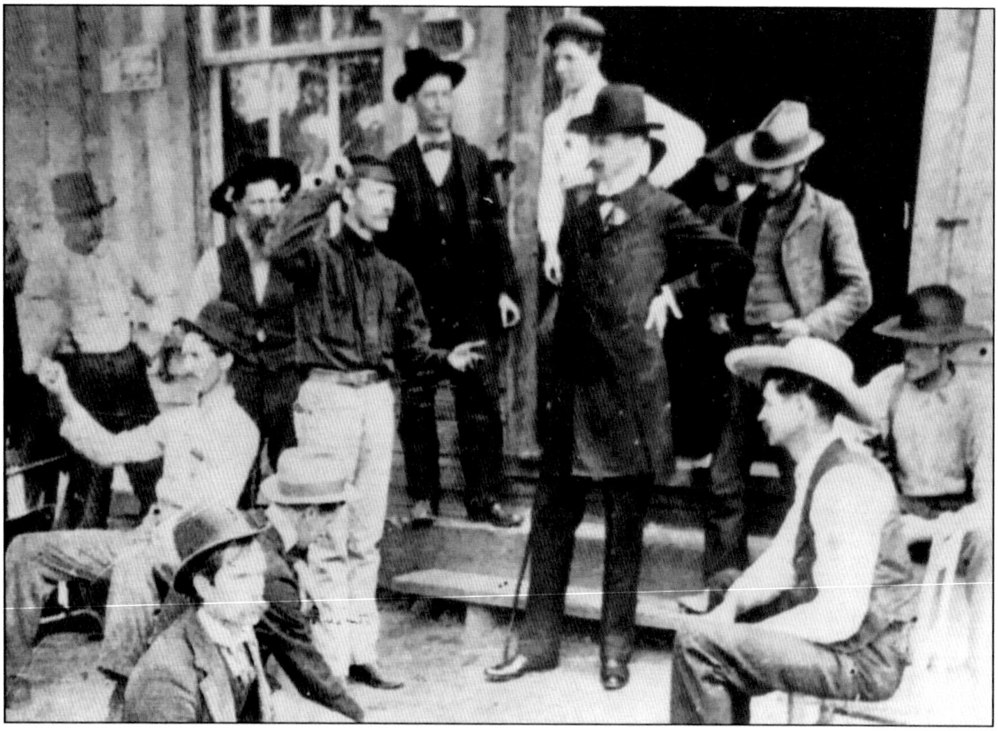

This early 1900s photograph shows a meeting of Conover businessmen at the Hunsucker store. Shown are James Rice, Eugene Smith, John D. Yount, unidentified, John Eckard, Bob Brady, John A. Isenhower, Sam Jordan, unidentified, Ed Herman, unidentified, and John L. Isenhower.

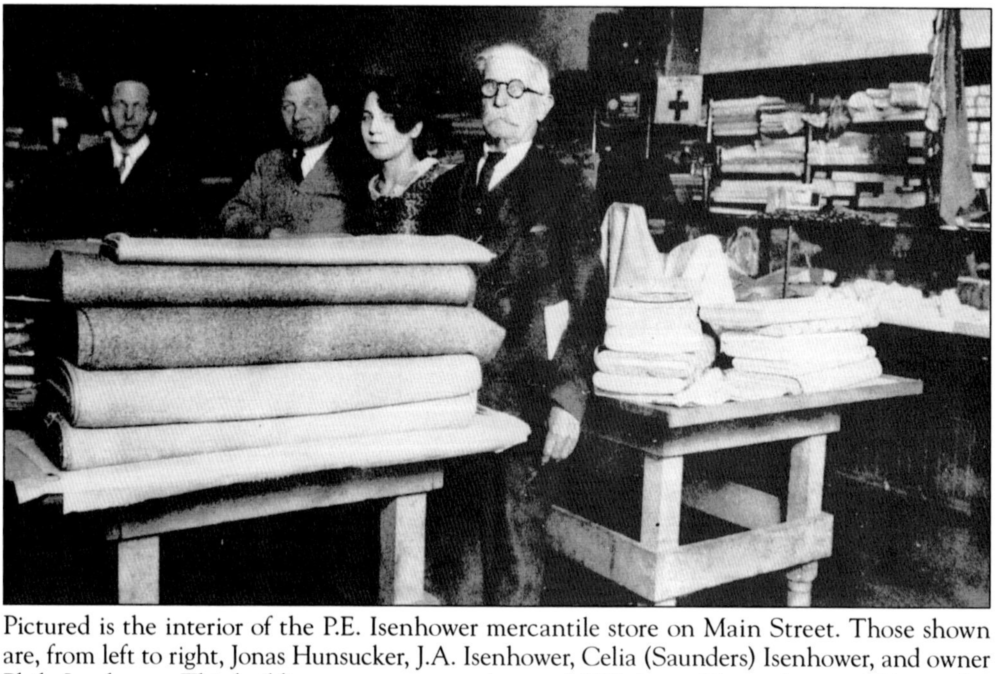

Pictured is the interior of the P.E. Isenhower mercantile store on Main Street. Those shown are, from left to right, Jonas Hunsucker, J.A. Isenhower, Celia (Saunders) Isenhower, and owner Philo Isenhower. This building was constructed around 1917. Jonas Hunsucker would leave this employment and open a Sinclair Service Station at five points in Conover.

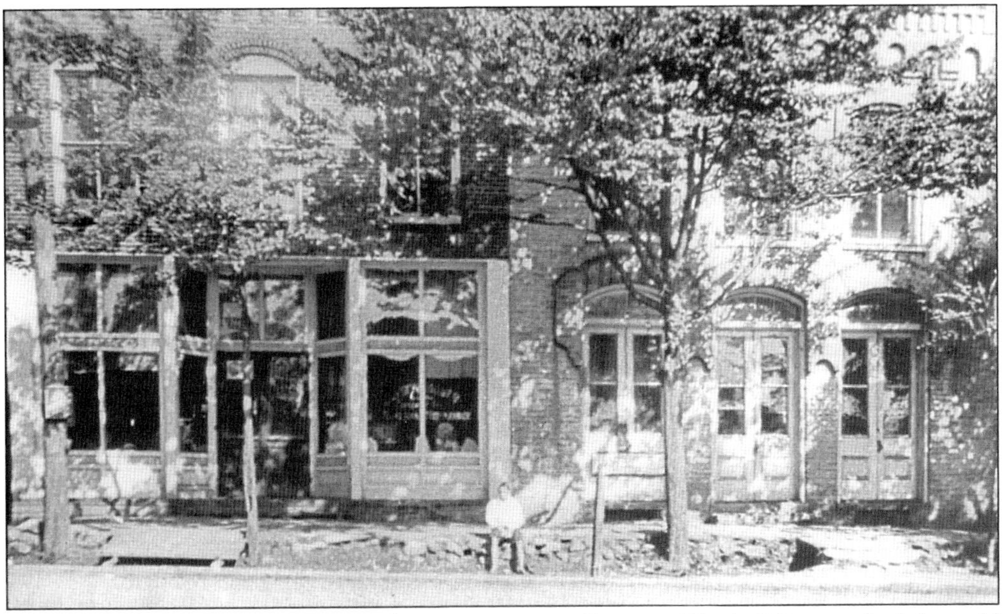

The Philo Isenhower stores were two business stores in Conover. The building on the left would adjoin the other by a common doorway along the wall. Isenhower owned both buildings. He was first married to Margaret Stine. To the union, seven children were born. She passed away in 1929. In 1931, Isenhower married Sophronia Stine Hefner.

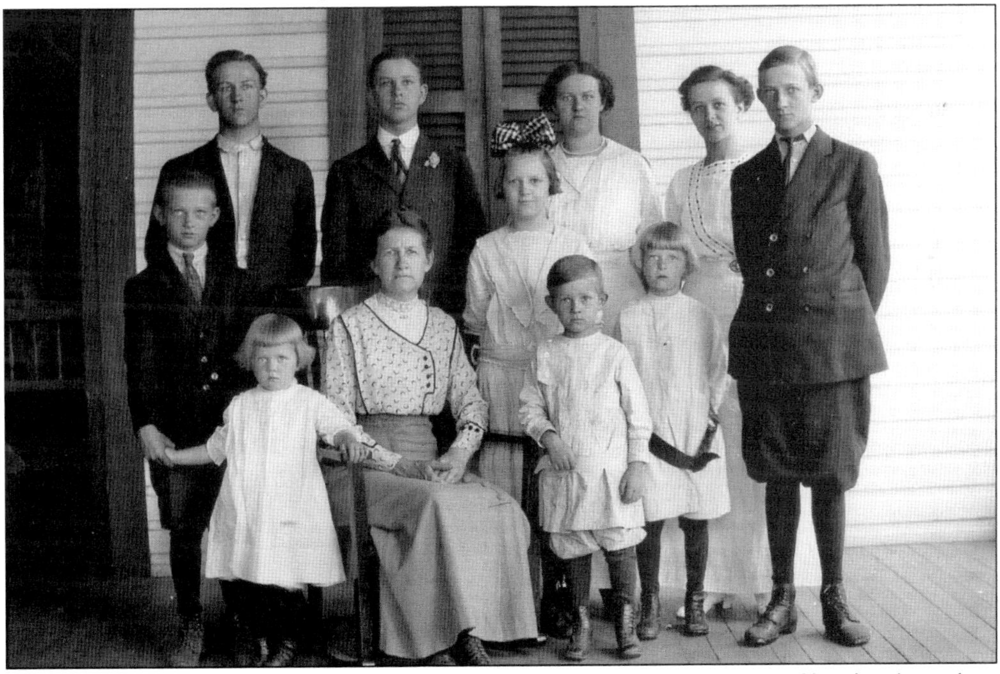

G.E. Moehlmann, a noted Conover photographer, took this early picture of his family at their new home on Third Street Southeast. Pictured from left to right are (first row) Ruth, Minnie (mother), Frederick, Henrietta, and Ernust; (second row) Gerhardt (Jim) and Margaret (with bow in her hair); (third row) Walter, Gustov (Gush), Gertrude, and Clara. This family photograph is on permanent display in Conover city hall.

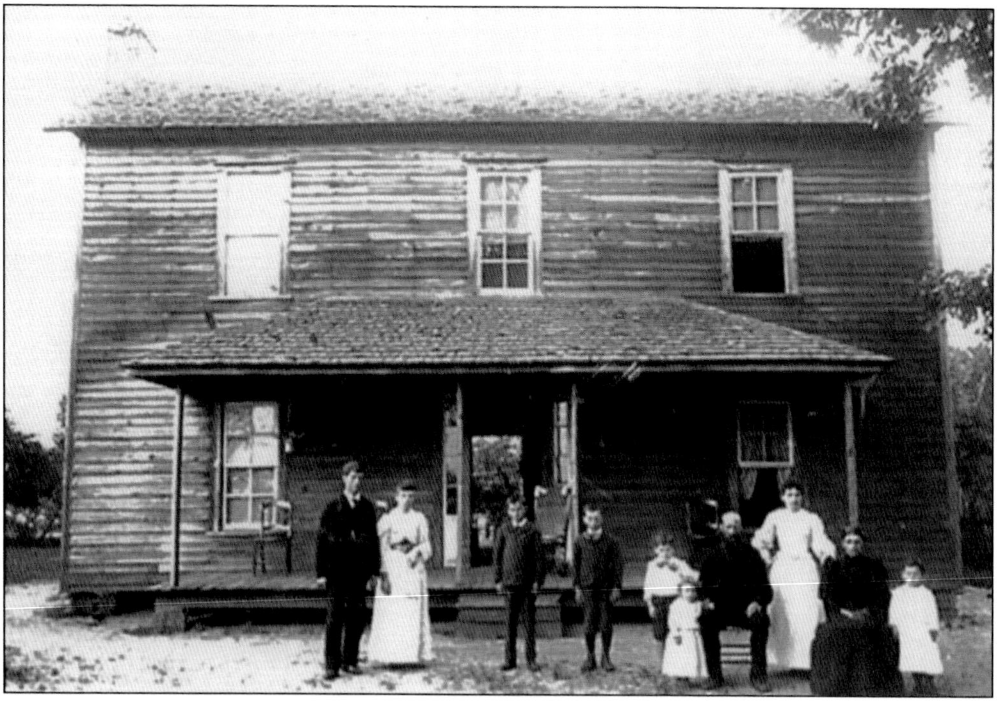

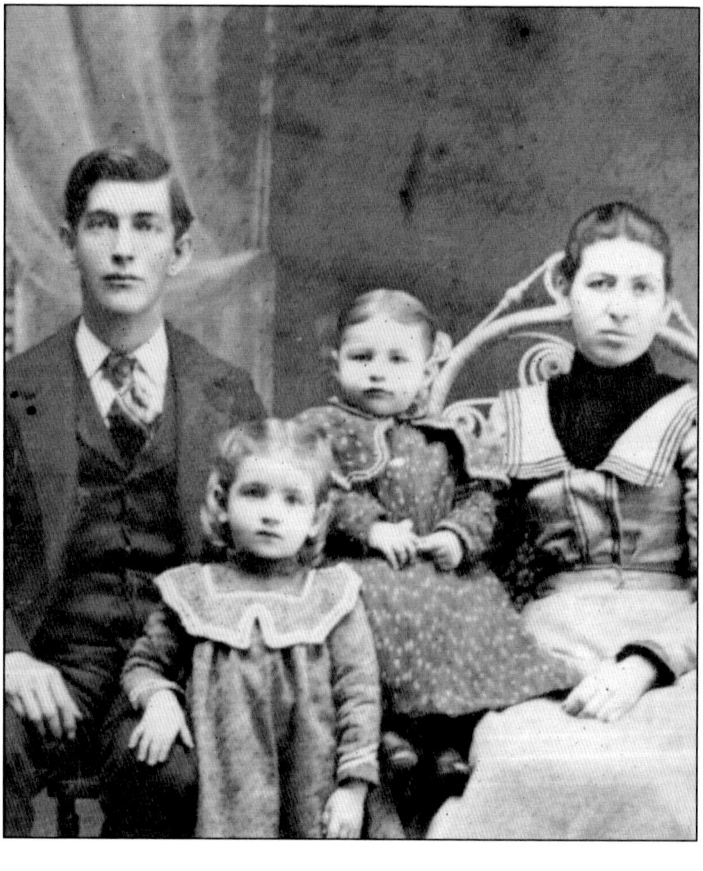

This photograph is of the Adoephus D. Herman family. Pictured from left to right are C.R. Brady and wife Eudora (Herman) Brady, Wilburn, Carroll, Robert, Preston, Adoephus Herman, daughter Alice, Ellie Miller Herman (wife), and son Perry. The home place was located beyond Southern Furniture Company, between the two large oak trees.

This is an early C.R. Brady family photograph. Shown from left to right are Charles R. Brady, daughters Edna and Olive, and wife Dora (Herman) Brady. Children to be born later would include another girl—Lula—and four sons: Clifford, Walter, Harvey, and Charles.

Charles R. Brady served as mayor of Conover and was a Catawba County surveyor at the age of 21. He designed the layout for the water and sewer system for the newly founded town of Conover. He was the second male child born in the town. He also served as chairman of the county commissioners and was a strong leader in the state Republican party. He was president of Hickory Handle Manufacturing Company and Conover Furniture Company.

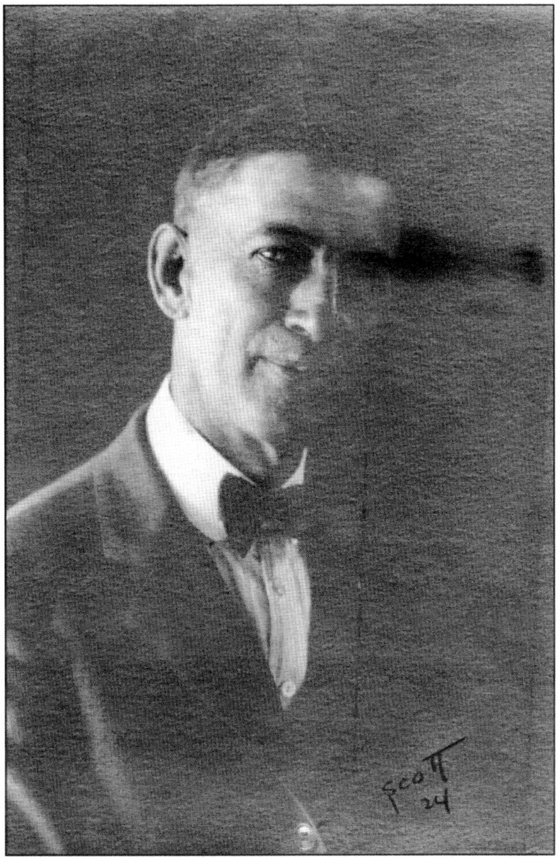

The Hickory Handle Manufacturing Company began in 1891 with the making of school desks and hickory handles. Principal officers were C.R. Brady, P.E. Yount, Jonas Hunsucker, A.F. Lail, and Ed Haupt. In 1928, Preston Yount and Robert Herman bought the handle business and moved it across the railroad tracks to what is today Conover Chair Company. The lady in the foreground is Lula Brady (Barker) going to work at her father's business. The new business later became Conover Furniture Company.

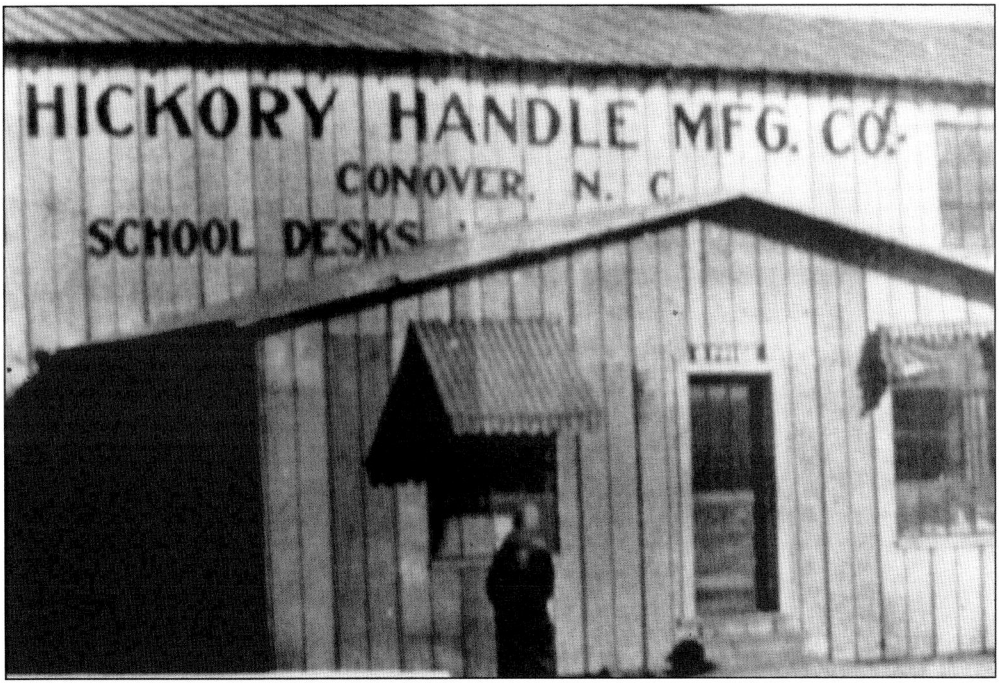

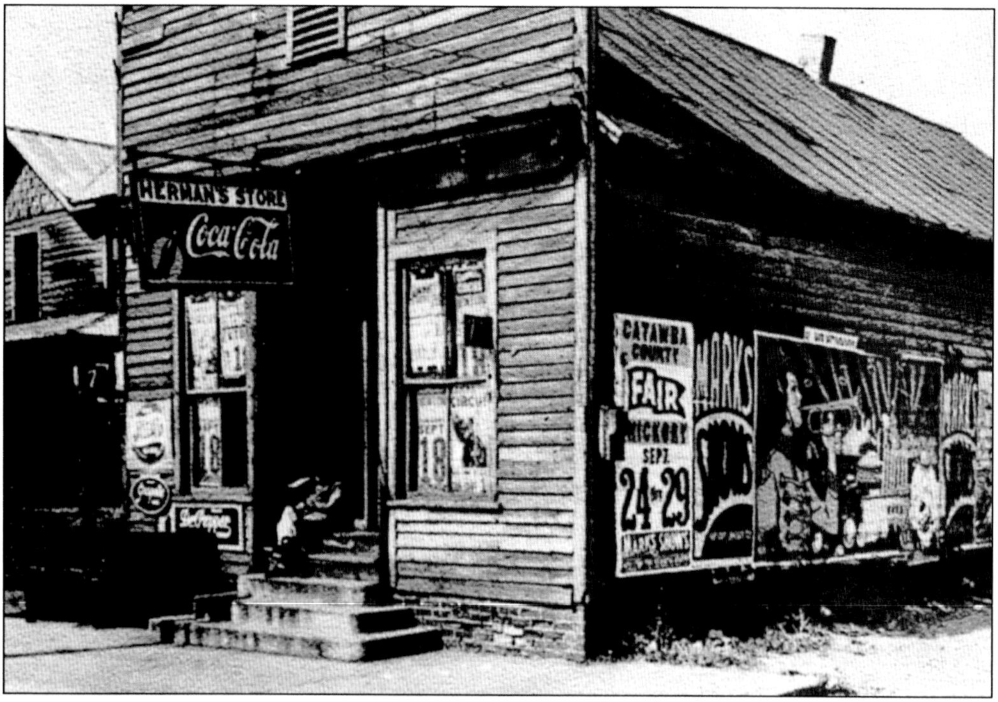

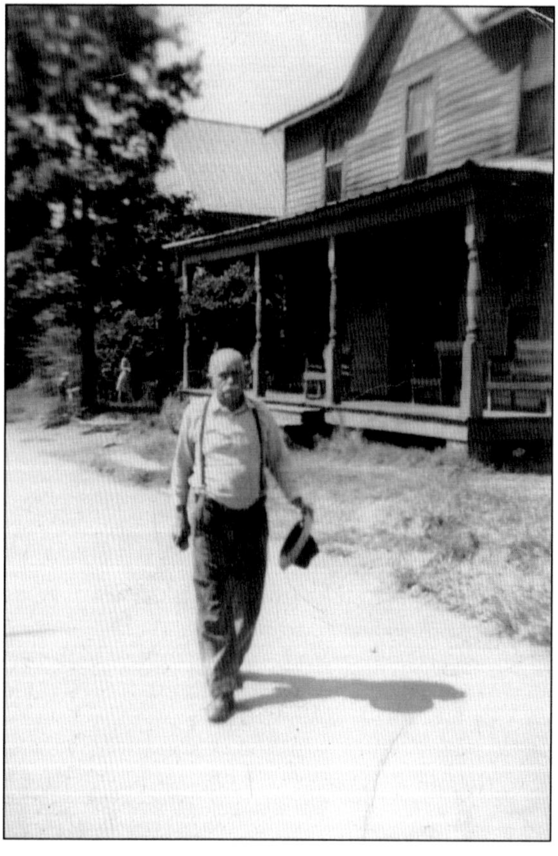

The Ed Herman Store stood on Main Street in Conover. This longstanding landmark was where the BB&T Bank is now. The boys at Concordia College would go here for sandwiches. Once, the boys ordered some cheese sandwiches. On the counter was a hoop of cheese, upon which sat a small mouse. When seeing this, Herman smacked at the mouse and said, "Git off there, don't you see I have customers!" The little mouse landed in the pickle barrel but lived for another day of cheese hunting.

Shown is Ed Herman, owner of the Ed Herman Store. Herman lived in the large, red brick Herman home next to the railroad. Rain or shine, he would pack a little red wagon with homemade sandwiches and an ice-filled peck bucket of soft drinks and pull the wagon into the Conover Furniture Company work areas at lunch for the employees. He was the only outside vendor allowed inside the plant.

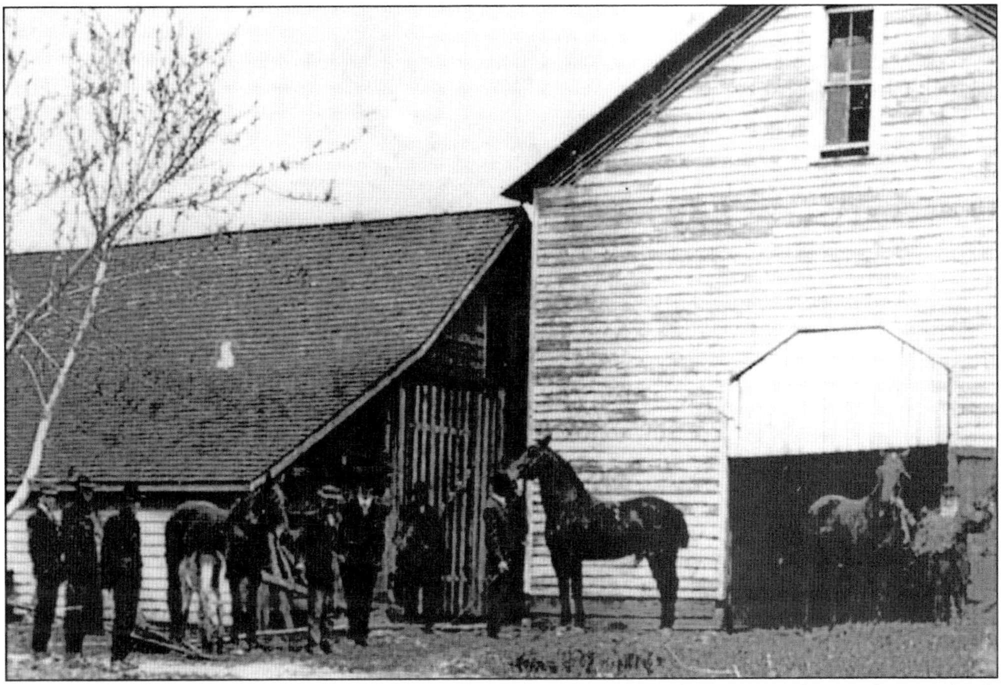

Saturday morning horse sales were attended by some buyers at the P.E. Isenhower barn, which was located just off Second Avenue in Conover. It was the custom in those days for men to visit sales for the buying and selling of livestock. Buggies were also for sale.

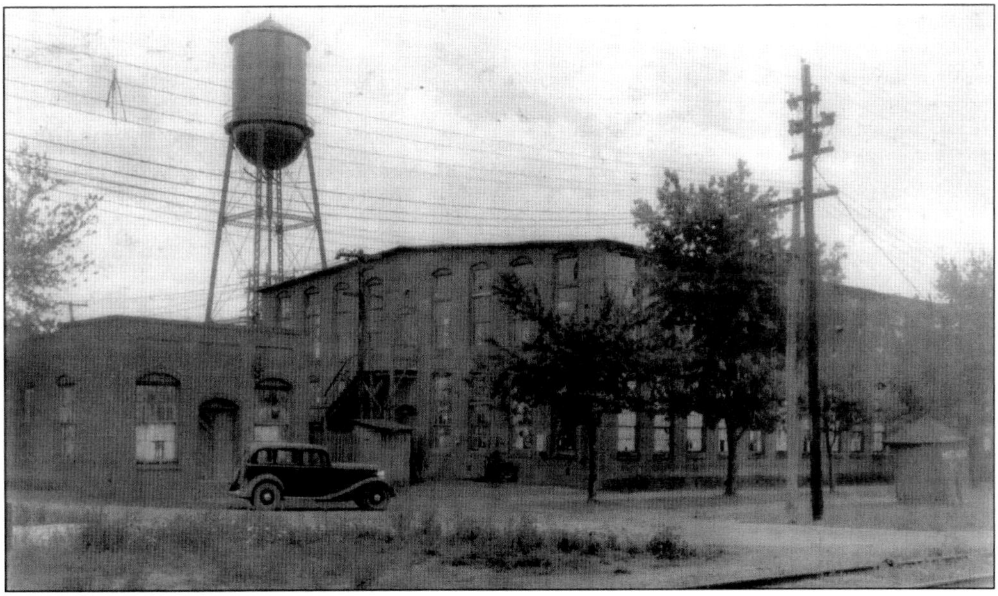

In the 1920s, the J.A. Yount Cotton Mill was located near the Superior Oil Company. It was a cotton-spinning mill and warehouse. J.A. Isenhower later purchased the operation from Yount. On the grounds were 21 mill houses built for the employees. The Isenhower brothers Joe, Sam, and Jim would collect the rent money from the dwellers. During the Depression years, the spinning machines were sold for scrap. The building later became home to the Old Dominion Box Company business. It is now closed and serves as a warehouse for furniture.

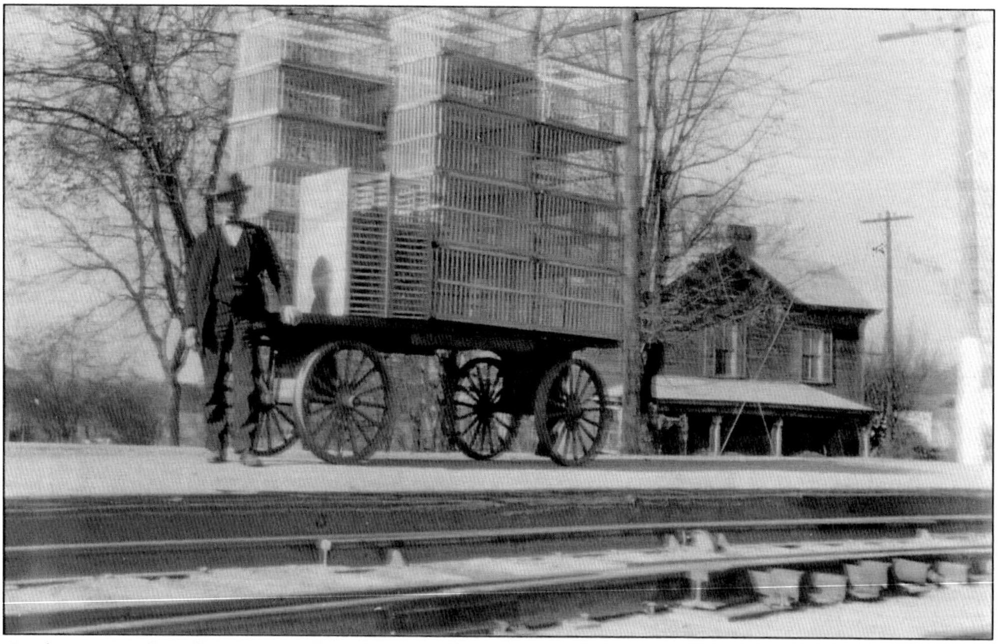

At the new railroad station in Conover stands Bob Brady, owner of Conover Furniture Company, waiting for the noon train to load newly built chicken coops onto the express cars. Scrap wood was often used to produce new products.

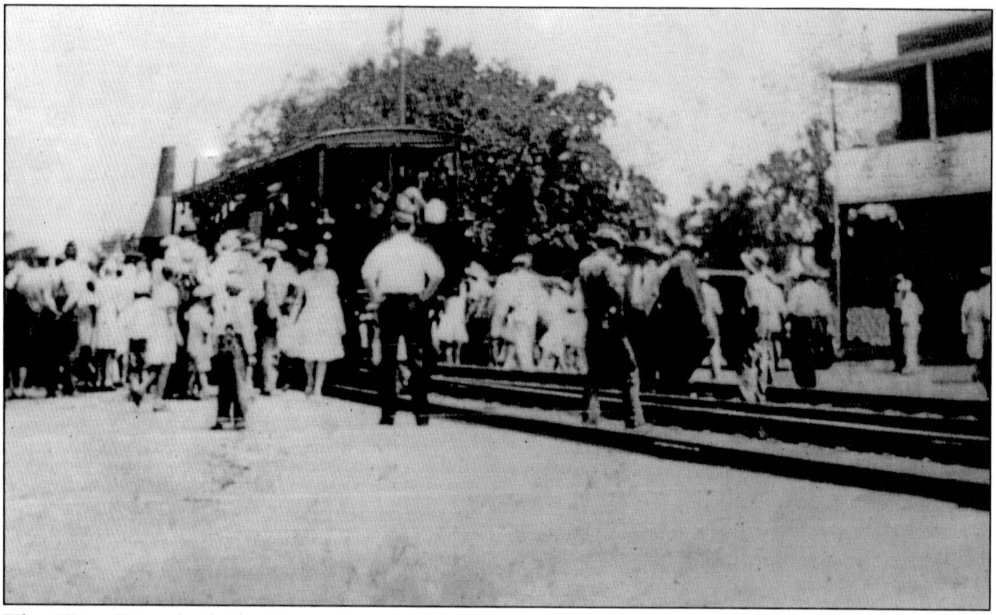

The "Best Friend of Charleston," a replica of the first locomotive in the United States, visits Conover Station on June 22, 1929, on its way to Hickory. Steaming out of Spencer under its own power with two antiquated passenger coaches and an equipment car, it is on a tour of the Southern Railway system. In charge of the train is Arthur White, general road foreman of engines out of Charlotte. The Spencer crew included conductor E.E. Yates, engineer H.L. Coburn, fireman W.E. Hippert, and flagman Carl Stout. The stop in Conover caused a lot of excitement to view 100 years of railway transportation.

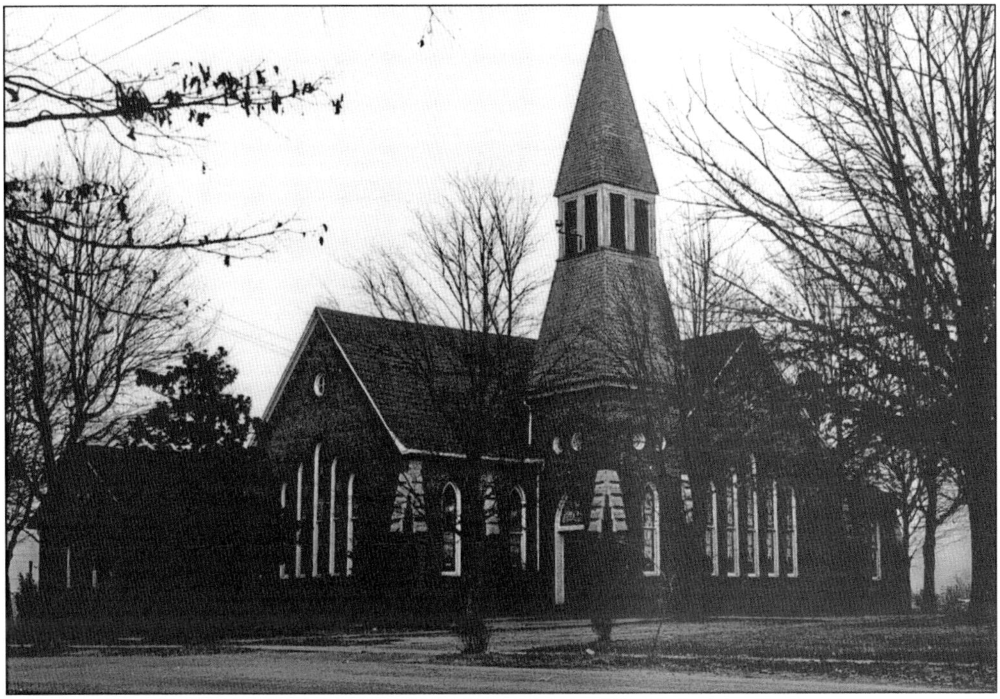

Concordia Lutheran Church had its beginnings with the old Concordia College, which was formed in 1877 at St. John's Lutheran Church outside of Conover. The primary mission of the college was for education and preparatory studies for men going into the ministry. No doubt the worship services were held from the beginning in the assembly hall of the college, but Concordia congregation was not officially in existence until it was accepted into the Tennessee Synod in September 1878.

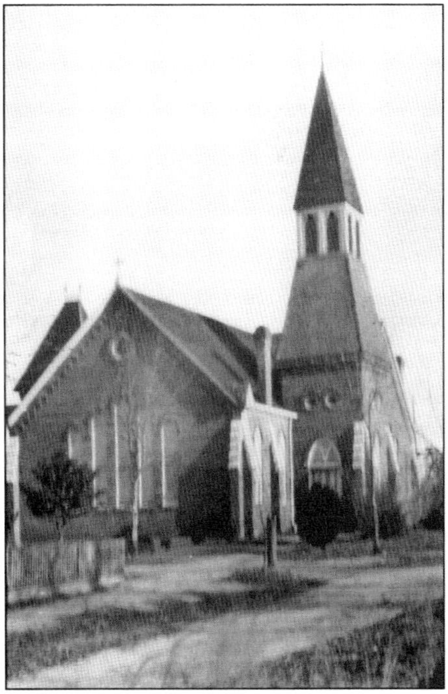

In 1878, the little congregation of Concordia had only about 100 members. Pastor R.A. Yoder, who was a professor at Concordia College, was the founding pastor of Concordia Lutheran Church. In 1894, the Concordia congregation took over the operation of grades one through seven from the college. That was the beginning of Concordia Christian Day School. Grades eight through the first two years of college were continued at Concordia College. The school was postponed in 1933 because of the Depression. In 1935, fire destroyed the main assembly building of Concordia College; it never reopened. But in 1946, the school opened in a new building on the grounds of Concordia Church and once again offered a Christian education to the children of Concordia and the surrounding community.

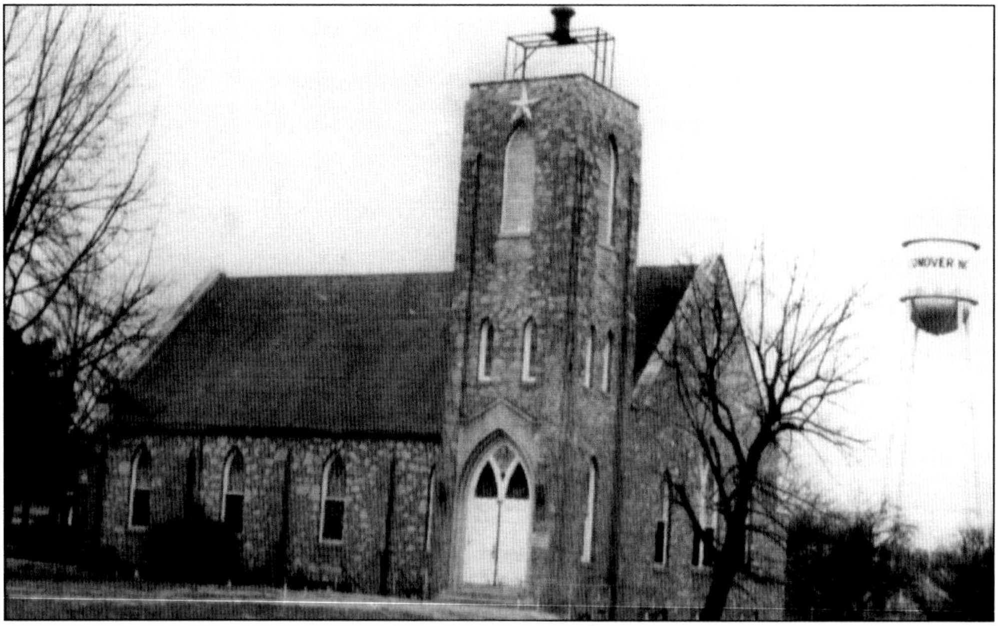

Trinity Reformed United Church of Christ in Conover has a long, rich history of over 120 years. It can trace its roots back to the Reformed and Lutheran meetings, which in the 1700s worshipped under the name of St. John's Church, located two miles northeast of Conover. Trinity Church was officially organized in 1892 under the leadership of Dr. Jacob C. Clapp, who was president of Catawba College in Newton. The first church built was a brick structure.

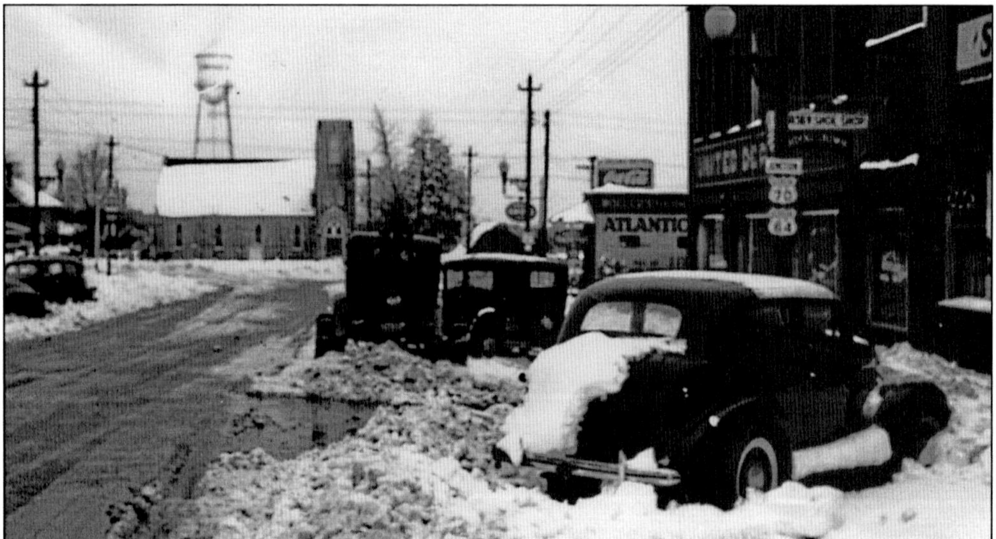

In 1935, the previous Trinity Church was replaced with the more familiar edifice in the heart of downtown Conover called the new Rock Church, so named because it was constructed of quarried stone. Trinity church is in the background in this 1940s snow scene in downtown Conover. The United department store would later be the home of Setzer's Supermarket. Trinity Church has always had the visibility of the community in mind with outreach programs and the famous Trinity Men's Barbecue that begun in 1950. A new brick structure was built in 1953, and the Rock Church became a community building for civic programs and even housed the fire station.

Two

Businesses and Industry

The only drugstore on Main Street in the 1930s was Conover Drug Company. But it was not the first. Around 1910, Peter Smith would be the first pharmacist in a building at the site of what is now Bowman Drug Company. Pharmacist A. Boyd Kunkle would be the first tenant of a new Conover drugstore across the street. Upon Kunkle's departure for Statesville, Coley Yoder came up from the Central Drug Company in Newton, along with his wife, Marie, to lease the business. Paul Yount would join them as did a young pharmacist named Billy Price, who later purchased the business. Price would build a new, modern drugstore on the site of the new post office. Pictured from left to right are Paul Yount, Coley Yoder, Billy Price, and Marie Yoder. Employees Nancy Isenhower and Stine Isenhower would jerk some sodas.

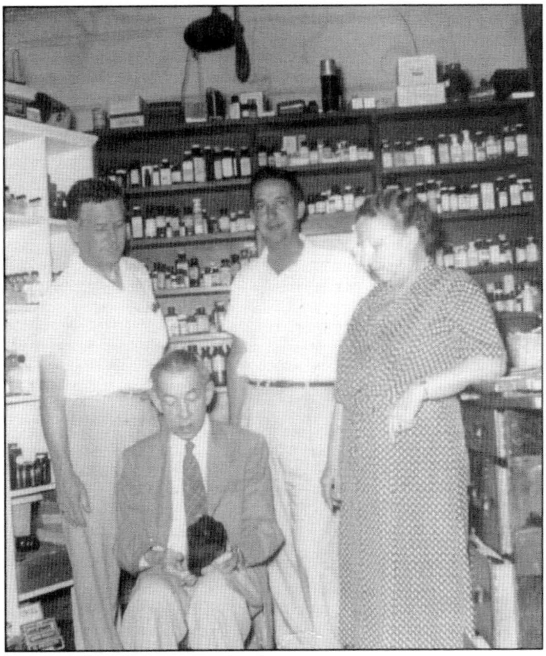

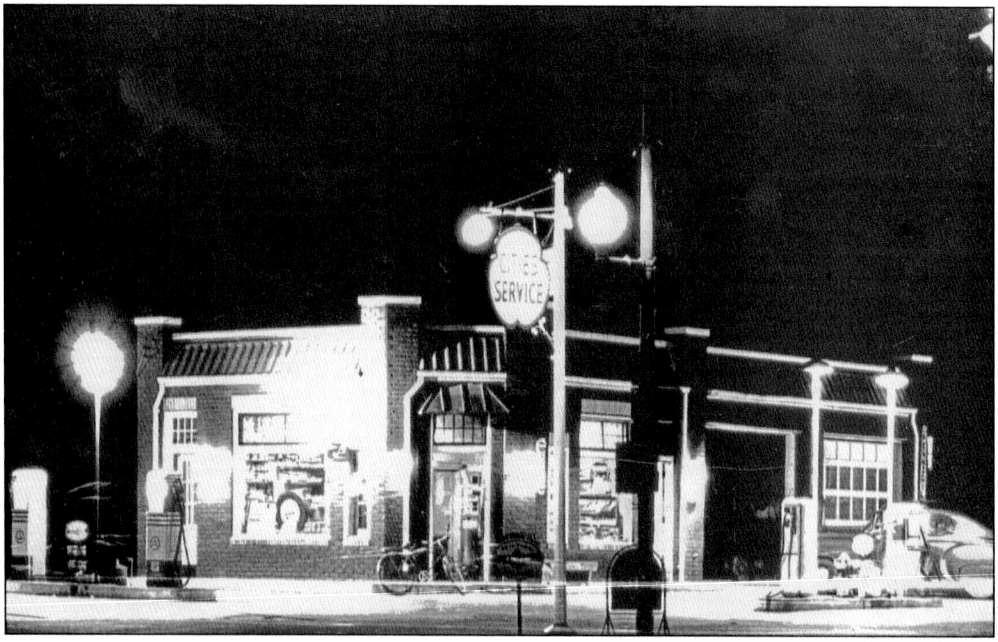

At five points in Conover, Cities Service Station was operated by Olin Winters and Bud Hollar and later was a Phillips 66 station operated by Hal Hollar. It is now a Pure Oil station. The station was the afternoon drop-off point for the local *Hickory Daily Record* newspaper delivery boys.

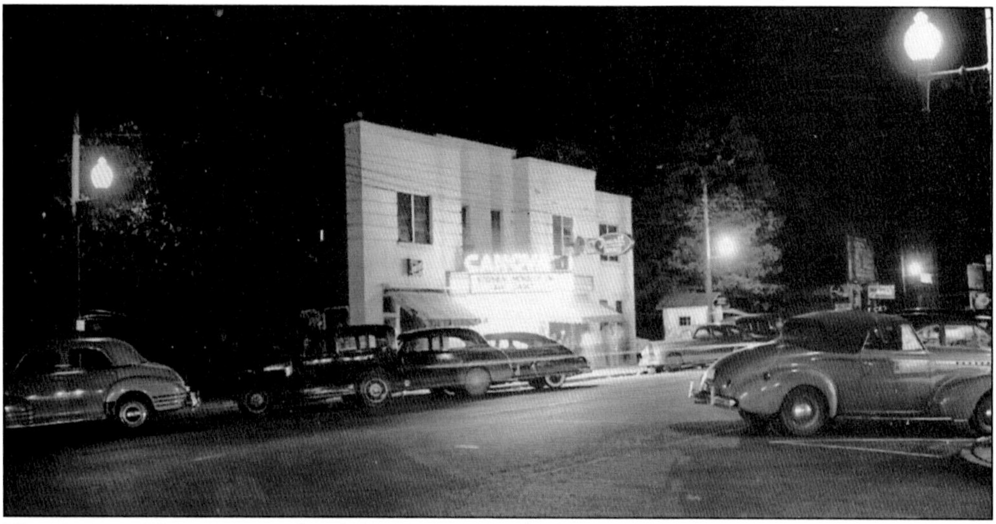

The Canova Theater opened in May 1941; it was built by V.O. Sipe, of Conover, and designed by Robert Clemmer, of Hickory. It was leased to Colonial Theaters of Valdese and operated by Kenneth Benfield. In 1941, the theater was awarded the title of Fourth Best in the Nation. Hal Haupt was the first manager, followed by Don Holler and Harry Whisnant. It was air-conditioned, vast, spacious, and unique in design. The balcony would also include a cry room for mothers with crying babies. Every other seat on the aisle was a loveseat, especially built for two. The admission prices were 9¢ and 25¢. A late show was screened on Saturday nights. Bank Night was on Wednesday nights with a drawing for a cash prize for a lucky ticketholder. The theater closed in the early 1970s. Wallace Perry Sr. was the last manager. The *Ten Commandants* was the last movie to be shown. The Conover-Newton Bus Line would bring in patrons from the outlying areas.

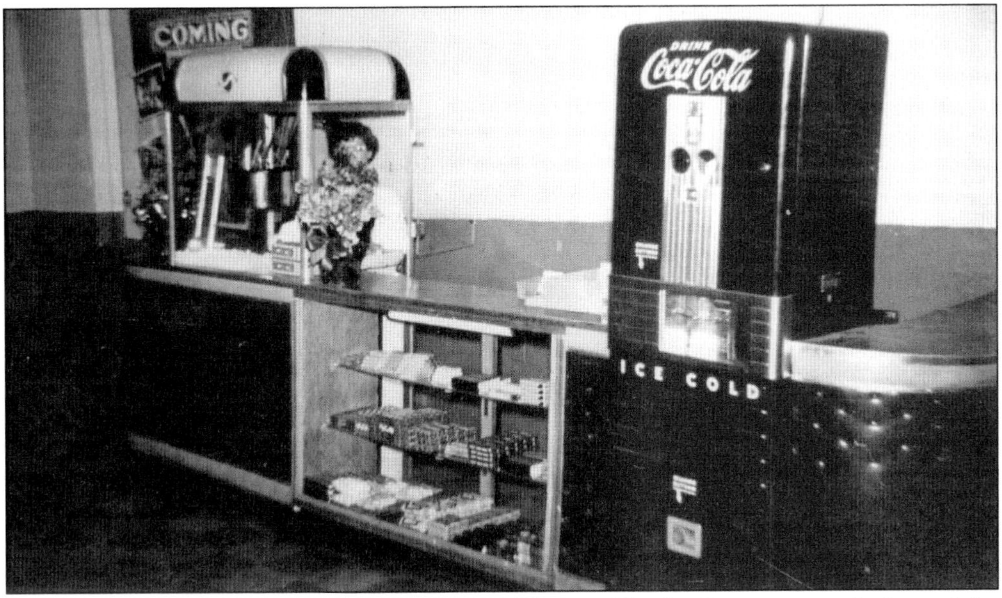

This is the new concession stand at the Canova Theater. Charles Simmons was the boss of the popcorn popper. Ann Brady Holt, Jean Alwran, Joy McCray, Janet Houston, Phillis Turner, and many other Conover boys and girls would work the snack stand. Changing the marquee was the job of Walter Griggs, Max Bowman, and Joe Dale Bolick. Bobby Spencer, Boyce Holler, Melvin Shull, and Jim Bogle would be employed as projectionists. Stine Isenhower, Bill Watts, and Ronald Kaylor also worked there as ushers, having been thoroughly trained in the use of a flashlight.

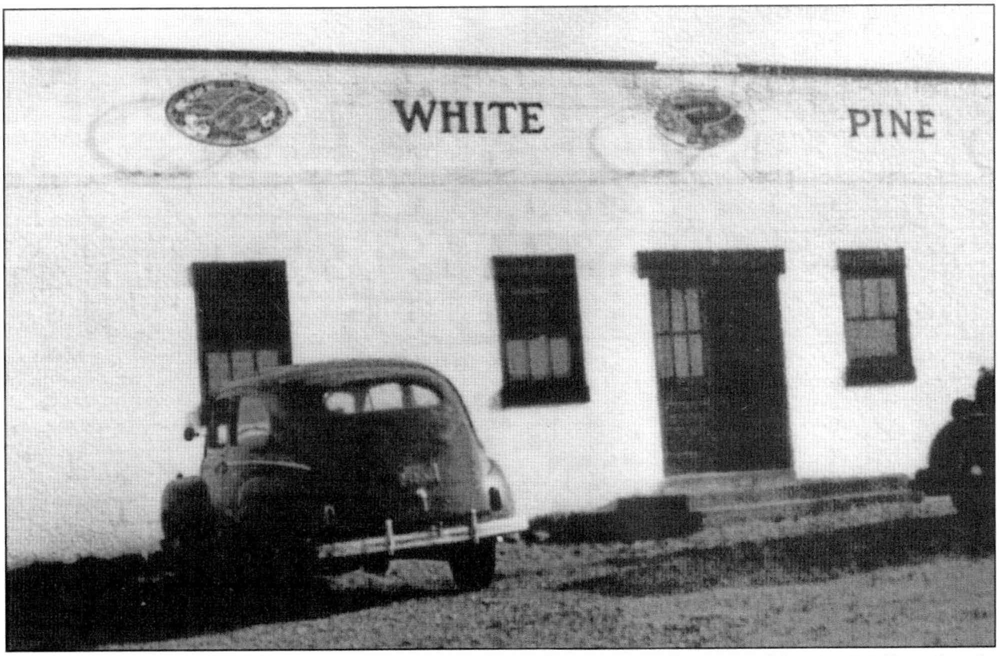

The legendary White Pine Club was built in the early 1940s and operated by the McGee family for many years. Dining and dancing with live bands on the weekends were great times for the patrons. Delicious dinners were served after church on Sundays. A Saturday-night menu special was the club steak.

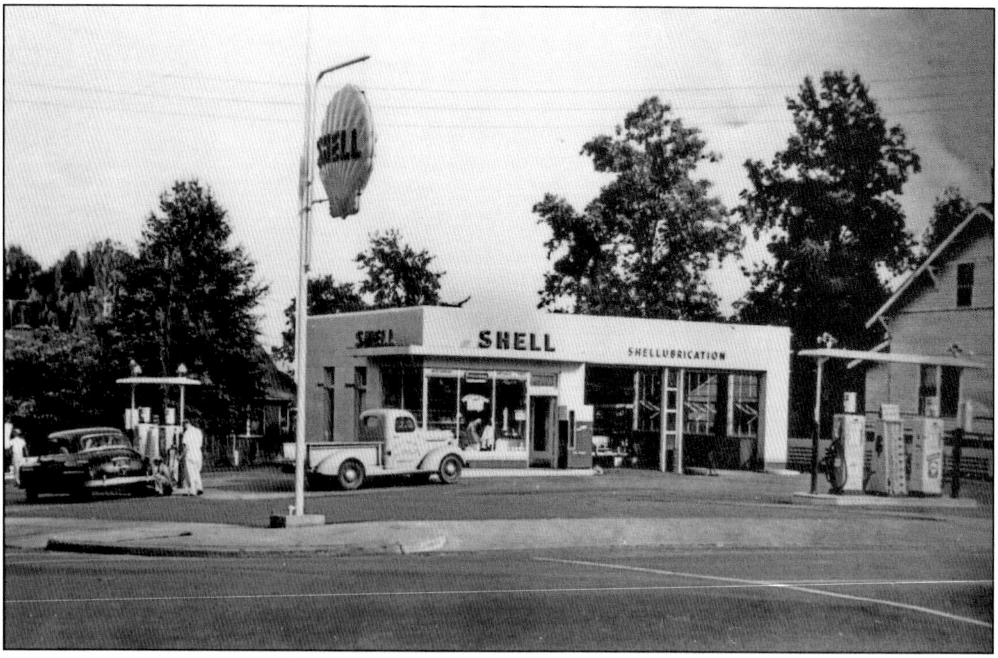

L.A. Yount and Tommy Rockett operated this Shell station at First and Third Streets Southeast. It was later a lock and key shop and is now a used car lot. The Jack Abernathy home was on the right. Tommy served in the Army Air Corps during World War II, stationed in England.

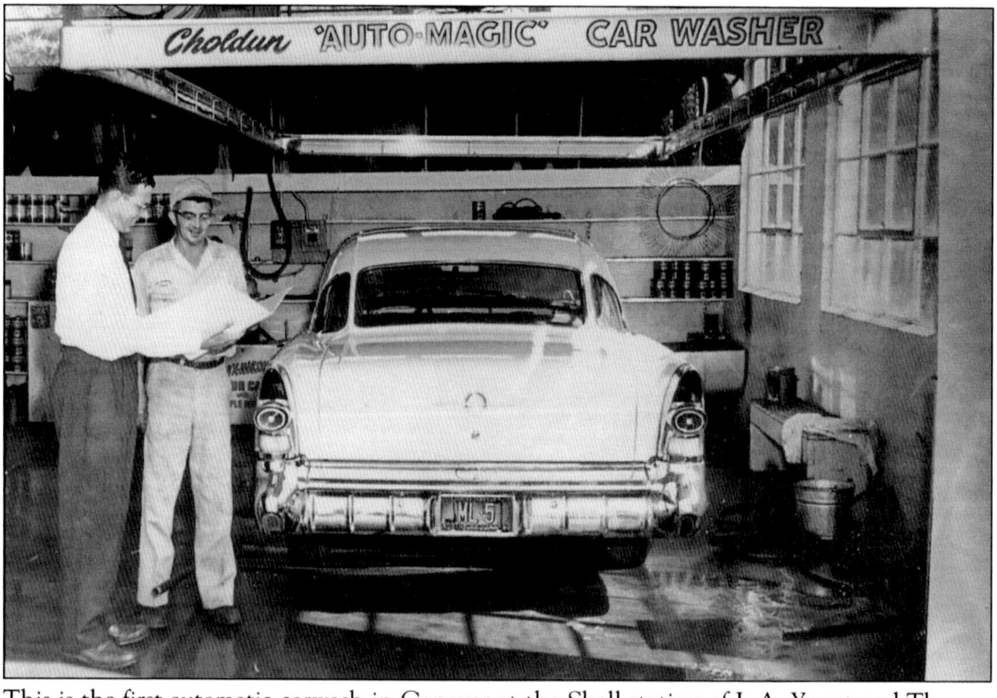

This is the first automatic carwash in Conover at the Shell station of L.A. Yount and Thomas "Tommy" Rockett. It was a simple contraption with a water hose connected to an electric motor that ran about on an overhead rail track—just soap and rinse! Rockett is shown here (right) with a salesman.

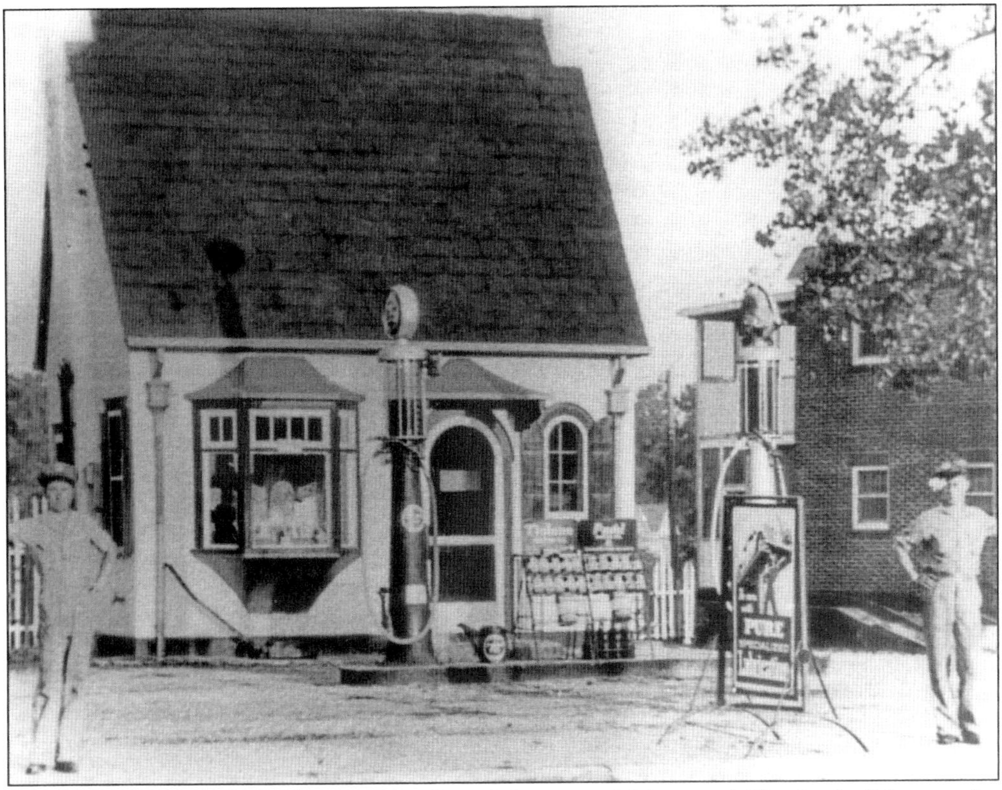

A very early business was the Conover Pure Oil station. Hubert and Charles Bolick were the operators. It is now the home of Conover Auto Sales. This uniquely designed building later housed a small hamburger and hotdog cafe.

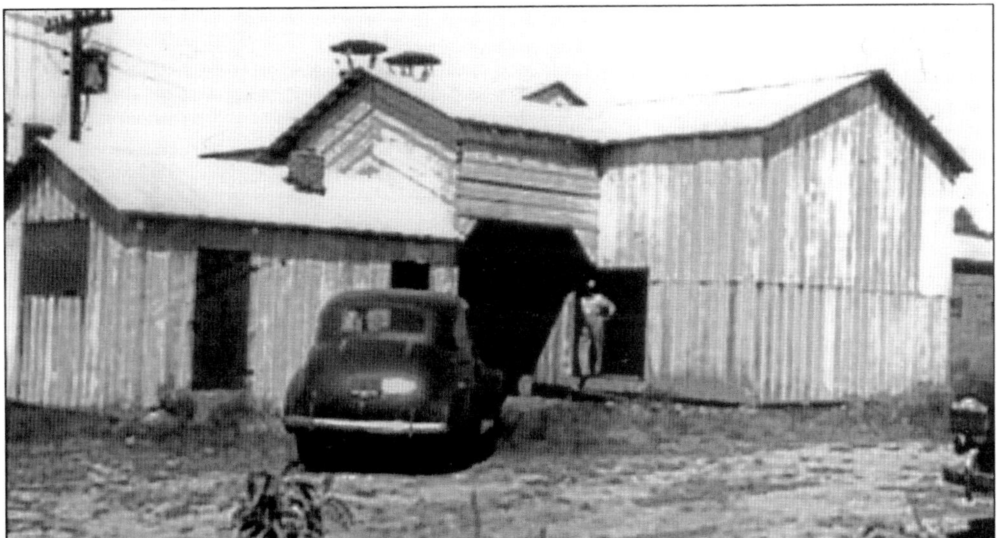

Around 1945, this cotton gin was operated by J.A. Isenhower and was located at the Interstate 40 bridge on the County Home Road in Conover. The family also operated a cotton gin on the site of the new post office. Conover was abundant with cotton fields. The Isenhower family would operate a bonded warehouse in Newton to hold these baled goods for market.

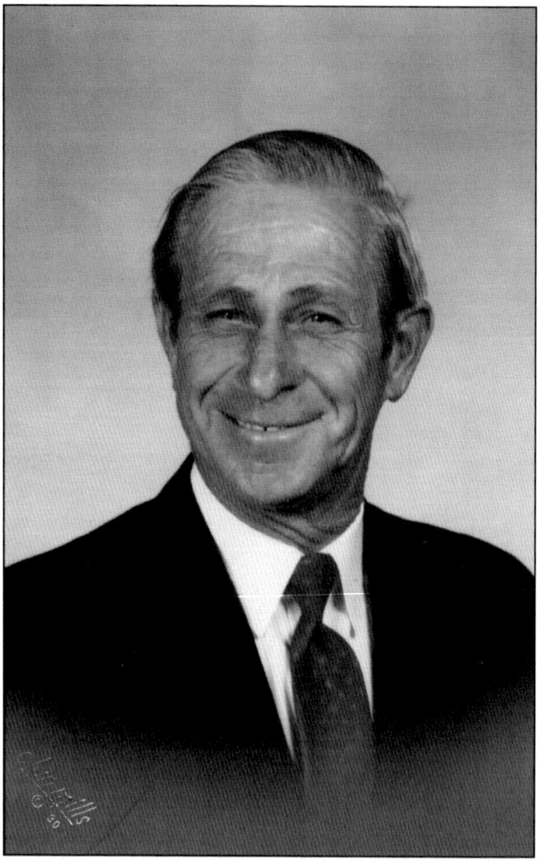

Neil Rowe and Pringle Killian operated the Conover Roofing and Sheet Medal Company. The business was first located on Main Street in a building vacated by a textile business. Rowe and Killian were in business for over 30 years. This building was home to the first drugstore in Conover, which was operated by Peter Smith. Neil was married to the former Joan Brown, of Hickory, and attended Concordia Lutheran Church.

Shown is the well-known Blue Mirror. It was built in 1948 by Miller Lynch, who had previously worked at Shady Grove. It was located on Highway 70 West on the right just past the Shell station. This road would be the new Conover-Hickory Highway. Many Conover boys worked on this project during the summer. Grady Hamrick was a flagman.

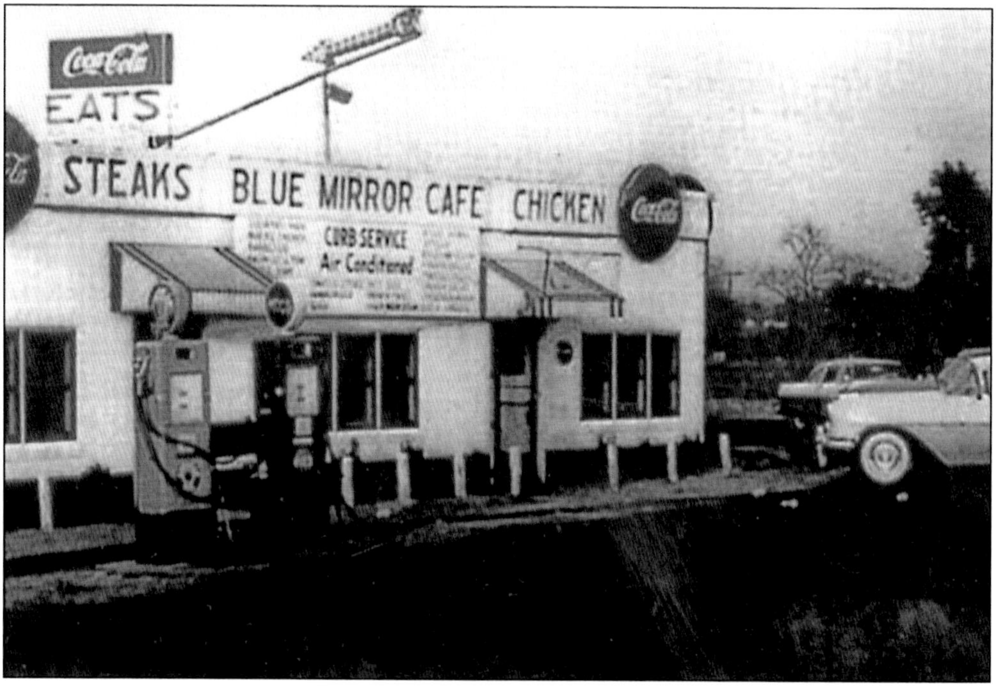

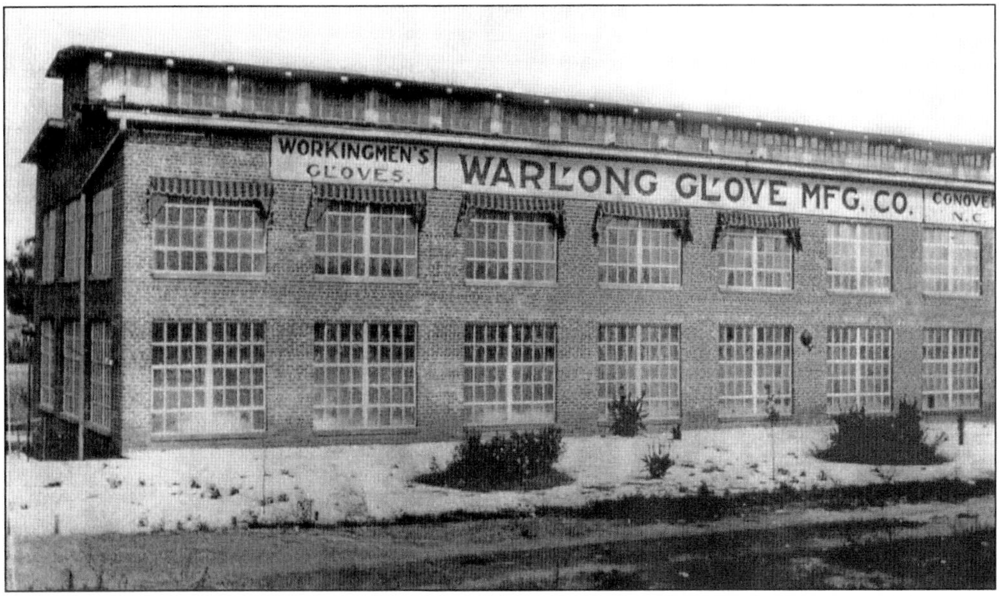

A.J. Shuford owned the Conover Knitting Company and Warlong Glove Company. These two combined factories had a great number of Conover men and women working during World War II. The property is now owned by the City of Conover for future redevelopment for multiuse for light rail and as a transportation hub in Conover.

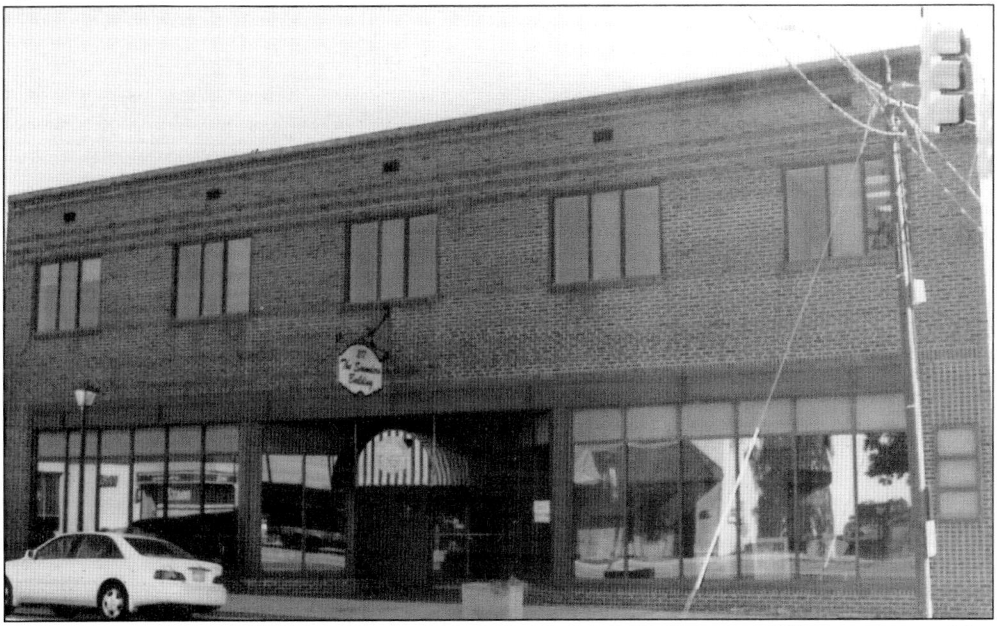

J.A. Isenhower built the Saunders Furniture Store in the early 1940s for T.W. Saunders and his son Walter. In the 1920s, T.W. Saunders and Van Commodore Drum operated a funeral home in the upstairs of Conover Drugstore and later in the old Setzer's Supermarket building, complete with an elevator. Later, Walter Saunders would operate the new retail furniture business in a large brick building now called the Saunders Building. Drum would build the new Drum Funeral Home in Conover across from the Conover Graded School. Walter Saunders was the first fire chief of Conover.

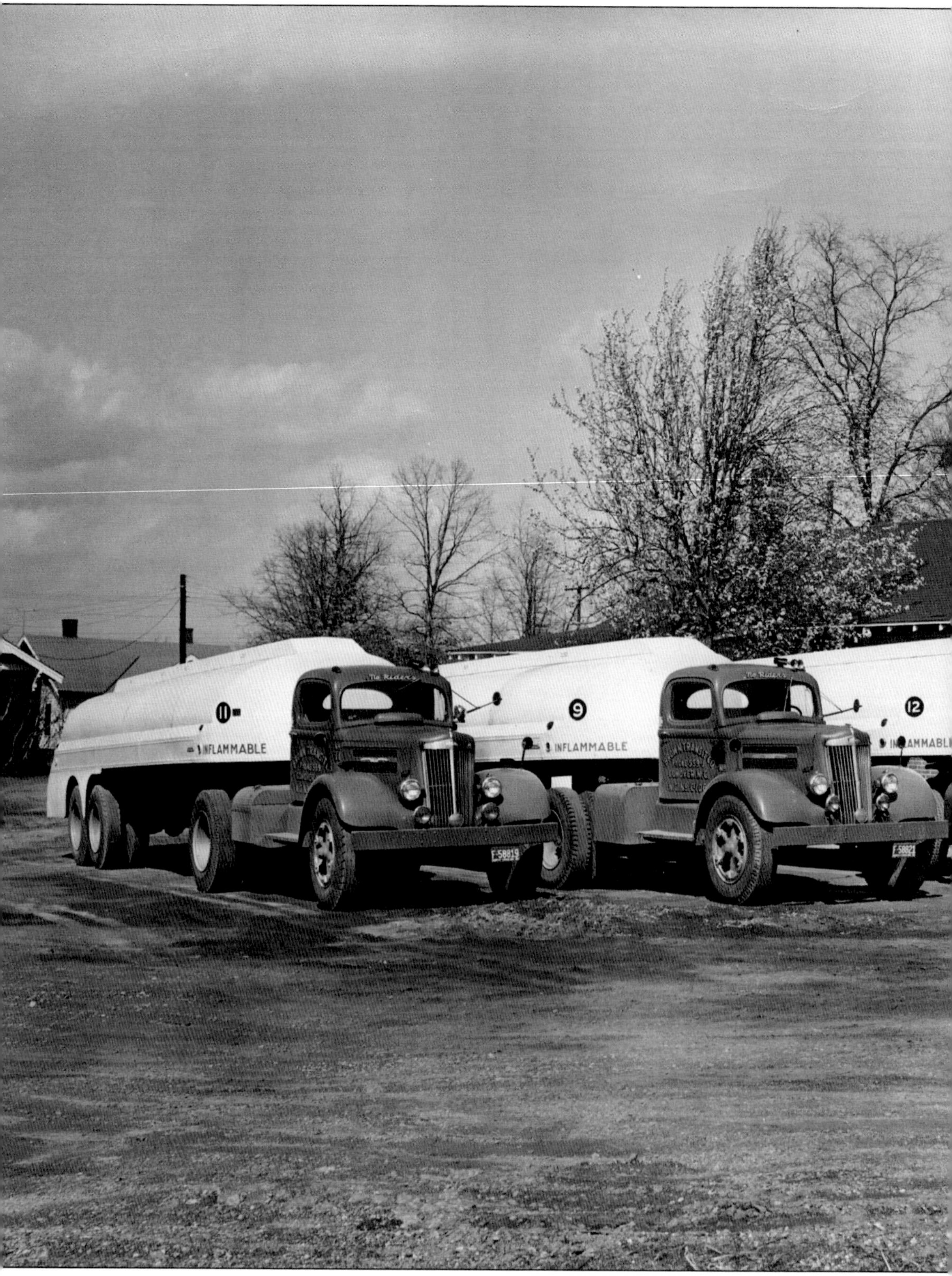
11
INFLAMMABLE
9
INFLAMMABLE
12

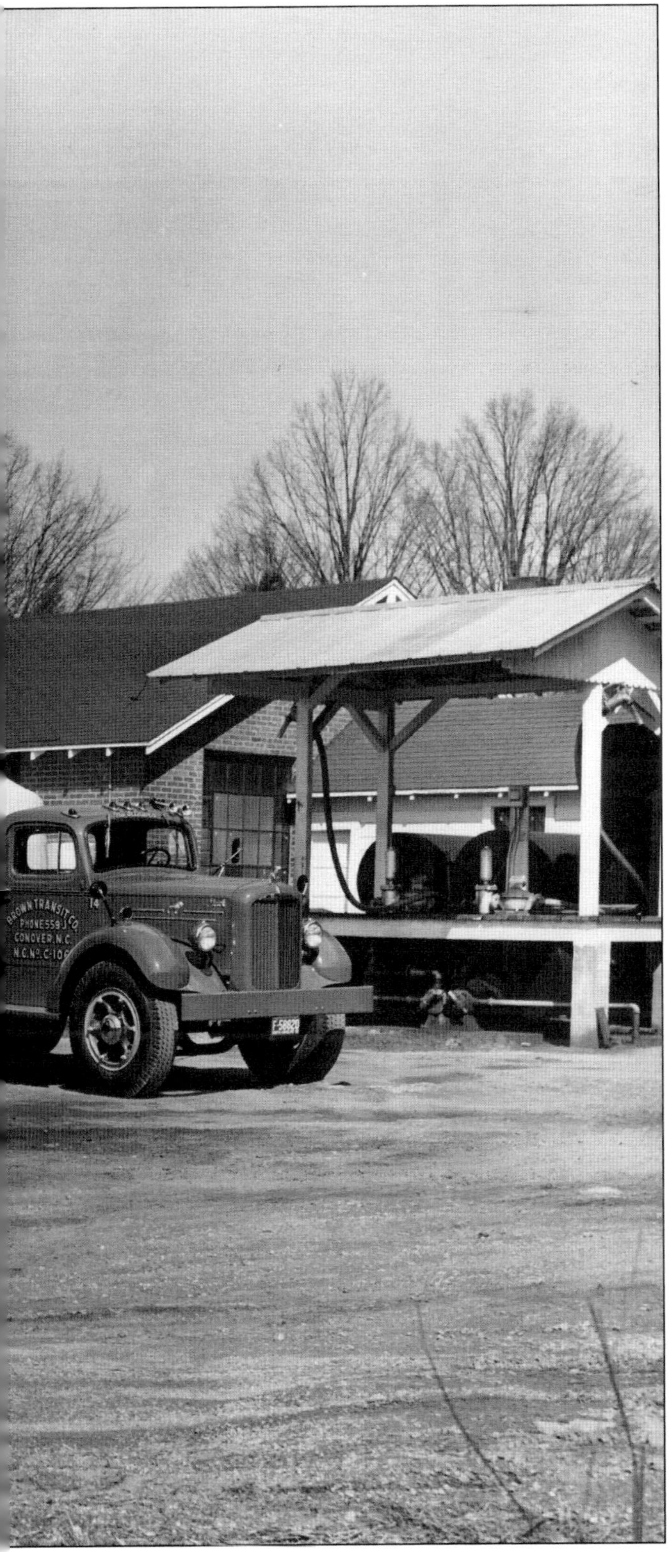

Pictured here are the transports of Brown Oil and Transit Company of Conover, which was owned and operated by Floyd K. Brown Sr., former mayor, prominent civic leader, and lifelong member of Concordia Lutheran Church. Brown Oil and Transit Company was a major Shell Oil distributor and dealer for nearly 40 years. During World War II, the transit company held military contracts for vital fuel delivery from the ports at Wilmington to various military bases in the state and to the Steel Creek storage facility in Charlotte. Brown's son Johnny and Johnny's son Eric continue to manage the Brown Oil Company business. This 1952 photograph shows the fleet of Mack-built transport tankers.

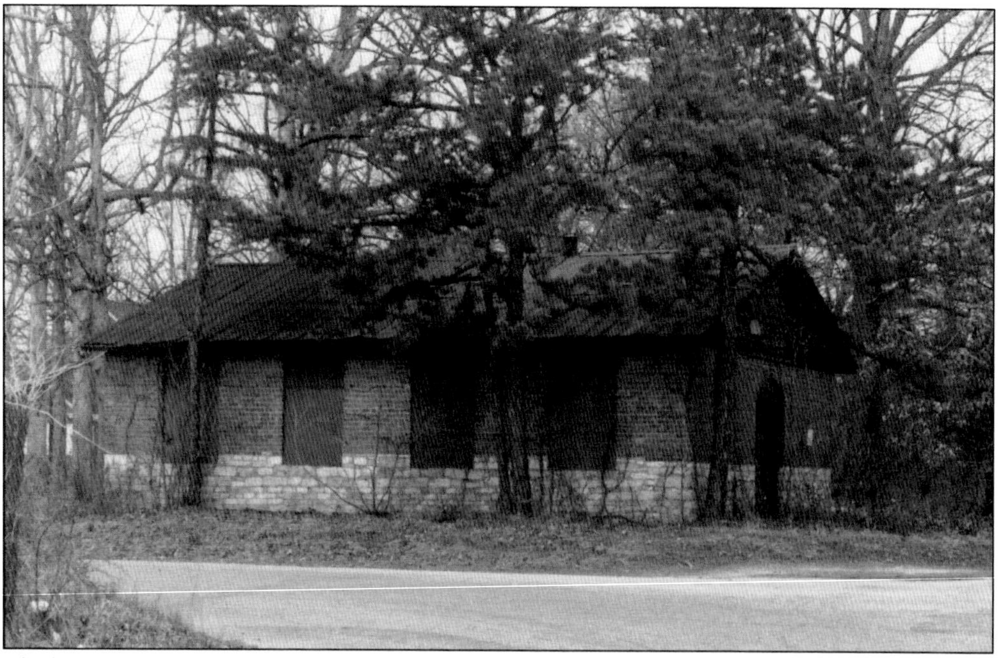

The last remaining remnants of the Jerome Bolick Buggy Shop are located in the Bolick historical district. The first steel-spoke buggy wheel was invented here. From the upholstery of buggy seats came the creation of Southern Furniture Company. A history of the Bolick Buggy Company is on display at Conover City Hall.

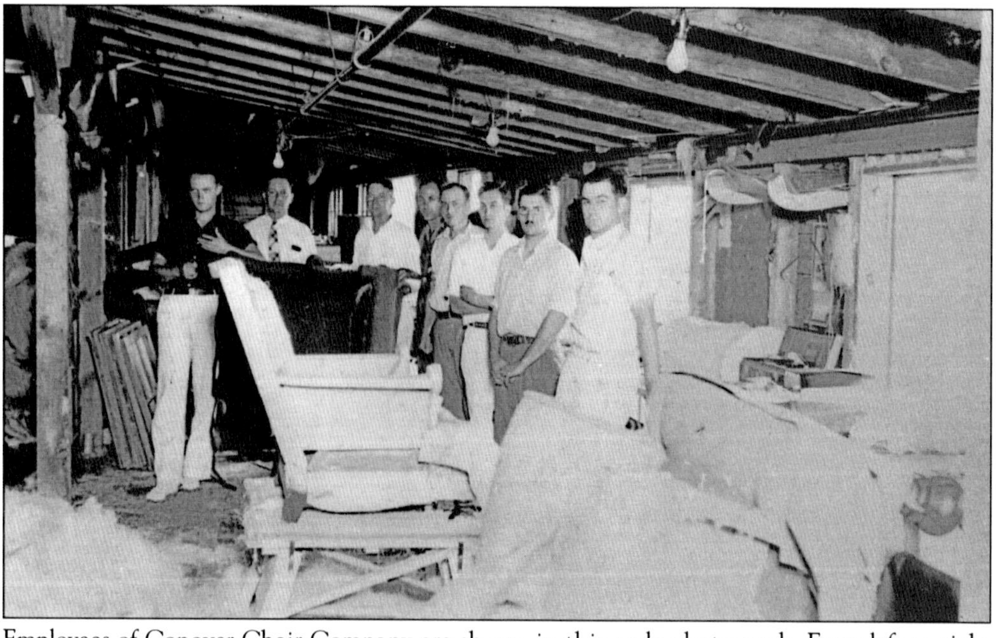

Employees of Conover Chair Company are shown in this early photograph. From left to right are Jim Shook, Alvin Bolick, Earl Bolick, Guy Little, M.L. Mann, Ralph Boston, Ralph Spencer, and Donald Kahill. Conover Chair was founded by 1927 by Alvin L. Bolick. Charles C.C. Bost, of York, South Carolina, married Luciphene Bolick, daughter of Alvin Bolick, in 1932. Upon the death of Alvin Bolick, Bost would become the new company president.

Pictured is Charles C.C. Bost. Conover Chair Company was formed in 1927 from the old Conover Mattress Company. Some men who worked there were Clint Bolick, Jack Shell, and Jack Bolick. It would produce a premium line of living-room furniture. Upon the death of Bost, his son-in-law Fred Sherrill would successfully manage the company for many years. The company was sold at Sherrill's retirement. The new owners were unsuccessful, and the business is now closed.

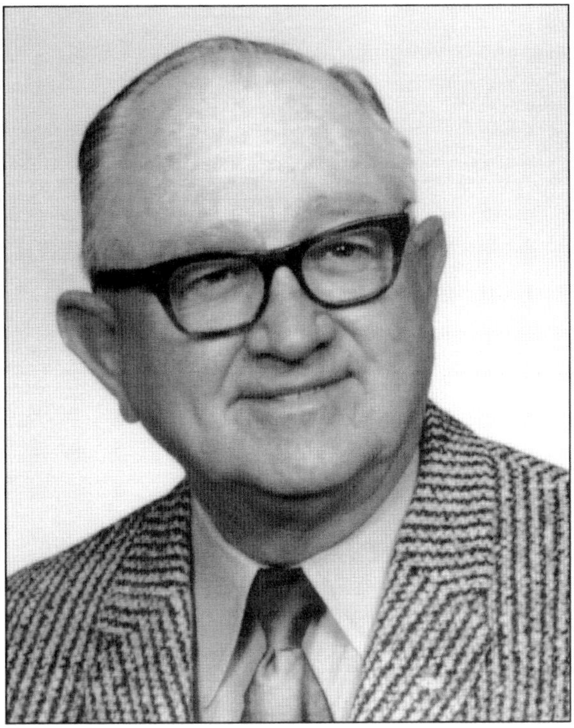

This is the Kenneth Herman Grocery Store in the early 1940s. This wood structure would stand for many years on Main Street next door to the new brick post office built by J.A. Isenhower. Herman was a prominent landholder. Herman would burn only one light and sell kerosene at the rear entrance.

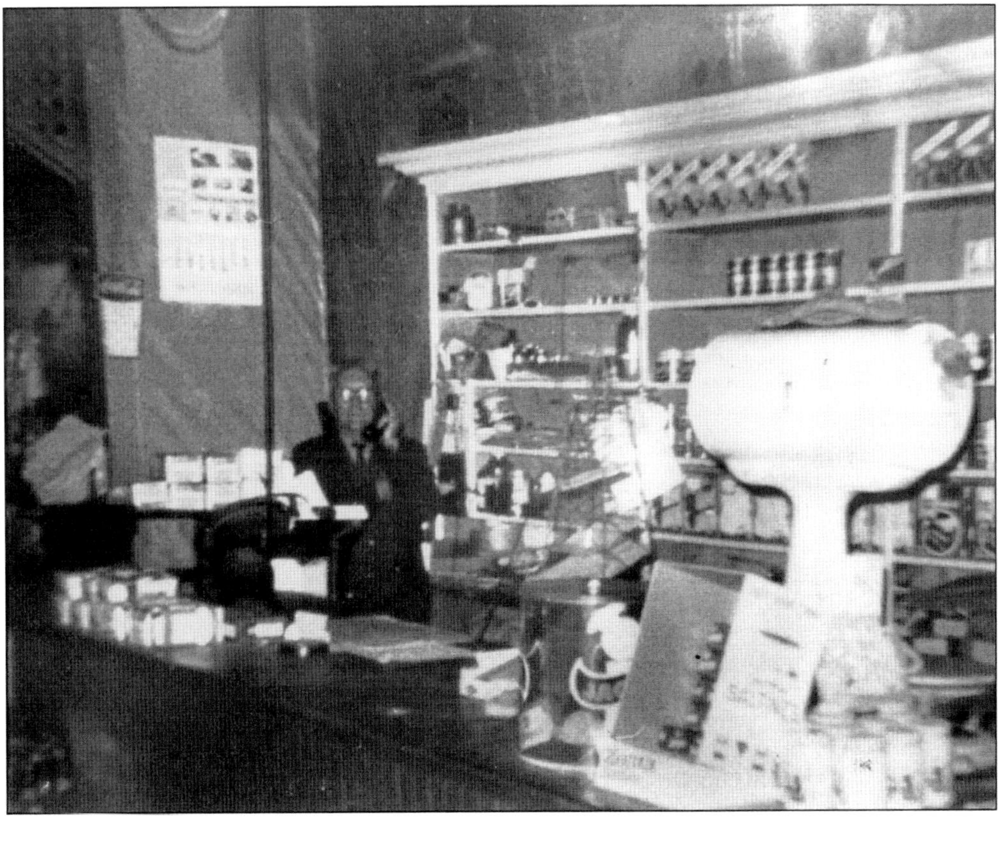

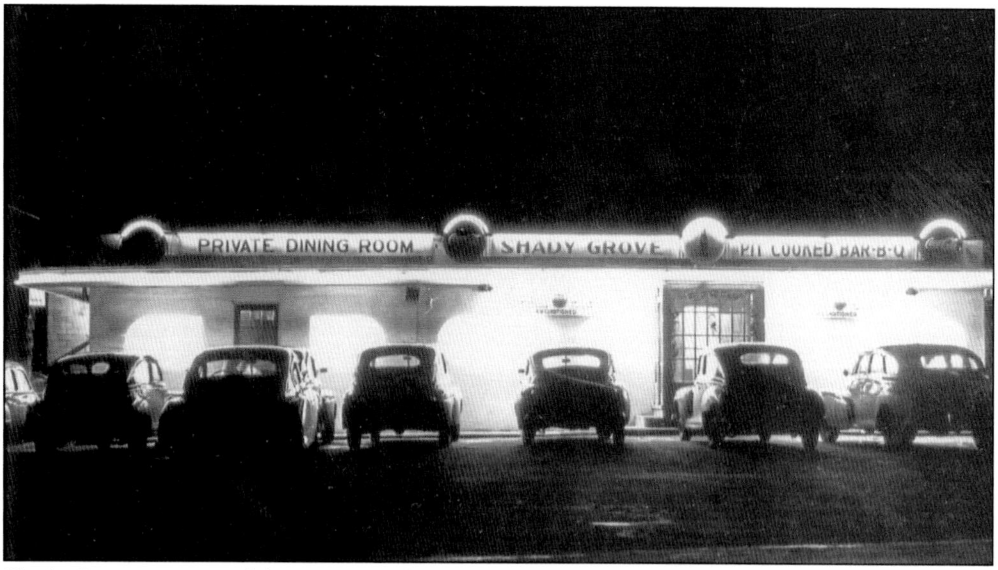

Shady Grove was one of the most popular restaurants in the area. It was built in 1925 by George Blackwelder, of Hickory, and Charles Everett Setzer. This was the "hang" for all area high school students and servicemen home on leave from the military. Onsite was a pet monkey in a cage. Once, a young Mona (Setzer) Moose was standing too close, and the monkey reached out and tore her dress off, leaving her mother to wrap her in her coat. Miller Lynch often worked the curb service. He later opened the infamous Blue Mirror. In a separate building in the rear was a skating rink. In the 1970s, the restaurant closed and passed into history.

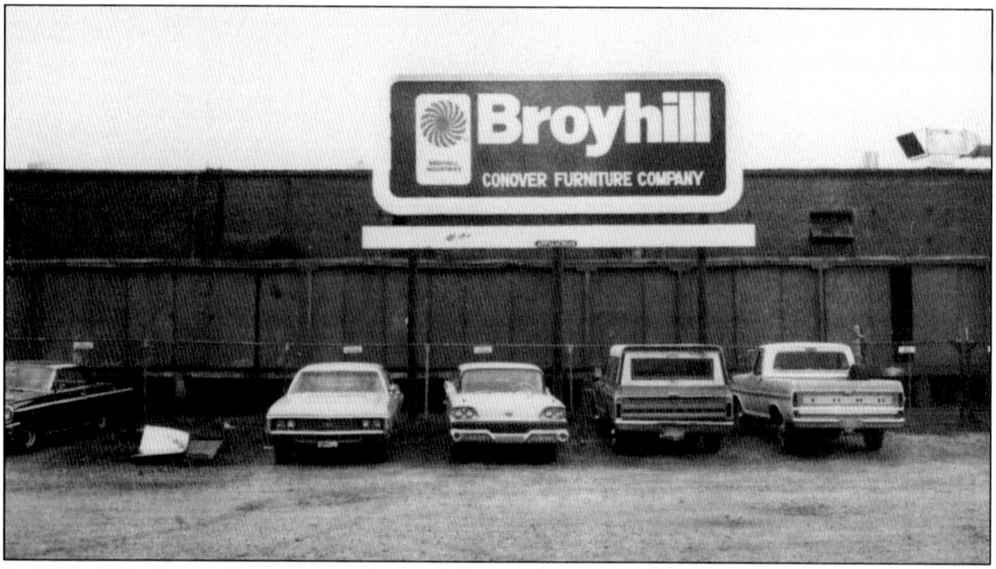

In 1919, C.R. Brady became president of the Hickory Handle Manufacturing Company in Conover, which built school desks, picker sticks, and hammer handles. He would later take sole ownership in the business and rename it Conover Furniture Company. The entire plant would be retooled to produce fine, high-end bedroom and dining-room furniture. The plant had the largest employee base of any plant in Conover. W.A. Brady and William J. Barker were the chief operating officers. After the Depression, the J.E. Broyhill Industries of Lenoir purchased the plant but kept the original name of Conover Furniture Company.

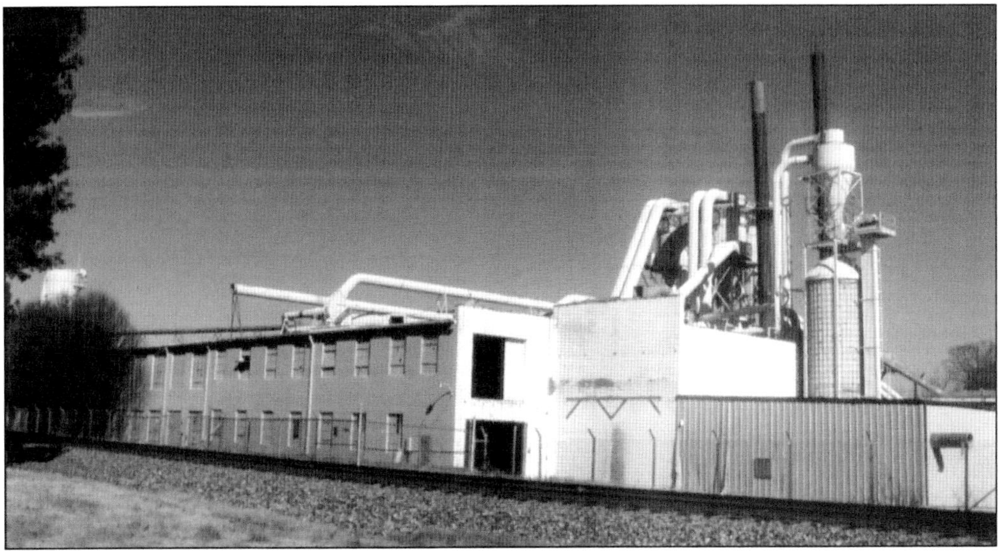

This is a photograph of the once mighty Broyhill Furniture Company in Conover. In the 1950s, Broyhill Furniture Company still carried the Conover Furniture Company name. It would work over 300 people for first shift. The United Veneer Company would occupy the old Conover Knitting (Warlong) building. Around 1945, Adrian Shuford Jr. built a larger new glove plant on Conover Boulevard, which later was sold to Gulf States Paper Corporation. It is now the Rock-Tenn Company, a paper packaging facility.

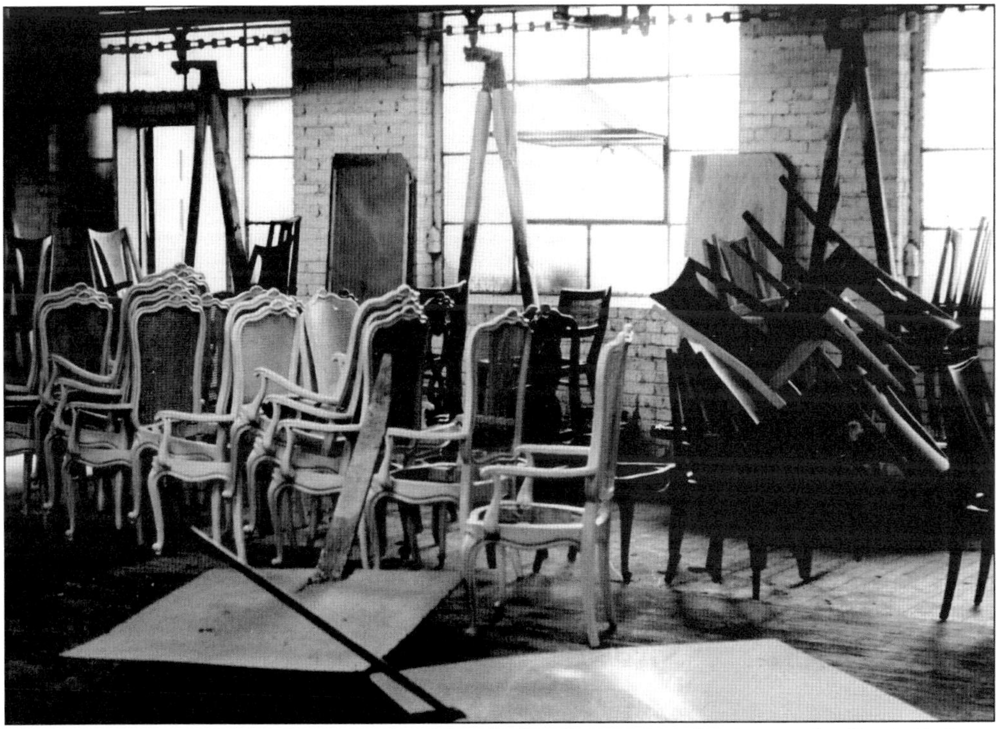

Chairs go along the line to be sprayed and finished and sent on to shipping at the Broyhill plant. Bedroom suites would also be finished in this manner. Over 900 chairs could be spray-finished in one day.

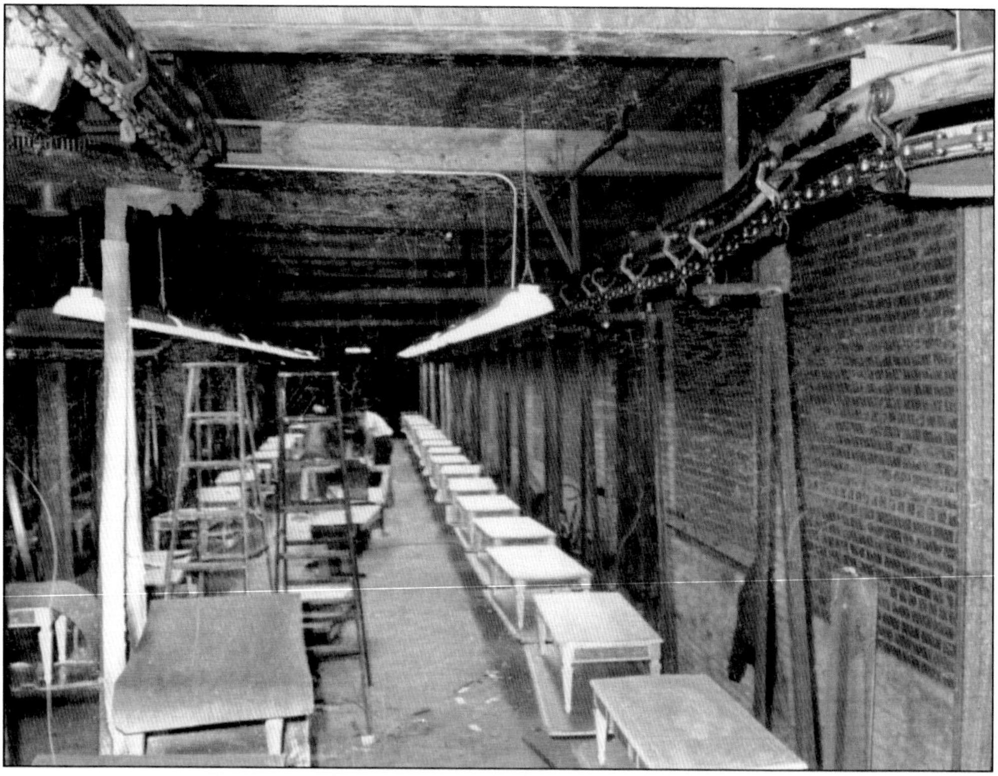

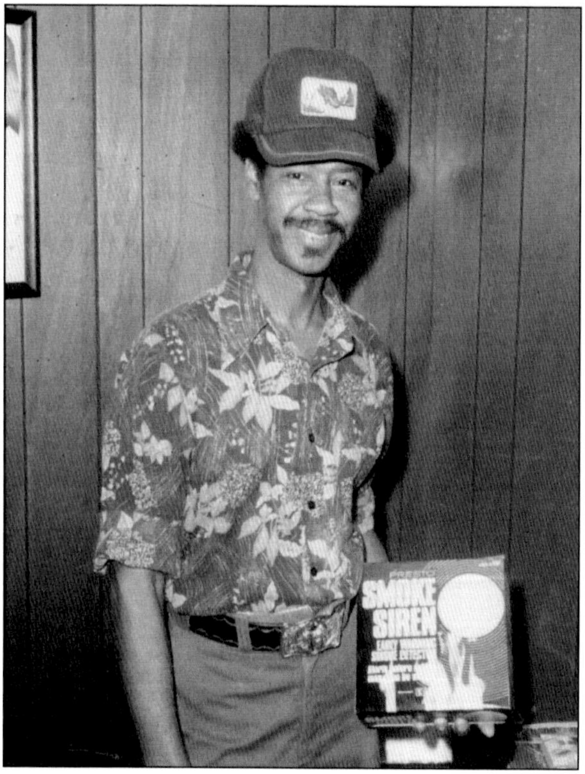

This is the Broyhill shipping department. Furniture would be packed and sent to New York, Chicago, and New Orleans showrooms and retail stores by rail and by truck. William Clarence Canrobert was the machine room foreman at Lenoir No. 2 in Newton from 1945 to 1950. He was Conover plant superintendent from 1950 to 1958.

Allen Ramsey was the finishing room manager. He was a resident of Conover and worked here for over 18 years. The old finishing and shipping department building was demolished in 2011. This building was constructed in the 1940s by the Herman-Sipe Company. The foreman for the project was Tolly Hedrick. Many young Conover teenagers were employed here during the summers.

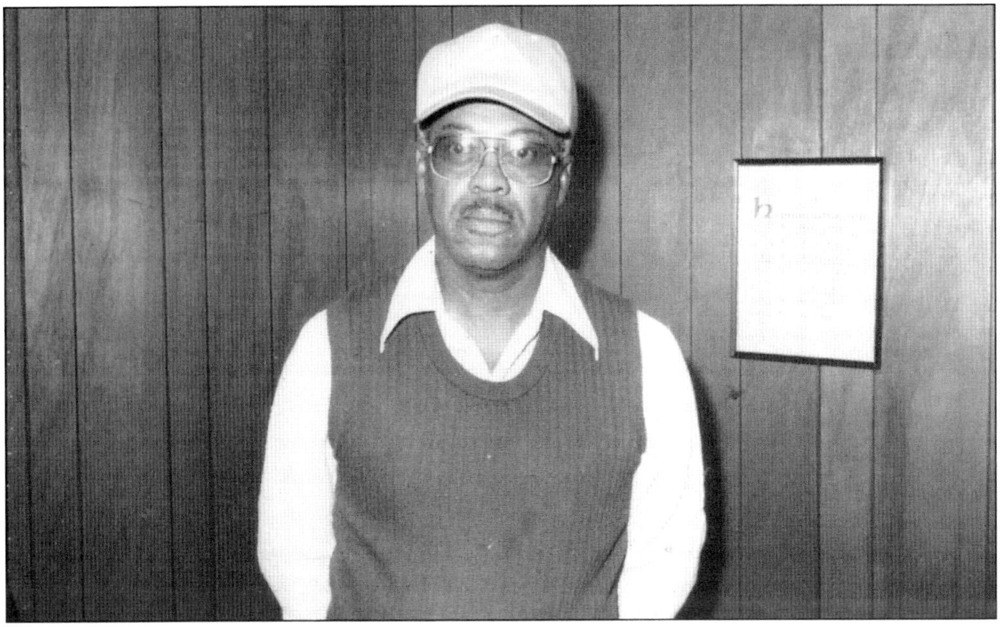

Ed Clark was well known and a lifelong Conover resident who worked at Broyhill most of his life. He loved to fish and play ball. He was also very active in his church. He is shown here at an awards presentation. Ed lived in the Southwest section of Conover.

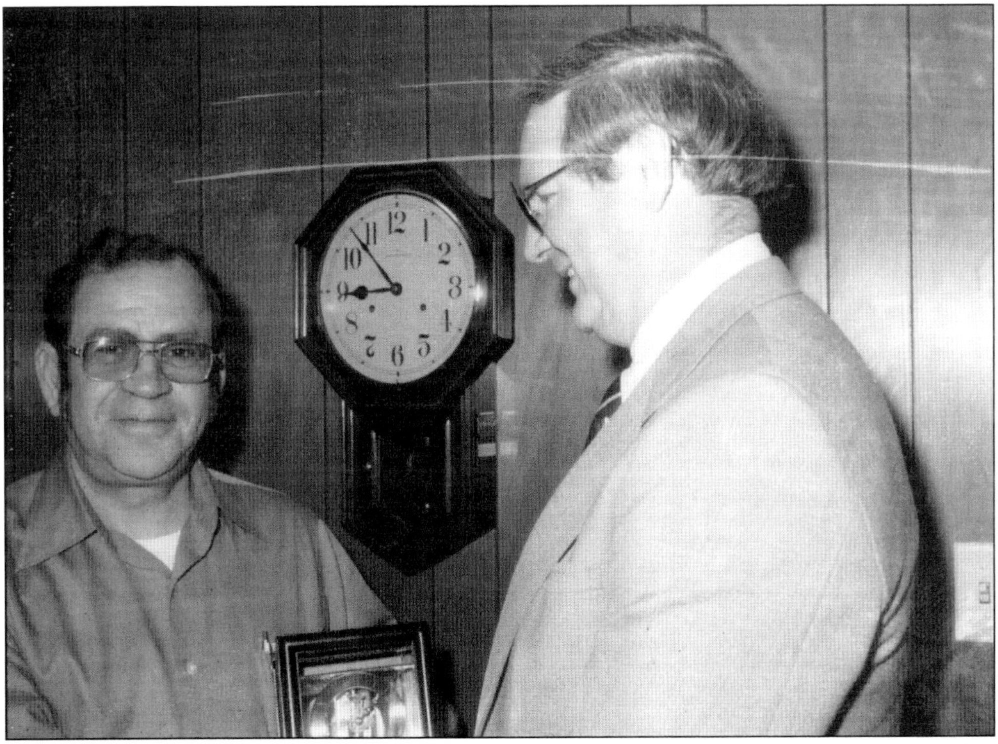

E. Kevette Wallace was supervisor in the finishing room at Broyhill for over 35 years. He attended Conover and Newton schools and lives in Conover. The finishing room building was torn down in 2011 to clear the grounds for the City of Conover's new Conover Station project.

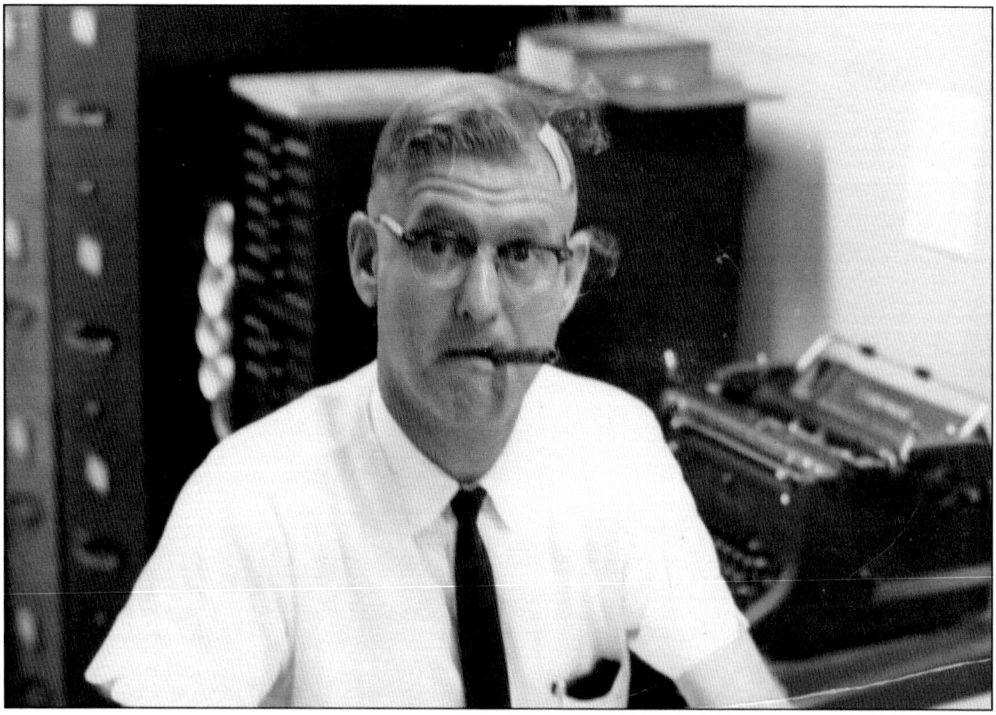

Cecil Darden was director of personnel at the Conover Broyhill plant. He was always a familiar face around the plant. He would arrange the parties and picnics during holidays.

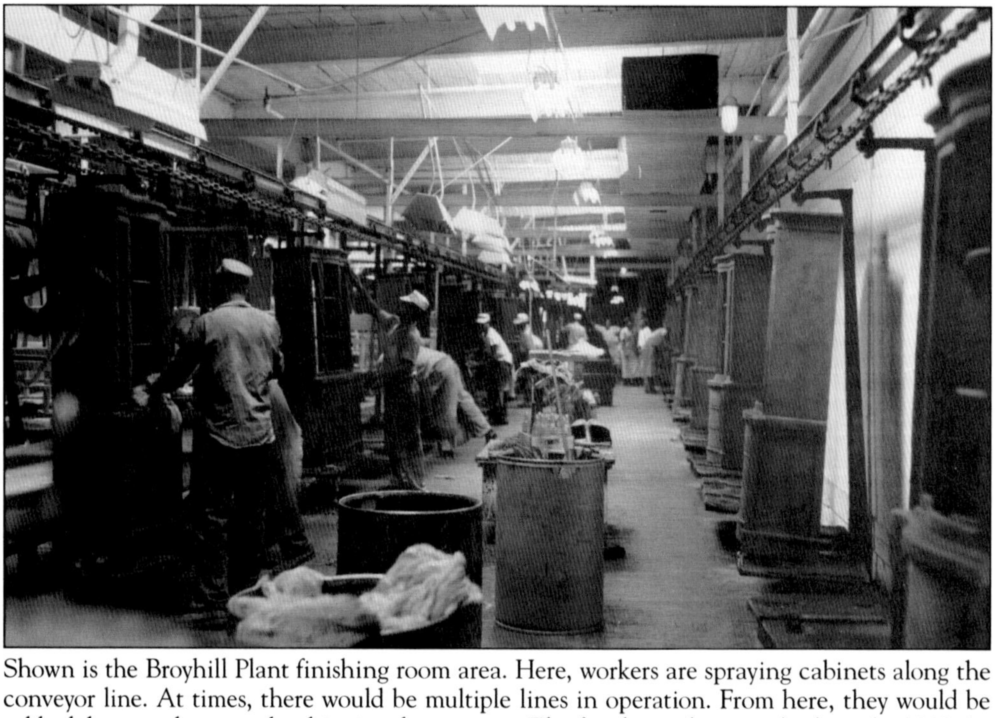

Shown is the Broyhill Plant finishing room area. Here, workers are spraying cabinets along the conveyor line. At times, there would be multiple lines in operation. From here, they would be rubbed down and sent to the shipping department. The finishing plant was built in the 1940s by the Herman-Sipe Company. Harvey Brady was in charge of the shipping department.

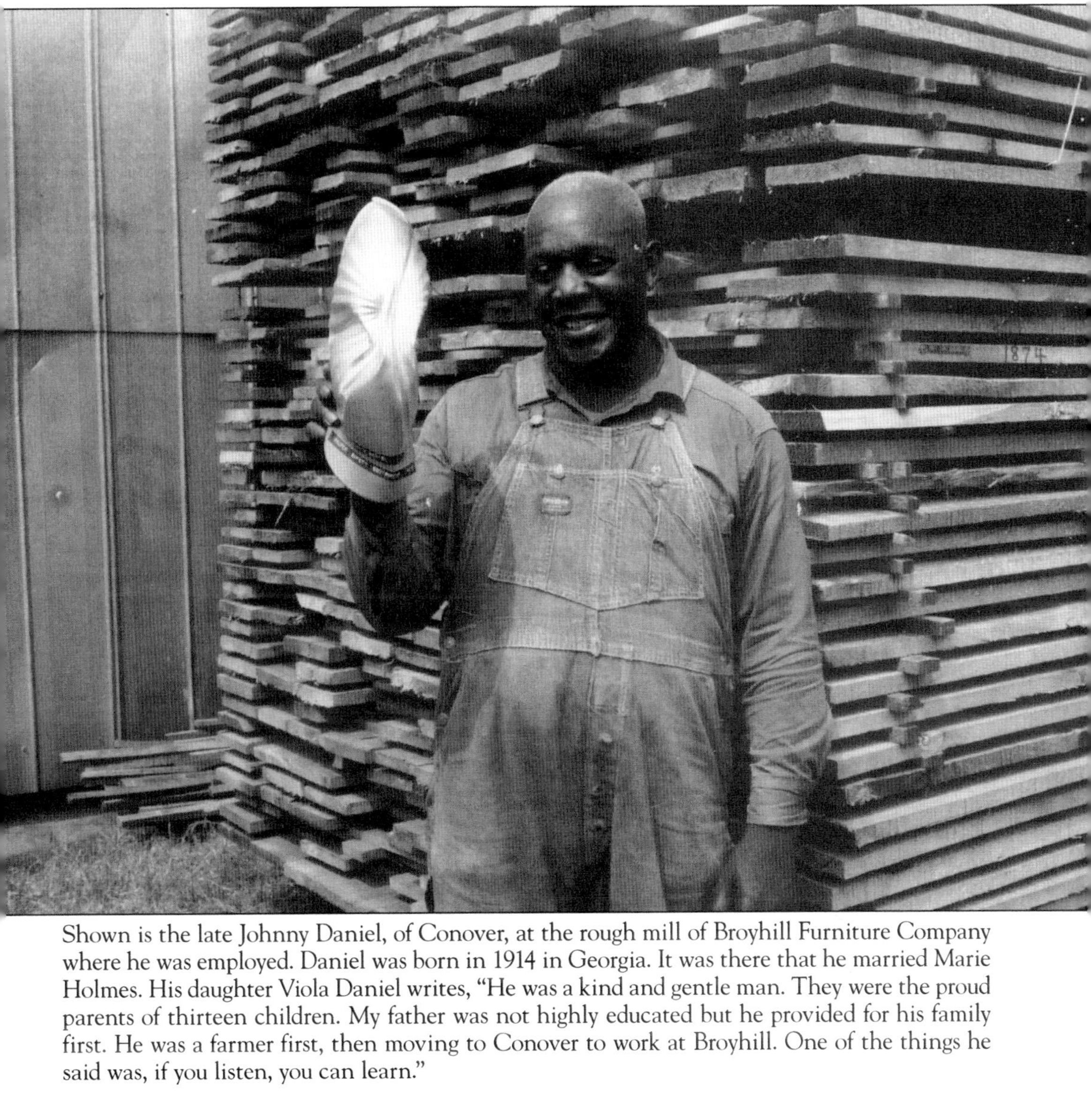

Shown is the late Johnny Daniel, of Conover, at the rough mill of Broyhill Furniture Company where he was employed. Daniel was born in 1914 in Georgia. It was there that he married Marie Holmes. His daughter Viola Daniel writes, "He was a kind and gentle man. They were the proud parents of thirteen children. My father was not highly educated but he provided for his family first. He was a farmer first, then moving to Conover to work at Broyhill. One of the things he said was, if you listen, you can learn."

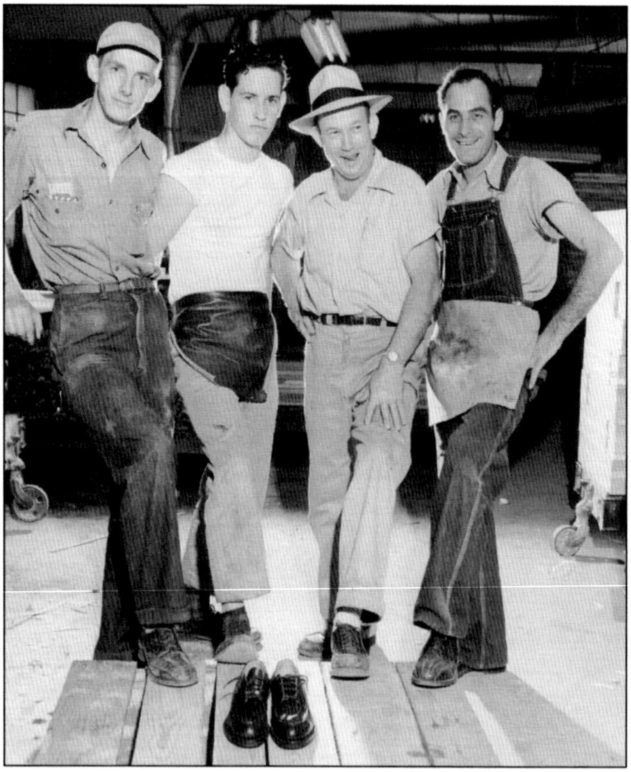

Employees at Broyhill look forward to wearing the new safety shoes. Pictured from left to right are William Arndt, Billy Powell, president of the Broyhill Furniture Corporation James Broyhill, and Ed Gibbs.

Shown here are members of a 1970s girls' softball team at the Conover Broyhill plant. From left to right are (first row) Mary Anton, Patsy Lail, Helene Forley, Kathy Baldwin, Jeannie Johnson, and Raynelle Miller; (second row) Cathy Smith, Kathy Misenheimer, Sandra Hedrick, Joannie Rippey, Betty Smith, and Margaret Setzer. Also on the team, but not pictured, is Daphne Lawence.

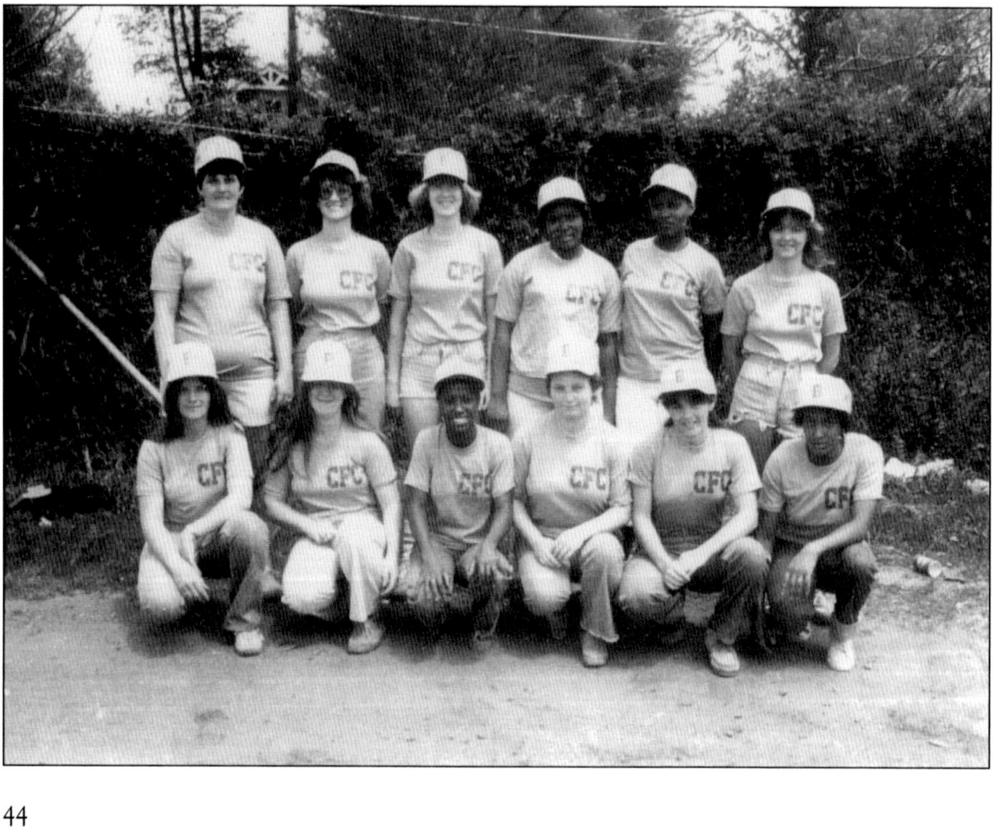

Three

NEWTON NEIGHBORS

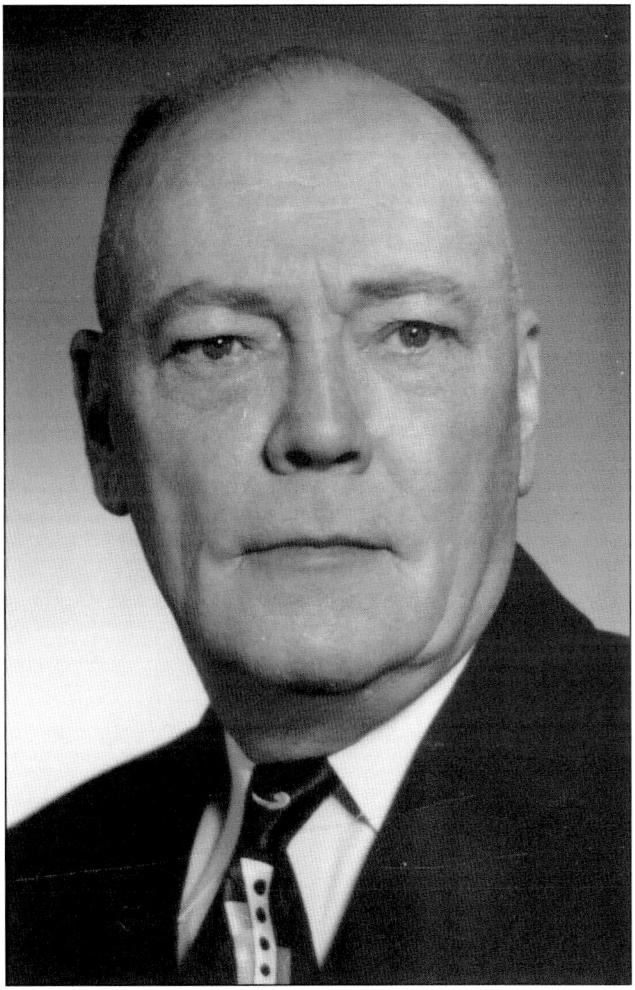

The names of Warlick, Morrison, Williams, McCorkle, and Mebane are synonymous with the newspaper publishing history of Newton. The first published paper in Newton was the *News Enterprise*. George Warlick was its publisher. In 1926, Charles Harden Mebane Jr. (pictured) became owner and editor of the second paper, the *Catawba County News*. With a consolidation with the third paper, the *Newton Observer*, the name was changed to the *Catawba News Enterprise*, making it the forth newspaper in the town. In 1948, Cyril Long Mebane joined the firm with his father, Charles H. Mebane Jr. With a final consolidation in 1954, the owners retained the names of the previous newspapers and named their new tabloid the *Observer News Enterprise*.

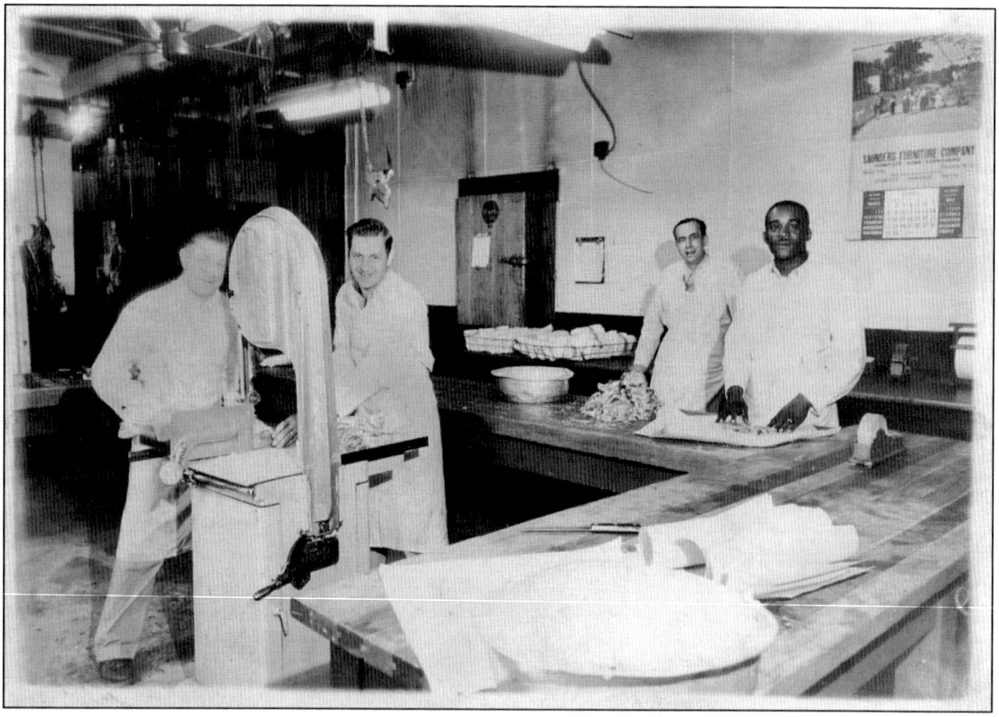

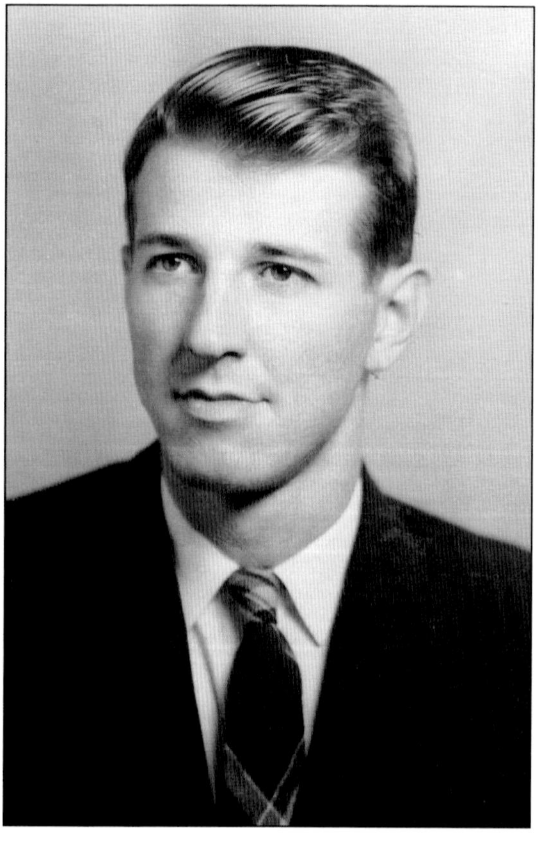

The Gaither Cold Storage business was established just off the square in Newton around 1945. This business would prepare and store customers' meats in numbered turnkey lockers in freezer storage for pickup at any time. Pictured from left to right are Guy Mauney, Paul Moose, Howard Kaylor, and Earnest Squarles.

Shown is the late Jesse Sigmon Jr., a popular Newton attorney. He was the son of the late Jesse Caleb Sigmon and Annie Killian Sigmon. He was a graduate of Lenoir Rhyne College and the University of North Carolina School of Law. He served as judge for the Catawba County Recorder's Court and as the attorney for the City of Newton and the Newton-Conover School Board. He was married to Nita Richie Sigmon. His daughters were Sharon, Rebekah, and Miriam. He and his family were lifelong members of Beth Eden Lutheran Church.

Well known and liked was this friendly Newtonian Ralph Jefferson Jones. He was married to Willie DeLorous Poole. Together, they had daughters Monteen and Patricia. He was staff manager with the Durham Life Insurance Company and retired after 35 years of service. As a lifelong member of the First Methodist Church, he held many offices within the congregation, including the advisory council and mission boards. He was a member of Lions International for over 50 years and received the Melvin Jones Fellowship Award. He was a charter member of the Newton Elks and member of the Catawba Valley Executive Club.

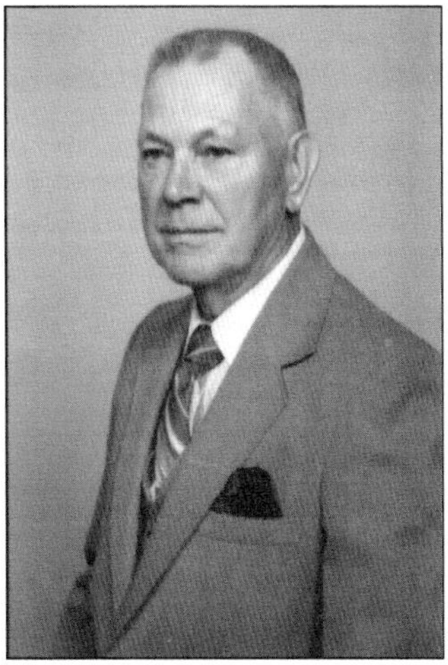

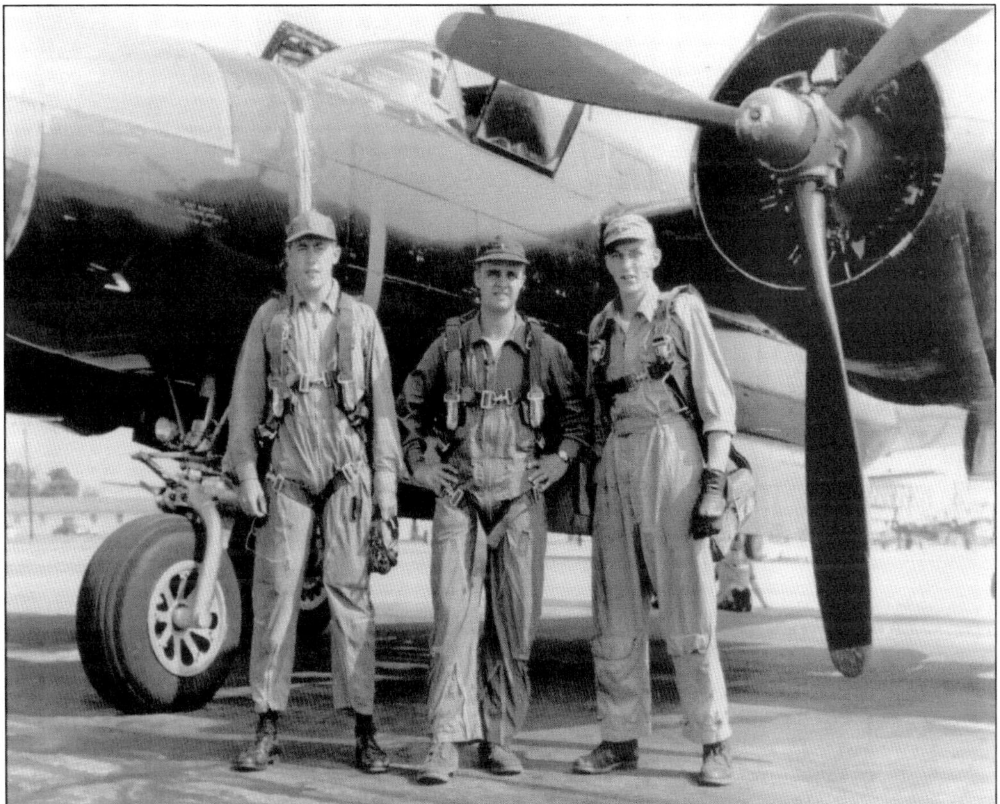

Jack Gantt was valedictorian upon graduating from Newton-Conover High School and joined the US Air Force Aviation Cadet Program. Gantt was commissioned as a first lieutenant. In this 1953 photograph is the crew with their new B-26 bomber at Shaw Air Force Base, South Carolina. Pictured from left to right are pilot John Buckley, of Newport News, Virginia; Gantt, navigator; and copilot Jim Jung, of York, Nebraska. This crew would be deployed to the Korean conflict in 1954. Jung would be killed in a test-flight crash in the late 1960s. Gantt later had duties with the national missile defense program. He would retire after some 30 years with the rank of major. He and his wife, Pat, reside in Newton.

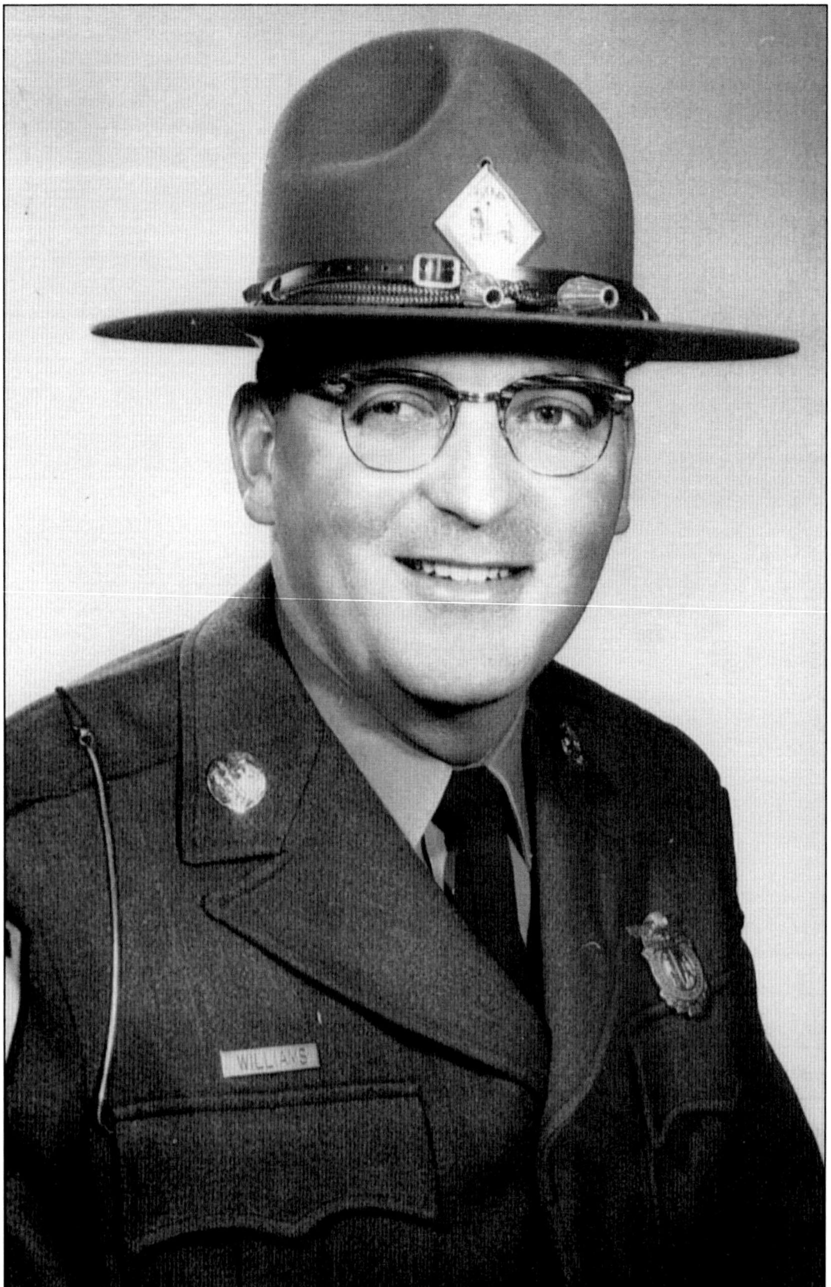

Pictured is Sgt. Harry Williams, of Newton, a veteran of the North Carolina State Highway Patrol. He was likely the most preferred among the other patrol officers. He always demonstrated the true ability of a "trooper." He was friendly, fair, and just. Williams and Jack Bass were the most influential persons in getting the placement of the totally new troop headquarters on the Smyre Farm Road south of Newton. The land became available from the Charles "Bud" Lofland family estate. Most of his service was in Catawba County. Having survived a nearly fatal wreck in 1959, he continued his duties with the patrol until his retirement. He and his wife, Sara, reside just south of Newton. Among the remaining youngsters of the 1950s, he is recognized as "the old guard."

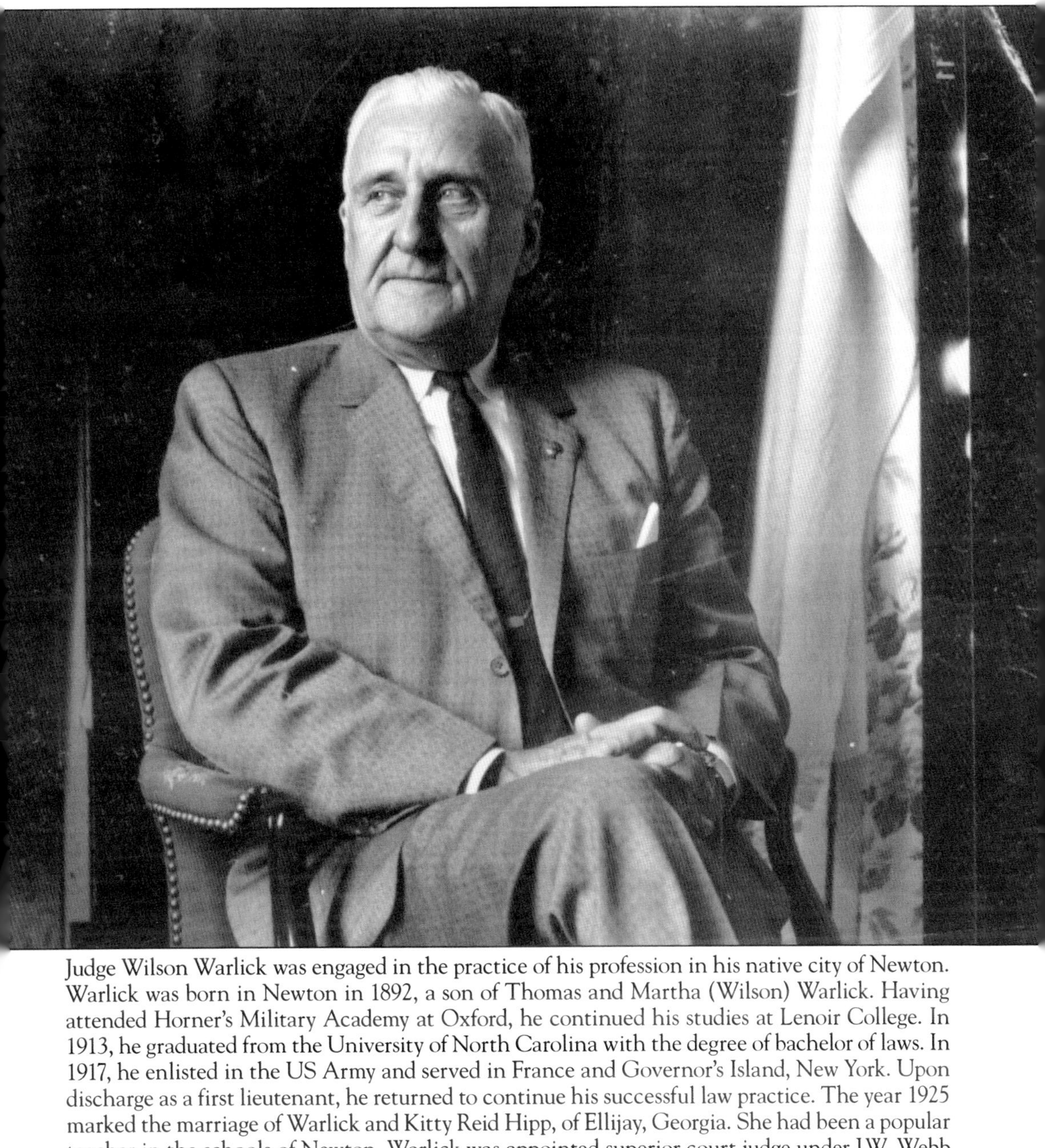

Judge Wilson Warlick was engaged in the practice of his profession in his native city of Newton. Warlick was born in Newton in 1892, a son of Thomas and Martha (Wilson) Warlick. Having attended Horner's Military Academy at Oxford, he continued his studies at Lenoir College. In 1913, he graduated from the University of North Carolina with the degree of bachelor of laws. In 1917, he enlisted in the US Army and served in France and Governor's Island, New York. Upon discharge as a first lieutenant, he returned to continue his successful law practice. The year 1925 marked the marriage of Warlick and Kitty Reid Hipp, of Ellijay, Georgia. She had been a popular teacher in the schools of Newton. Warlick was appointed superior court judge under J.W. Webb in the 1940s. Senator Hoey recommended Warlick to President Truman, and Warlick ultimately went to the federal bench, declining many offers at the capital level in Raleigh. A man of superior qualification and character, Warlick was praised by US senator Sam Ervin for his great knowledge of the law and his understanding heart. Former Newton mayor Loyd Mullinax stated that Warlick played a tremendous part in the growth and development of Catawba County. His son Thomas continues to practice law in downtown Newton.

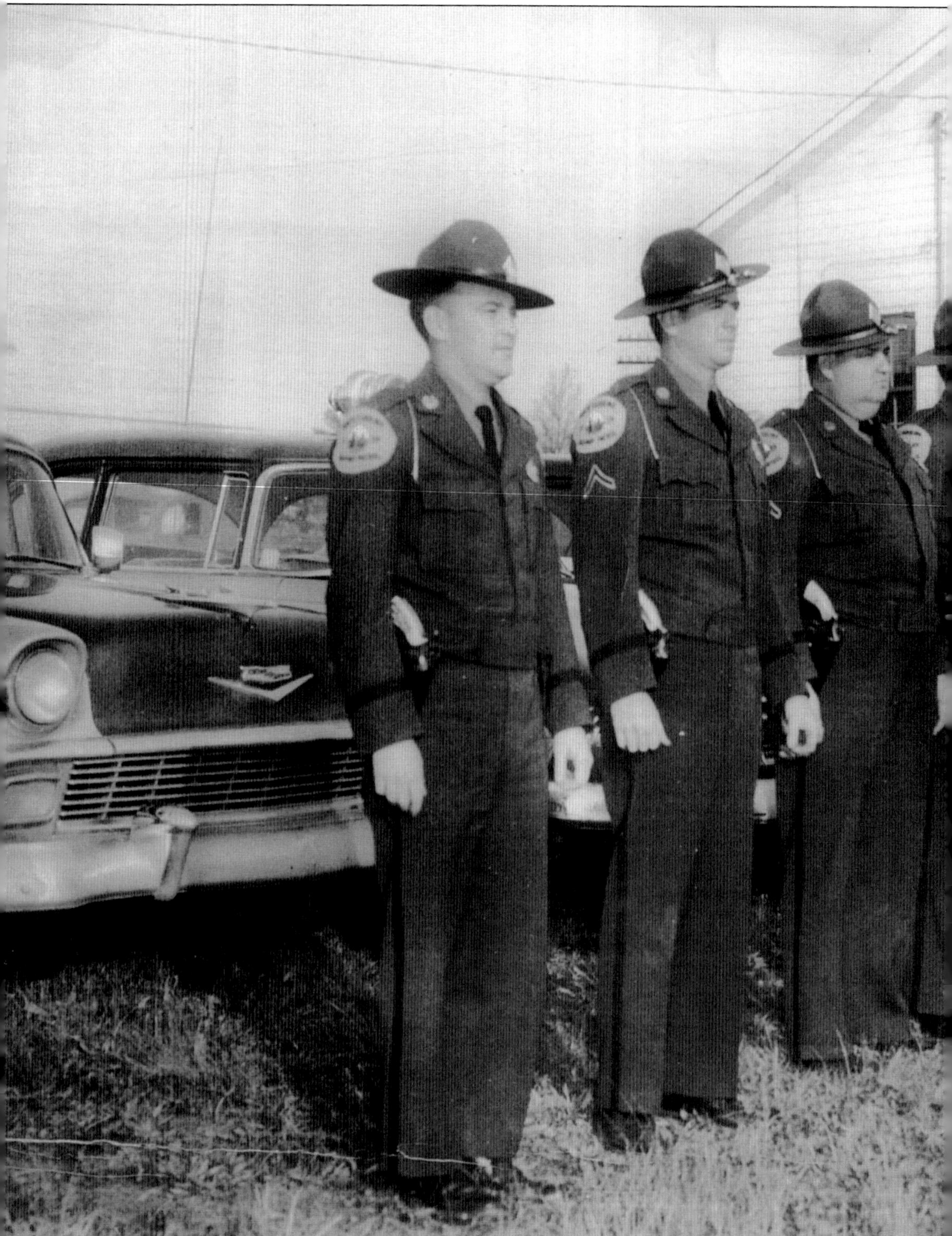

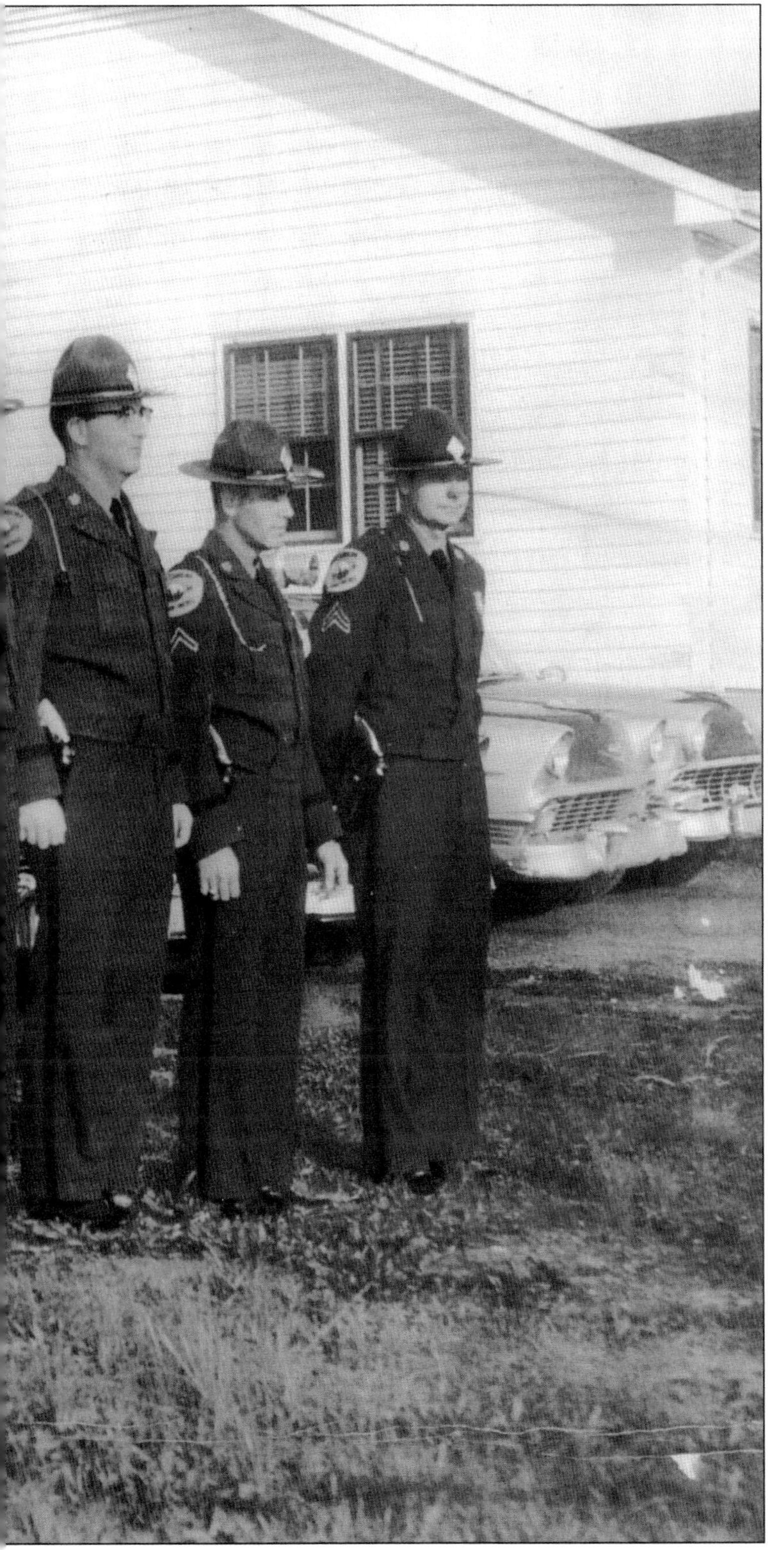

Shown are the 1956 North Carolina Highway Patrol troopers assigned to District Five, Catawba County, Troop F. This photograph was taken at the old wooden headquarters building across from the Hickory Motor Speedway. Pictured from left to right are Pfc. Bill Lundy, Pfc. Harry Hooper, Pfc. Matthew Simmons, Pfc. David Searcy, Pfc. Harry Williams, Pfc. Myron Lyerly, and Cpl. Hughes Hunt. Other troopers who served in Catawba County were Capt. Earl Greene, Sgt. Bonnie Walker, Pfc. Bruce Griffith, Sgt. John Brinkley, Sgt. Malcolm Ivey, Pfc. Robert Pope, Pfc. Ralph Ray, Pfc. K.E. Carroll, Pfc. M.E. Plummer, Pfc. J.L. Griffin, Pfc. Joe Rhoades, Pfc. Joe Bracy, Pfc. W.R. Beaver, Pfc. Dewey Butler, Pfc. A.L. Wright, Pfc. C. Bolick, and Sgt. Raymond Hansman.

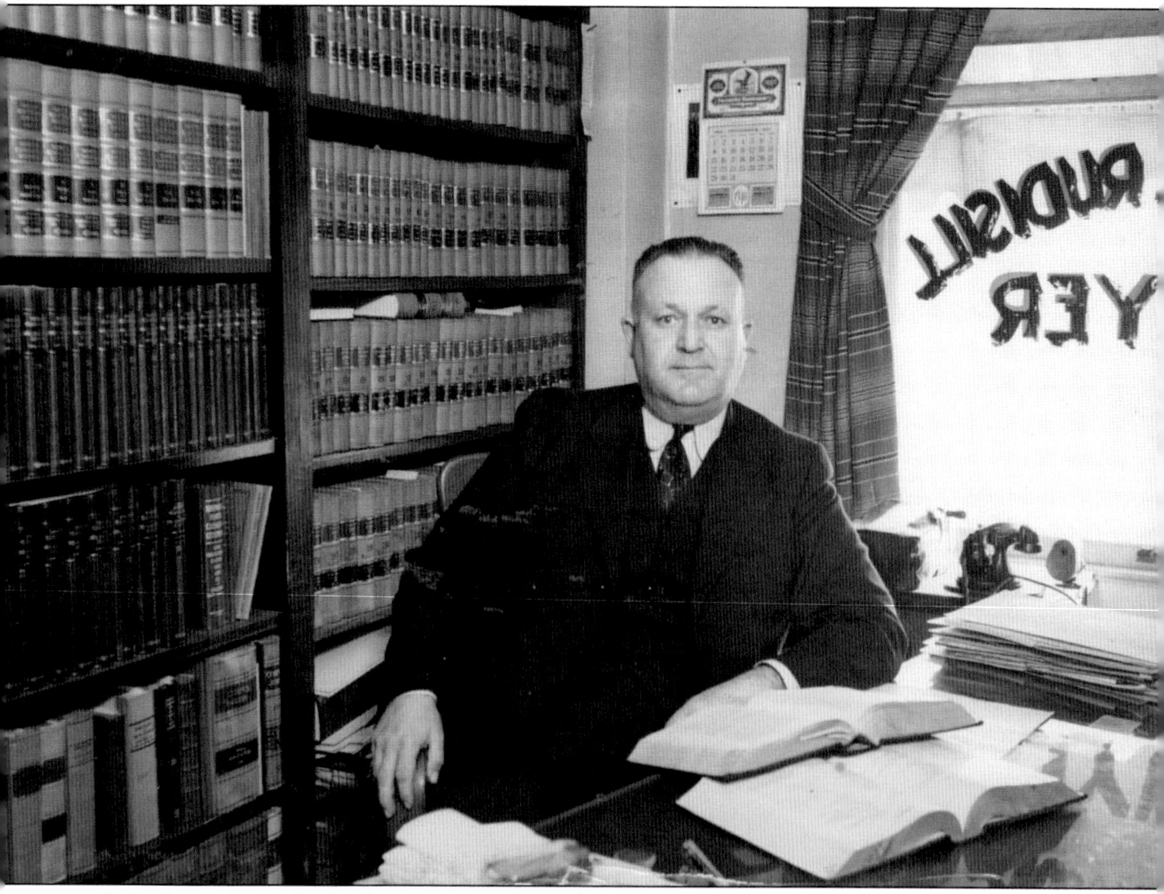

Judge Justus Coyte Rudisill was trustworthy and loyal to the cause. He was born in Maiden, North Carolina, in 1894 to Robert A. Rudisill and Julia Withers Rudisill. He was married to Olanthe Mill Rudisill and had sons J.C. Jr. and William Miller Rudisill. He was a graduate of Lenoir Rhyne College in 1916 and served in the US Army in World War I. After the war, he attended Wake Forest College and passed the state bar to practice law. He was the county attorney from 1926 to 1930. Governor Broughton appointed Rudisill in 1944 as a special superior court judge. He received appointment from Gov. Kerr Scott in 1949 as superior court judge. Rudisill would fill the vacancy of Judge Wilson Warlick, who stepped down to be a federal judge. He was elected superior court judge in 1950 for the 16th Judicial District. He served as secretary for Congressman A.L. Bulwinkle for one year. Rudisill said, "He wanted to be where you can be trusted and know your enemies." He retired in 1957. He was a member of Beth Eden Lutheran Church and served as superintendent of the Sunday school.

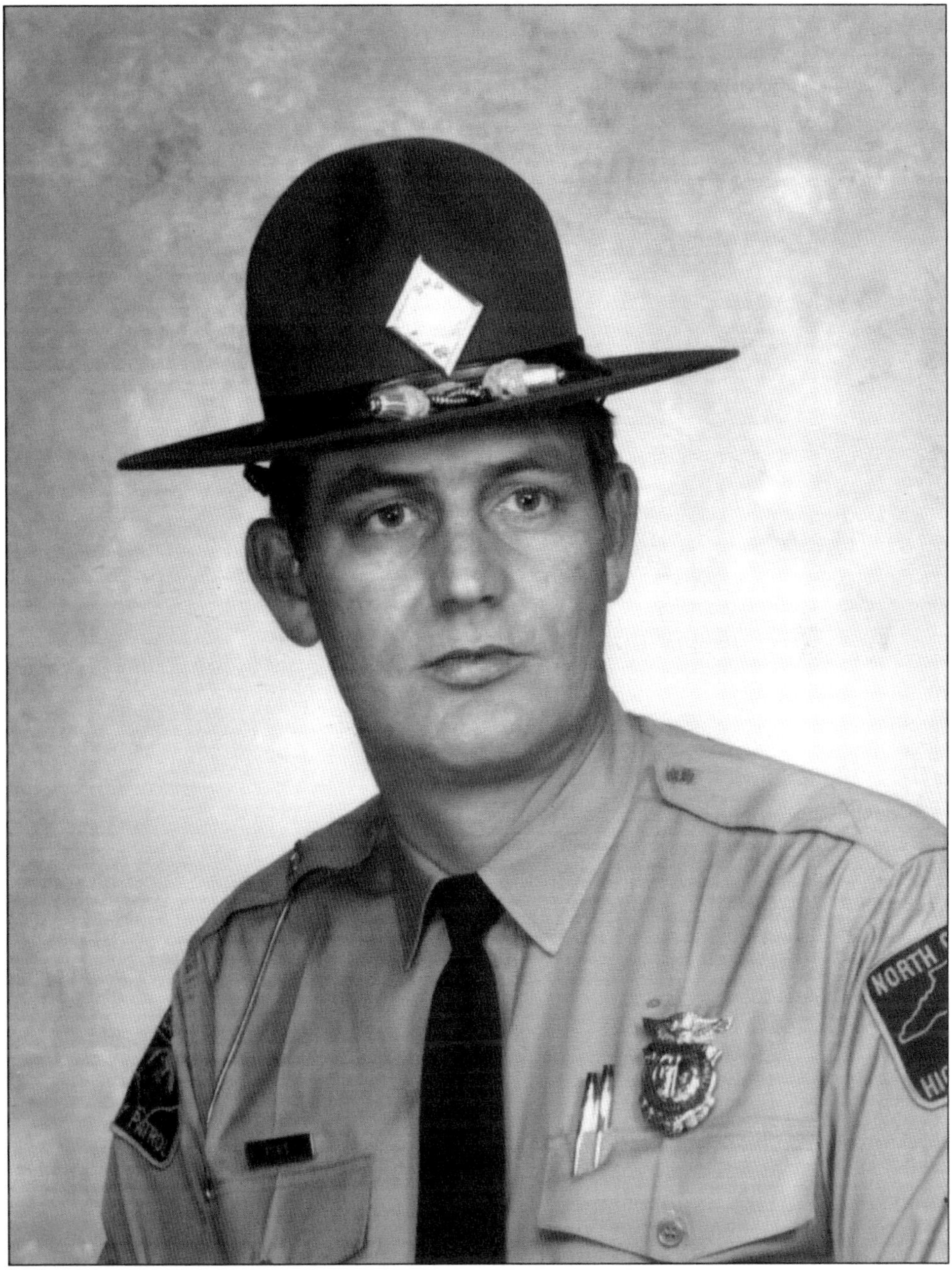

Shown is Robert G. Pope. This young officer of the North Carolina State Patrol came to Catawba County from Dunn, North Carolina. He attended North Carolina State University for one year, and in 1959, joined the US Army, serving with the 82nd and 101st Airborne Divisions, stationed in Germany during the Cold War. He joined the ranks of the Highway Patrol in 1959 and was stationed in Catawba County with Troop F. His assignment here would make him the youngest trooper in the county. In 1961, he married Mickie Janice Rockett. They were parents of two sons. Known to all as Bob, he retired from the patrol in 1984, after 25 years of duty. He then joined Western Steer Restaurants in 1986 in the quality control division and retired in 1998. He and his wife reside in Hickory.

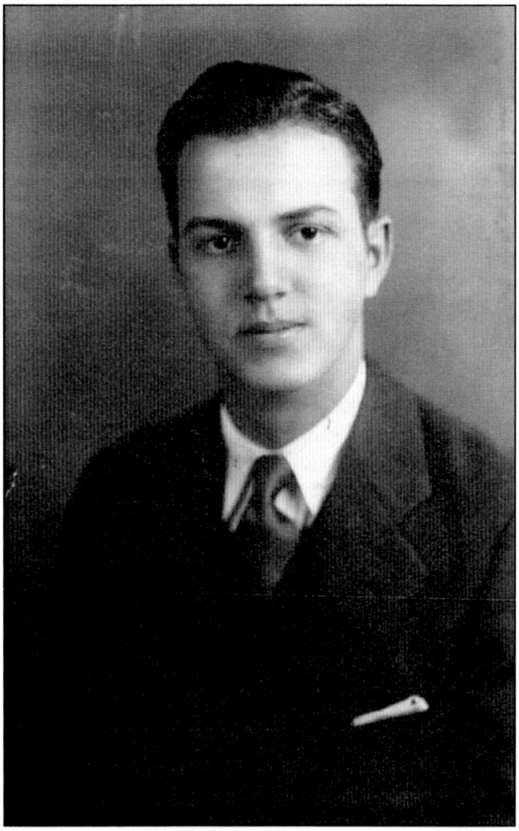

A most popular Newton dentist was Dr. Marshall. R. Barringer. He was the son of James and Jennie (Miller) Barringer. His office was above the H&W Drugstore. He was married to Mildred Phillips and had sons Robert and Donald. Dr. Barringer was a lifelong resident of Newton. Both he and his wife are deceased. They were members of Holy Cross Lutheran Church.

A friend to every student at the high school was the likeable custodian—and quite the harmonica player—Guy Sherrill. Pictured on lunch break are, from left to right Guy Sherrill, Sam Salmon, Billy Ray Kelly, Harley Bowman, and Bill Hester. Sherrill and his wife had 22 children.

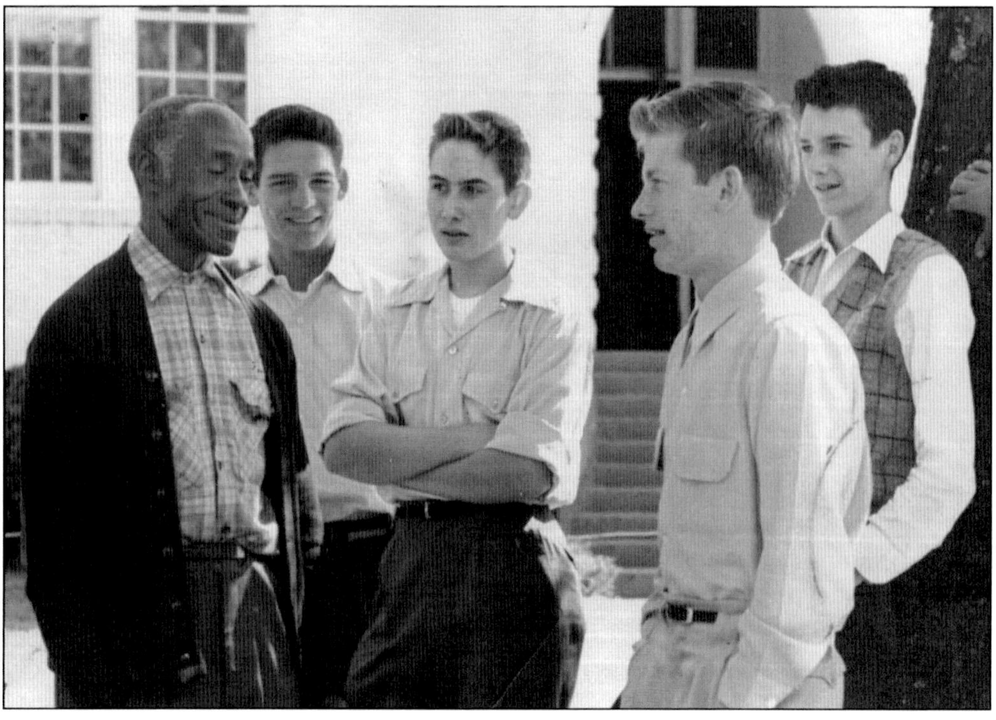

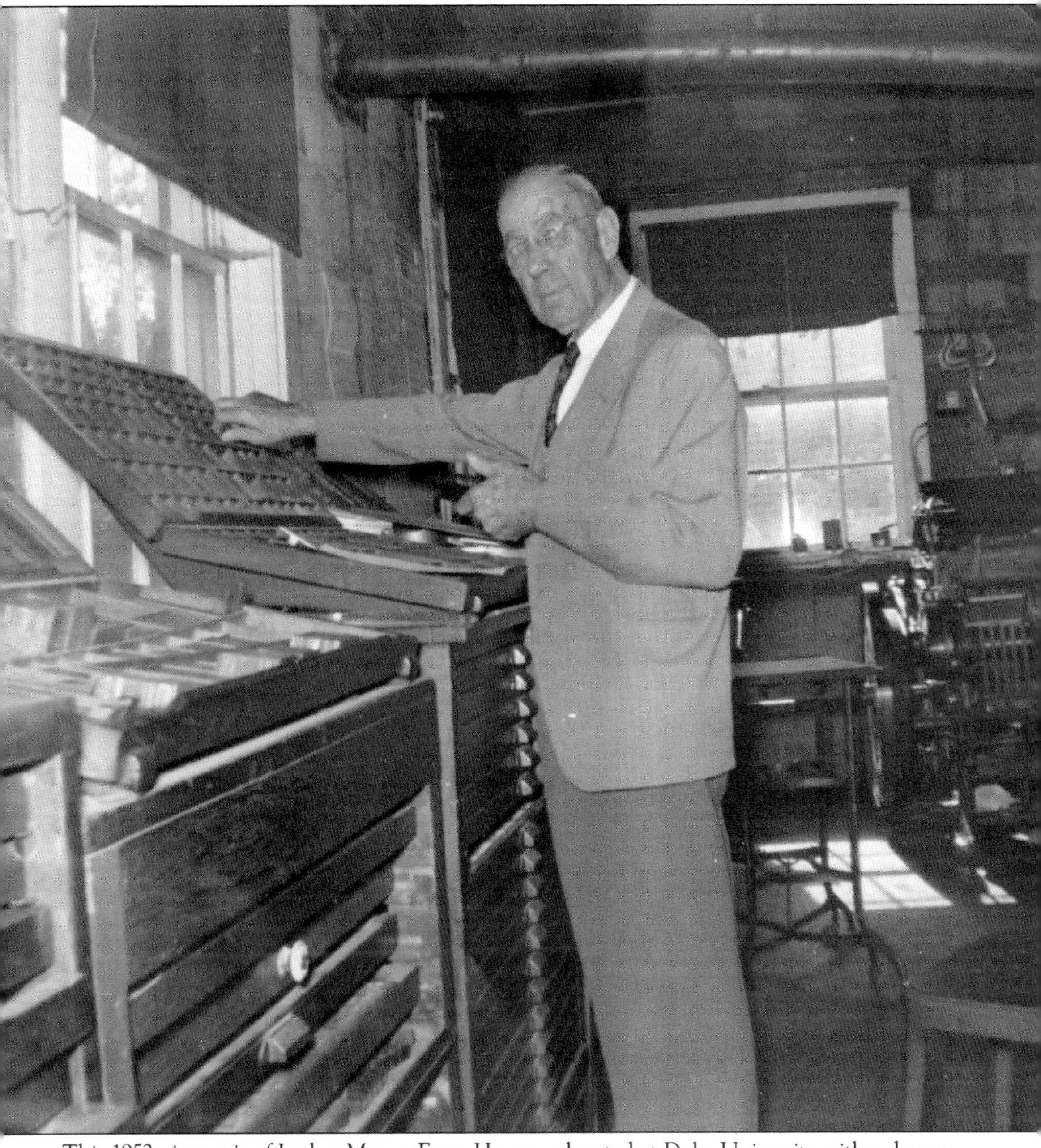

This 1952 picture is of Luther Macon Epps. He was educated at Duke University with a degree in education. He was the founder of Epps Printing Company in 1923. Epps also held positions as magistrate and superintendent of schools. He had five children: sons Macon, Charles, and Joe and daughters Lucille and Ruth. His son Joe now operates the company in Newton.

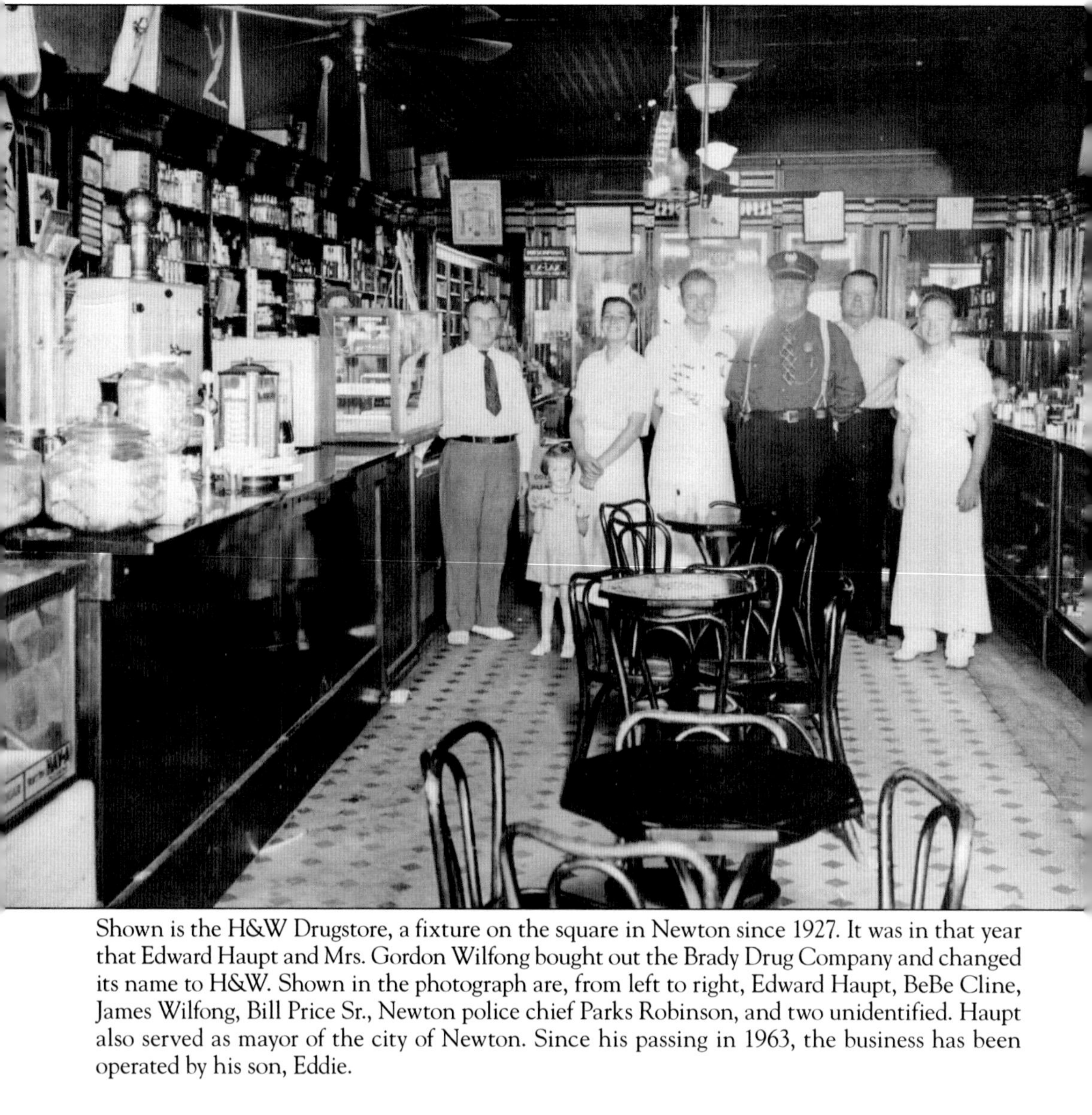

Shown is the H&W Drugstore, a fixture on the square in Newton since 1927. It was in that year that Edward Haupt and Mrs. Gordon Wilfong bought out the Brady Drug Company and changed its name to H&W. Shown in the photograph are, from left to right, Edward Haupt, BeBe Cline, James Wilfong, Bill Price Sr., Newton police chief Parks Robinson, and two unidentified. Haupt also served as mayor of the city of Newton. Since his passing in 1963, the business has been operated by his son, Eddie.

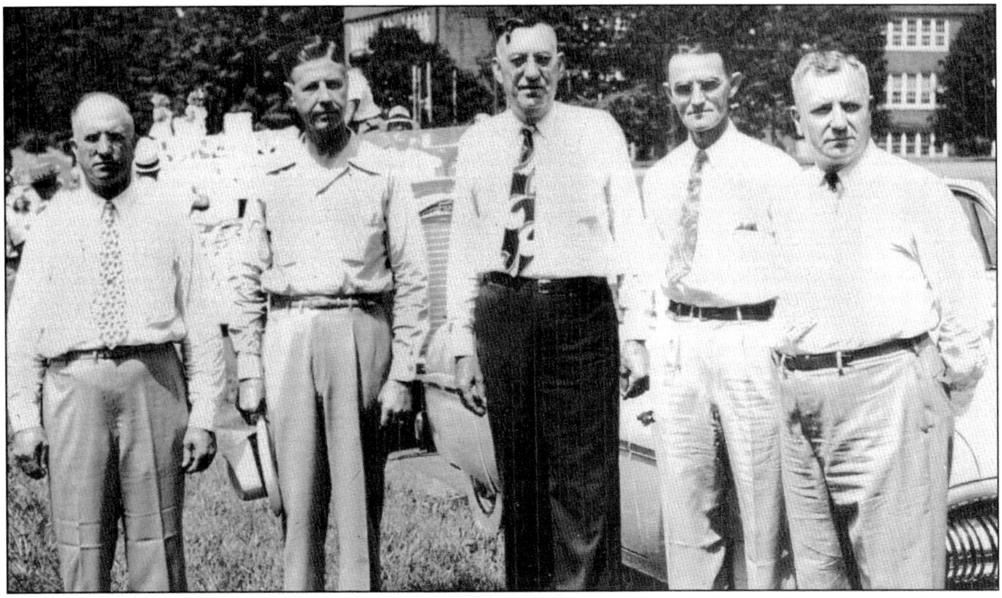

This is a photograph of the 1940 Newton Town Board. Shown from left to right are Ray Wilkerson, Lock Lorance, John Caldwell, Henry Gantt, and Mayor Edward Haupt. Absent are E.B. Clapp and D.M. Cloninger. Gantt had a combined service of 29 years with the City of Newton. He ran the ever-popular Gantt's Store, a little wooden grocery store on Caldwell Avenue. This was a well accepted hangout for grownups and children alike on the block. Gantt and his wife, Lill, had children Betty, Jack, and Nancy.

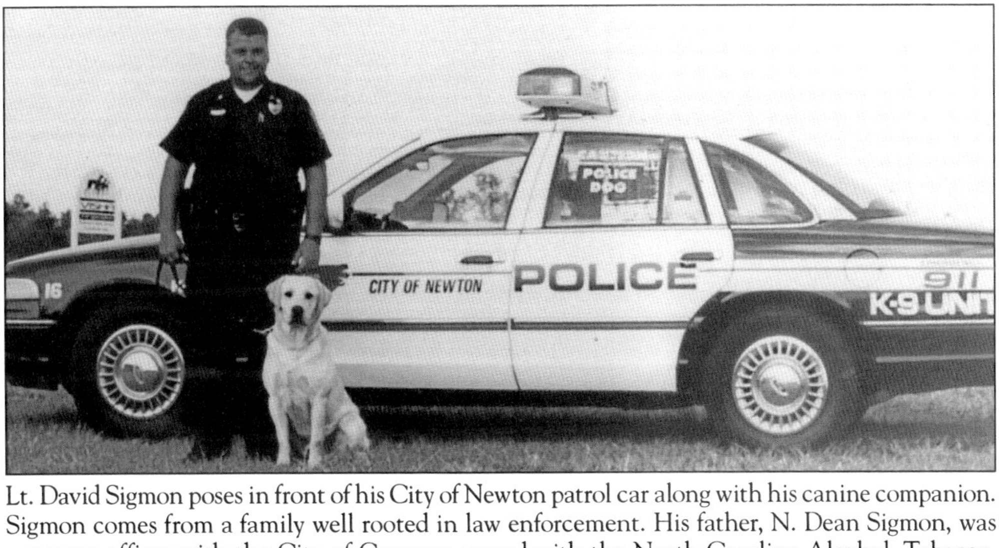

Lt. David Sigmon poses in front of his City of Newton patrol car along with his canine companion. Sigmon comes from a family well rooted in law enforcement. His father, N. Dean Sigmon, was a reserve officer with the City of Conover, served with the North Carolina Alcohol, Tobacco, and Firearms Division, the North Carolina State Highway Department of Motor Vehicles Enforcement Division, and received the Order of the Long Leaf Pine for his years of service. His uncle Eddie Ray Sigmon, now of Cary, was a former Catawba County deputy sheriff. He was in the US Marshal Service as the chief of the Southeastern District. His grandfather Harlan Sigmon served over 40 years with the City of Conover as the director of public works, with only one dump truck, a single road grader, and two helpers. He was also the chief of police for the city of Conover for 23 years.

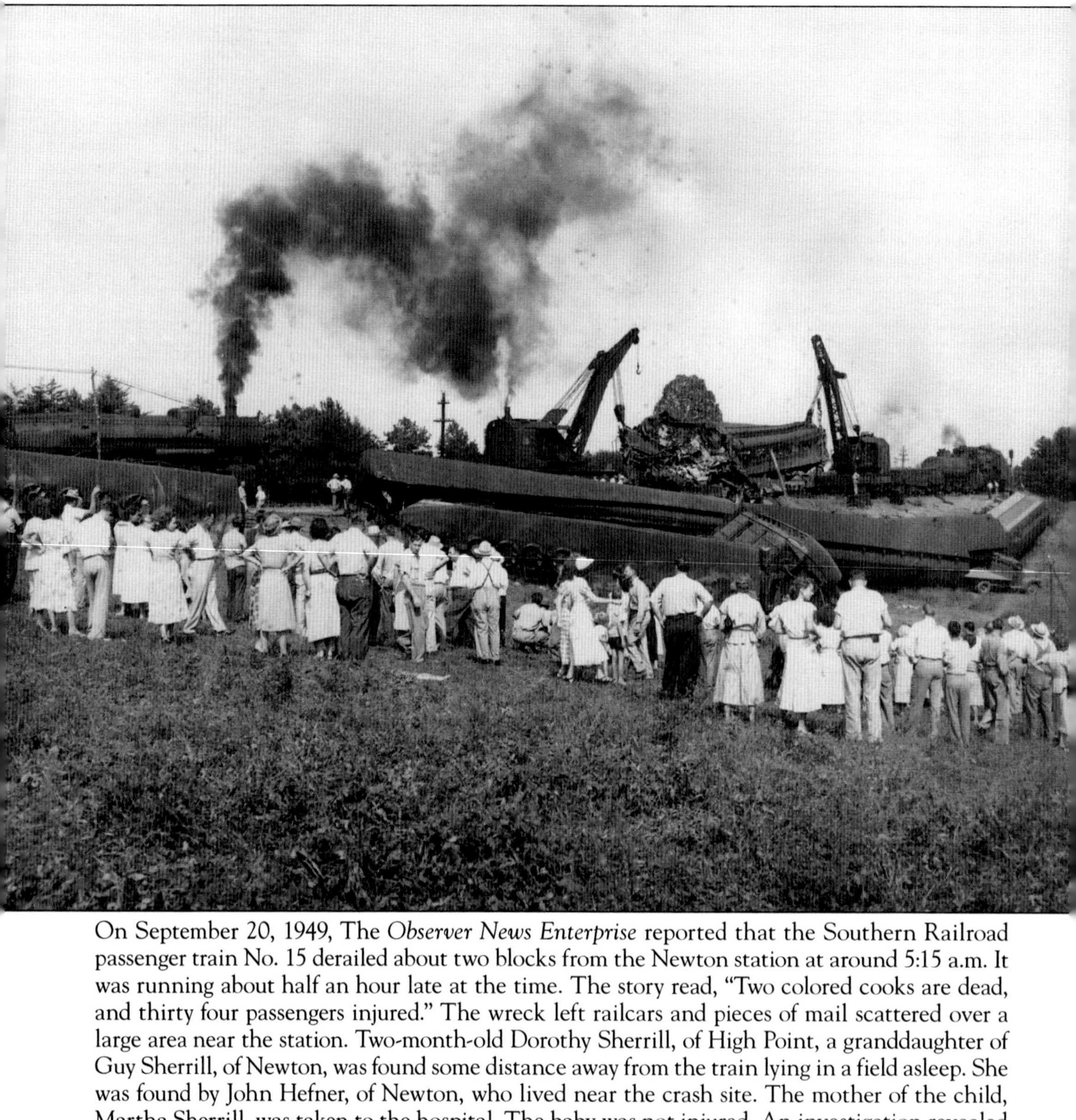

On September 20, 1949, The *Observer News Enterprise* reported that the Southern Railroad passenger train No. 15 derailed about two blocks from the Newton station at around 5:15 a.m. It was running about half an hour late at the time. The story read, "Two colored cooks are dead, and thirty four passengers injured." The wreck left railcars and pieces of mail scattered over a large area near the station. Two-month-old Dorothy Sherrill, of High Point, a granddaughter of Guy Sherrill, of Newton, was found some distance away from the train lying in a field asleep. She was found by John Hefner, of Newton, who lived near the crash site. The mother of the child, Martha Sherrill, was taken to the hospital. The baby was not injured. An investigation revealed that the train engineer was speeding at the time the train left the tracks.

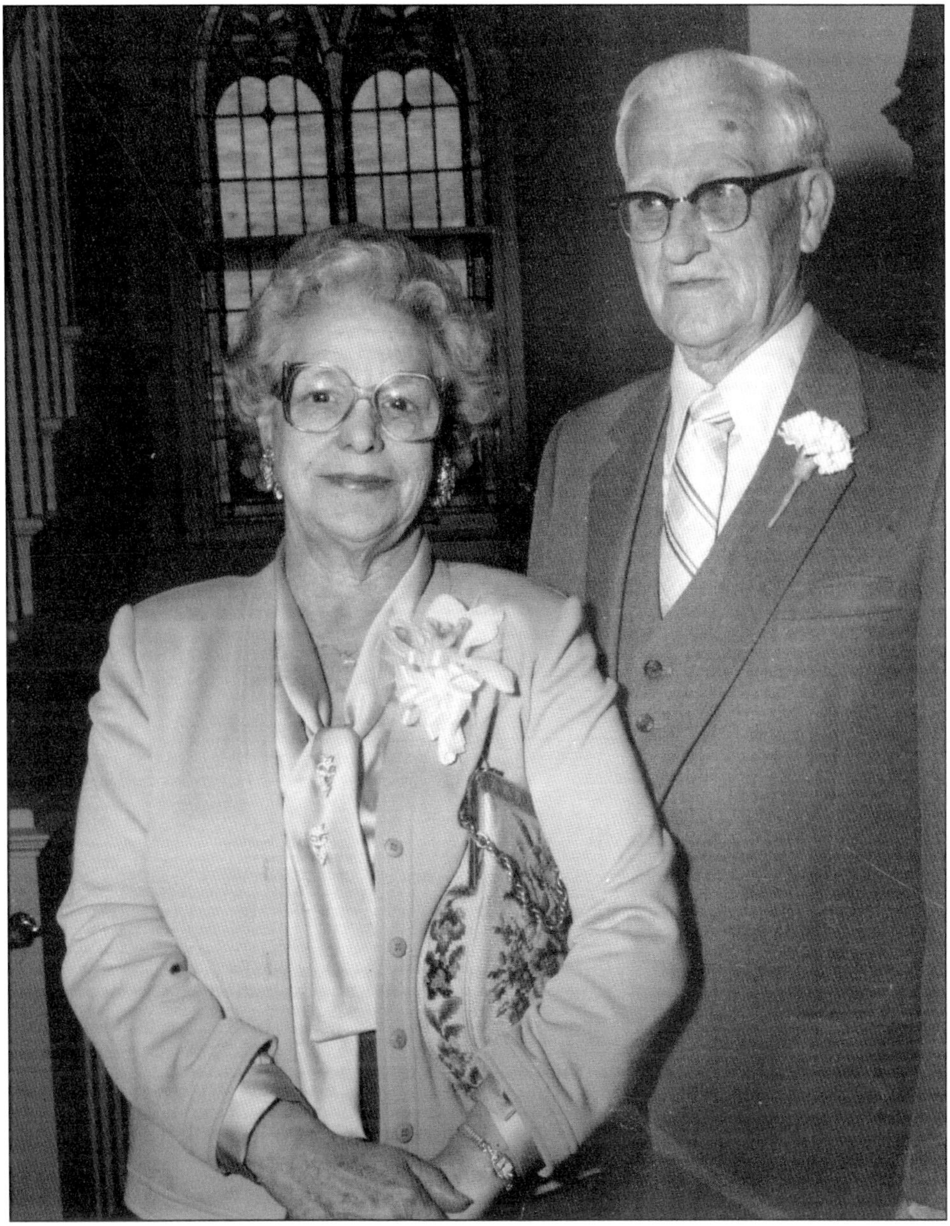

Need a toy for Christmas? Need a float for the Christmas or reunion parades? Many youngsters would visit their favorite five-and-dime store uptown to put that special toy on layaway and to view the trains on display. The person to see would be Robert Joezell and "Kat" Cline. Seems Joe and Catherine Cline just never grew up, always wanting to entertain the children and the public. And they did it very well. Newton-Conover folks needed good, attractive, built-to-travel parade floats. Through the years 1945–1980, Joezell, Catherine, and son Charles supplied this need through their company Cline's Floats. With parades in Johnson City, Asheville, Charlotte, Statesville, and many other cities, the floats would be built locally and hauled to their destination by drivers on time for the parade. Some of the drivers were Lewis Hollar, Bob Rockett, Charles Cline, and many others. Without the Clines and their drivers, Christmas would just not be the same. Both now deceased, the Clines were lifelong members of Calvary Baptist Church.

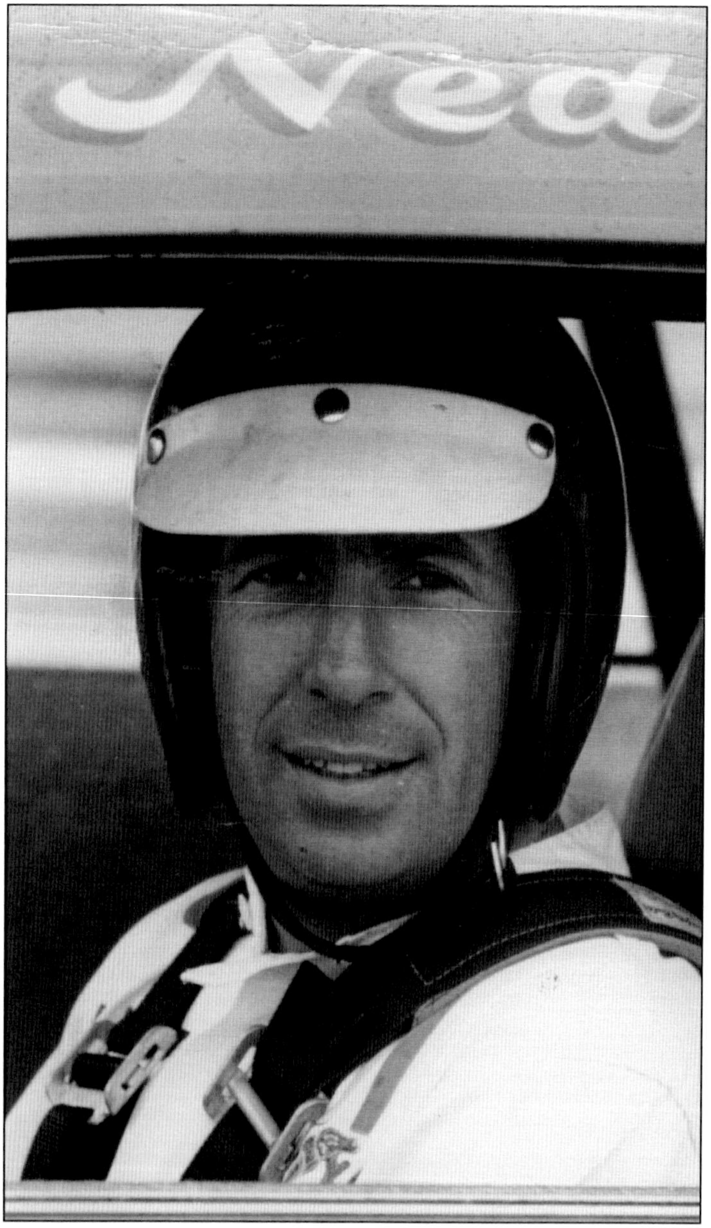

Ned Jarrett is a retired racecar driver and two-time NASCAR champion. He became known as "Gentleman Ned." An intense competitor, he is featured in national and international halls of fame. He was voted into the NASCAR Hall of Fame in Charlotte on the second ballot in May 2011. Jarrett was introduced to cars early in life. His father let him drive the family car to church on Sunday when he was nine years old. He helped at his father's sawmill at the young age of 12, but racing was always on his mind. His personal character was demonstrated when he made the decision to sell his 1961 Chevrolet to Wendall Scott, the first African American NASCAR driver who did indeed come to Newton to get the car. It was then that Ned changed to Fords. John Carl Ervin would later become crew chief for Ned and the number-11 Fords. Other members of his family are also related to the racing industry. Sons Dale and Glenn and daughter Patti also worked in racing. Ned and his wife reside in Newton.

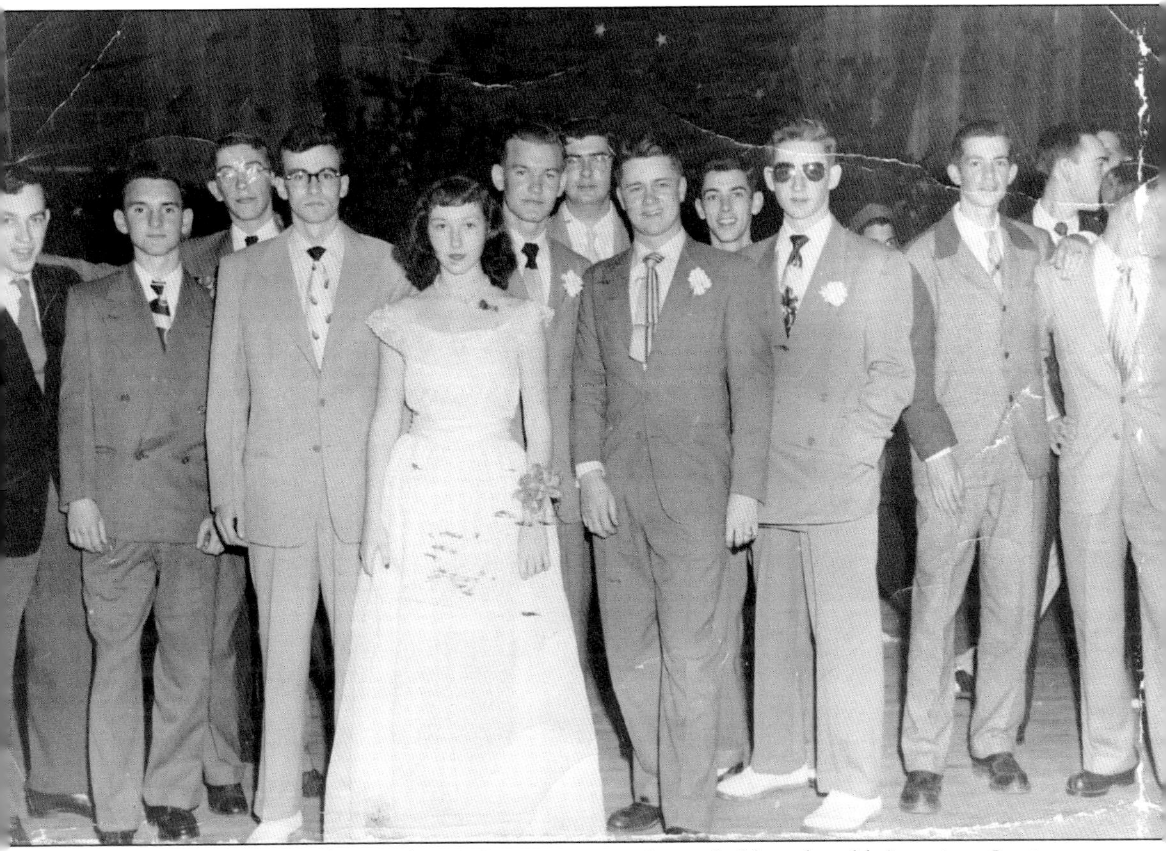

This photograph was taken at the 1949 junior-senior dance held at the old American Legion building. Pictured are, from left to right, Clyde Fisher, Louis Evans, William Smith, Joe Furr, Mabel Ann Pendleton, Ernest Sigman, Lewis Dale Hunsucker, "Sparkie" McSwain, Dwight Dellinger, Bobby Abernathy, Bill Zimptbaum, and Wayne Wilkinson. When the new gymnasium was built at the new high school, students would decorate the place with crepe paper and streamers.

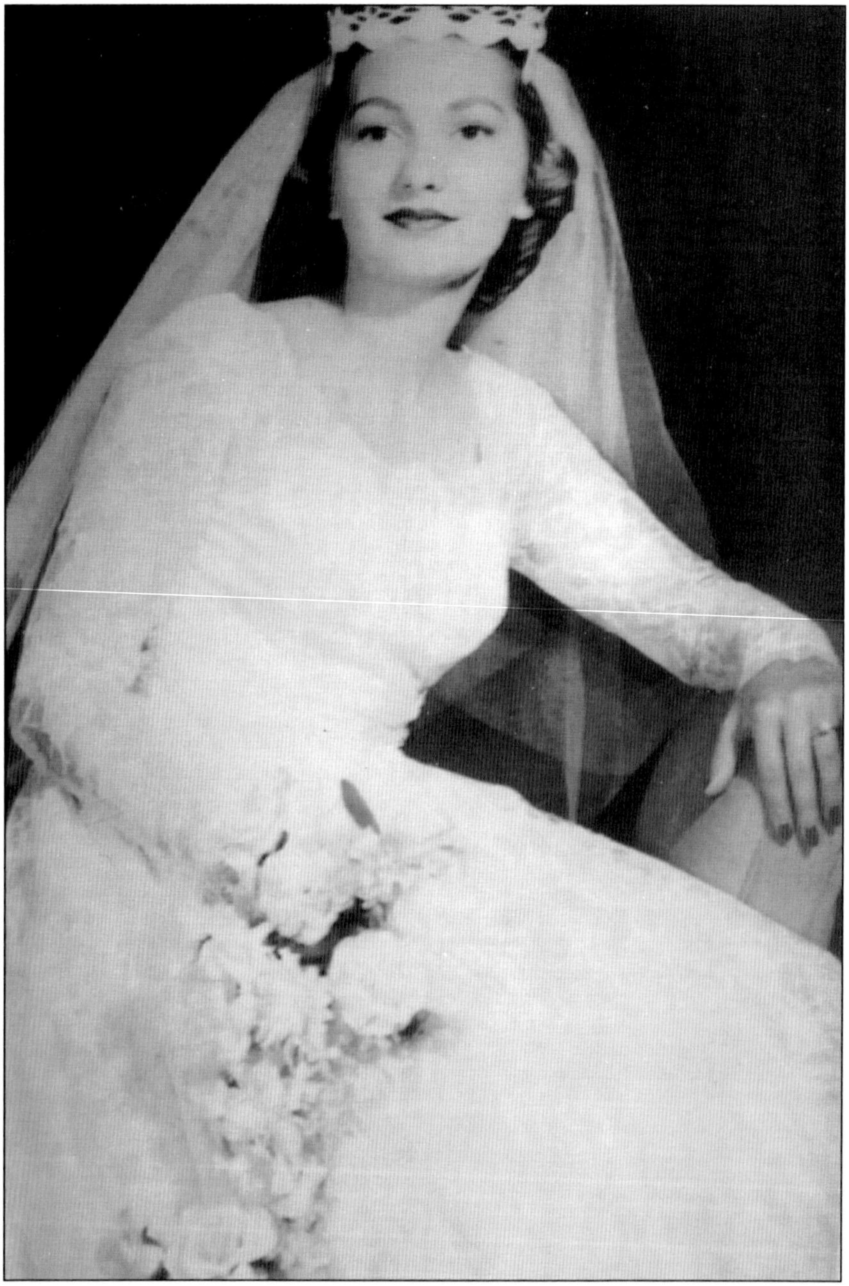

Pictured is Jane Coley Sigmon, of Newton. She was a graduate of Newton-Conover High School, and attended Catawba College and the University of Richmond and graduated from Lenoir Rhyne College. Jane was a most gifted teacher whose career spanned 35 years, having taught in High Point and Charlotte city schools, and culminating at Newton, Central, and Thornton Elementary Schools. She was known for her kindness and compassion to others. She had an innate ability to see the world through a child's eyes and was known for her unbounded sense of wonder. She was also a cheerleader at Newton Conover High School. She was a teacher of dance, a very gifted dancer, and loved the big band sounds. At the school dances, she was the desire of many young boys awaiting their time to take a turn on the floor with her.

Four

Our Town and Our People

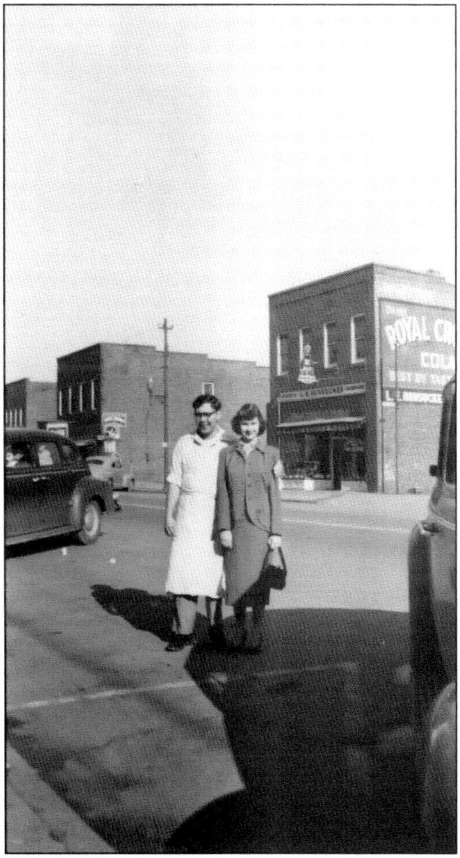

This 1940s photograph is of Charles Simmons and Joan Brown on Main Street. Both Charles and Neil Rowe worked at the Bowman Drug Company. Neil met Joan at the soda fountain and formed the friendship that would lead to their marriage. In the background is the L.E. Hunsucker Hardware business and beyond are the Conover Grocery Store and the Conover Drug Company.

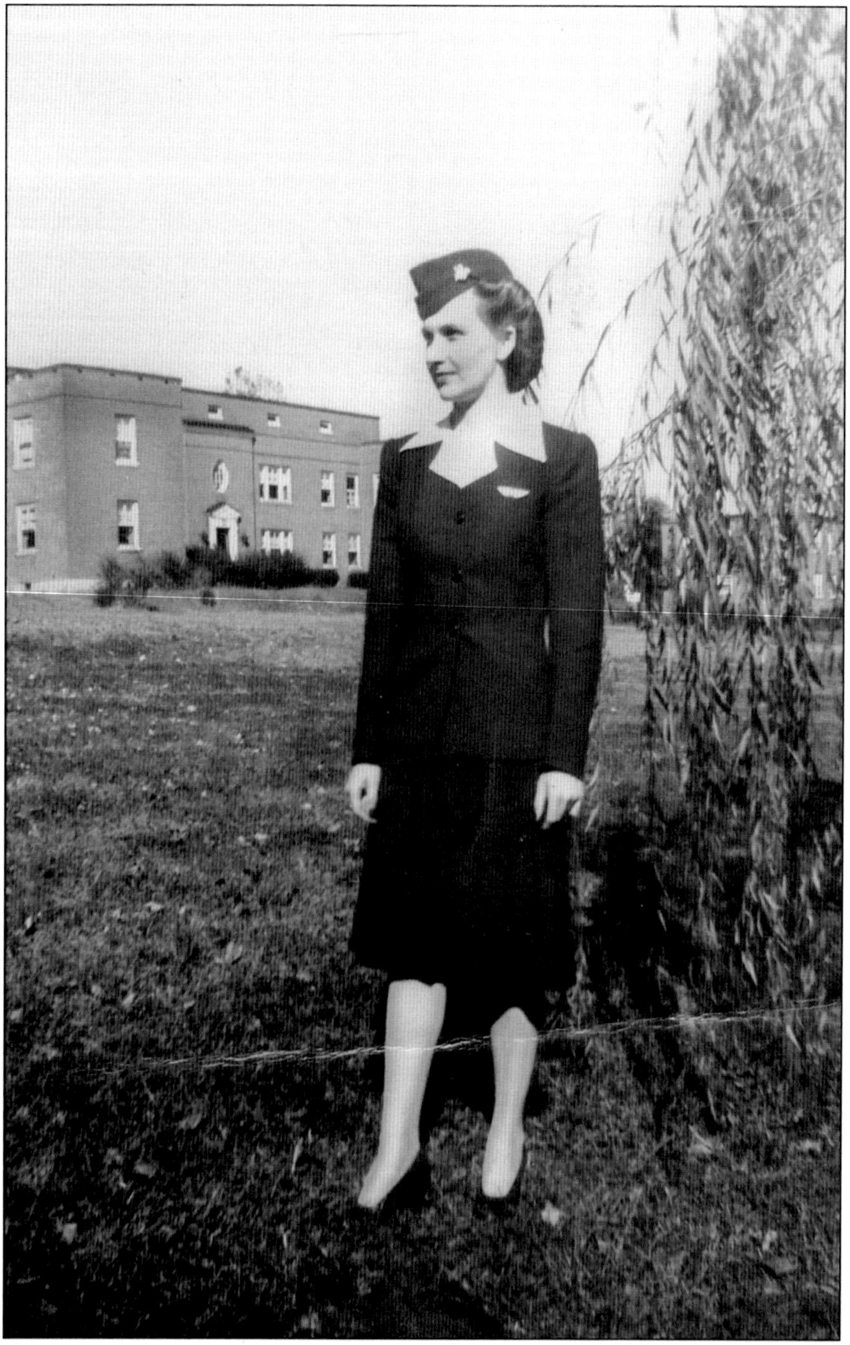

Most proud of her new American Airlines uniform is pretty Leannah Power, of Conover. She was the daughter of Mr. and Mrs. M.L. Power. Her father was a mail carrier for the town. During this time, her father's hours were cut, thus curtailing her schooling at Lenoir Rhyne. She was studying nursing at Lenoir Rhyne College in Hickory. In the early 1940s, while working at Bowman's drugstore, she read an advertisement in a magazine calling for young ladies with some college and studies in nursing to become stewardesses with American Airlines. She answered the advertisement and was immediately accepted. She would be stationed in California.

The man to see for worms or crickets or hunting goods would be Charles "Charlie" E. Simmons at his bait shop. He was one of the more successful businessmen of Conover. After a tour in the Army, he opened his own retail bait shop in 1956 in the old Conover City Hall building, which is now an automobile repair garage. The Catalpa worm was the favorite of the fishermen and would be sold on the street for a dime each. In 1969, he opened the more spacious Charlie's Bait Shop across from Ralph's Cleaners, under the big orange ball of Phillips 66.

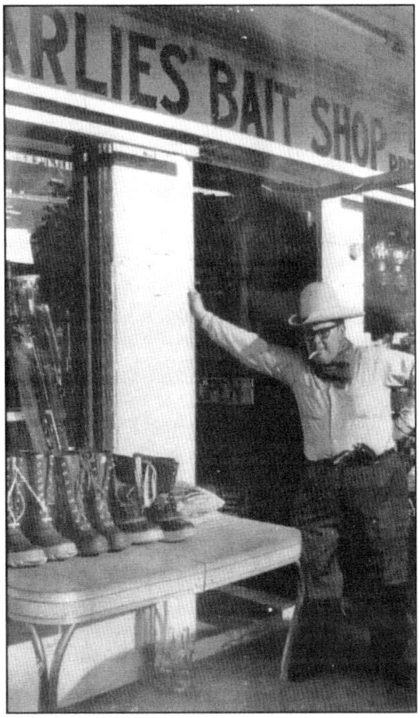

Shown is the original Charlie's Bait Shop. It opened in 1956. This store would become well known throughout the Southeast. This building was once the town hall of Conover and the Conover Fire Station. Walter Moehlmann was the town clerk at this time. Charlie retired in 1995. He was the first person to sell mountain-grown Christmas trees from a lot in town. He was also the chief operator of the popcorn machine at the Canova Theater. At times, locals may see him still working at Big Lots in Newton. He and his wife, Pat, reside in Conover.

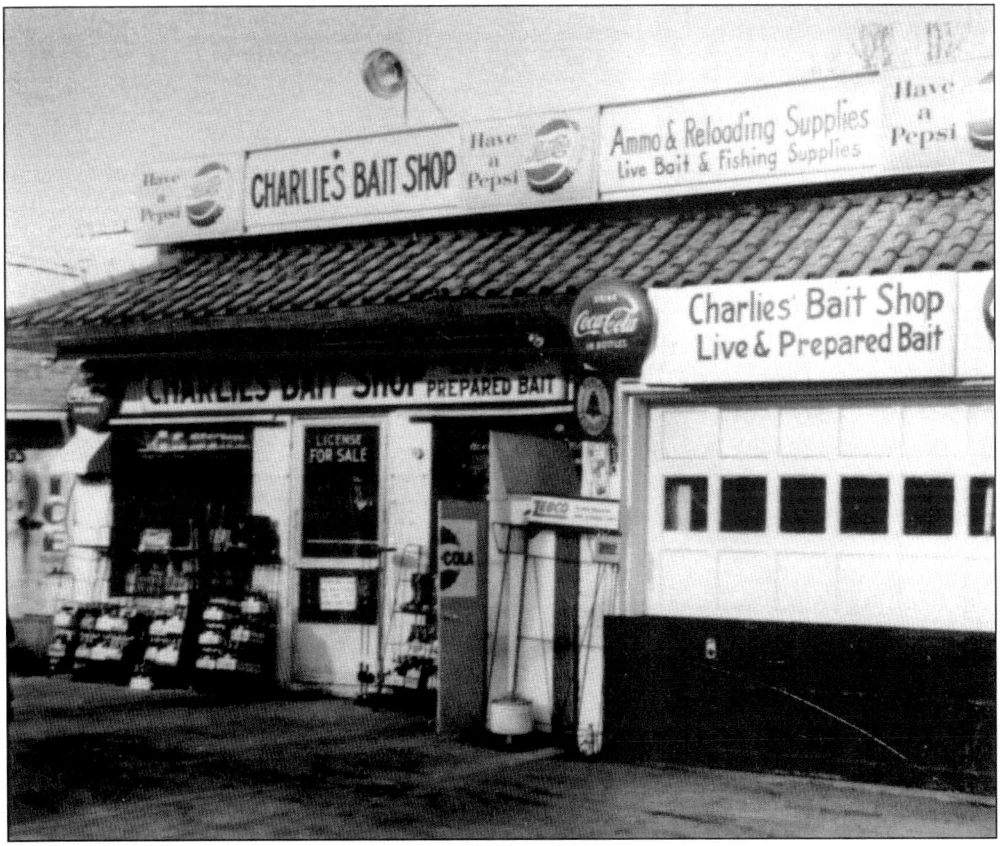

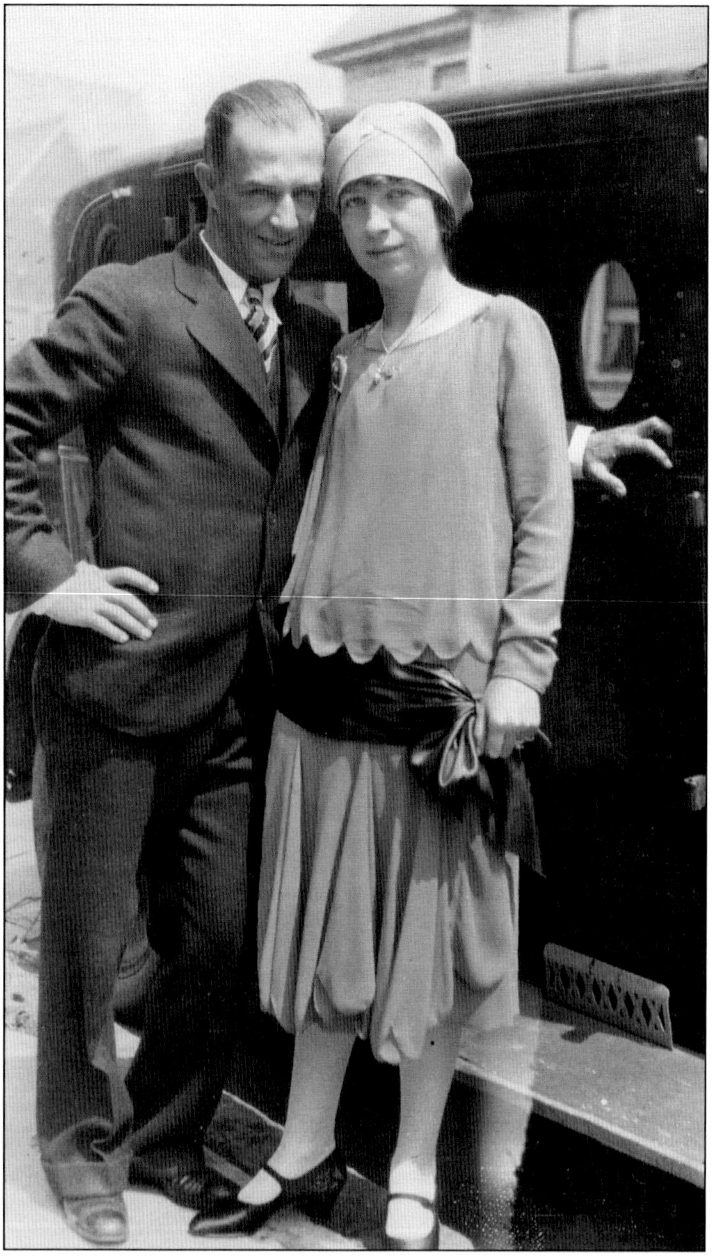

William J. Barker and wife, Lula (Brady) Barker, are pictured on their honeymoon in New Orleans. They are the persons to whom this book is dedicated. William "Bill" Barker was born in June 1898 in New Orleans to J.W. Barker and wife, Maltilda. Bill attended Concordia College in Conover and the Lutheran Seminary in St. Louis, Missouri. He returned in 1928 to Conover and married Lula Brady, daughter of C.R. Brady. He and his brother-in-law Walter became vice president and secretary (respectively) of Conover Furniture Company. Walter Brady would attend to the business at the Conover plant, while Bill would travel, setting up showrooms for products in New Orleans, New York, and Chicago. Later, with partner James "Lefty" Lingle, he would form Piedmont Distributors of the Carolinas in Charlotte. Lula Barker also attended Concordia College. Both were lifelong members of Concordia Lutheran Church.

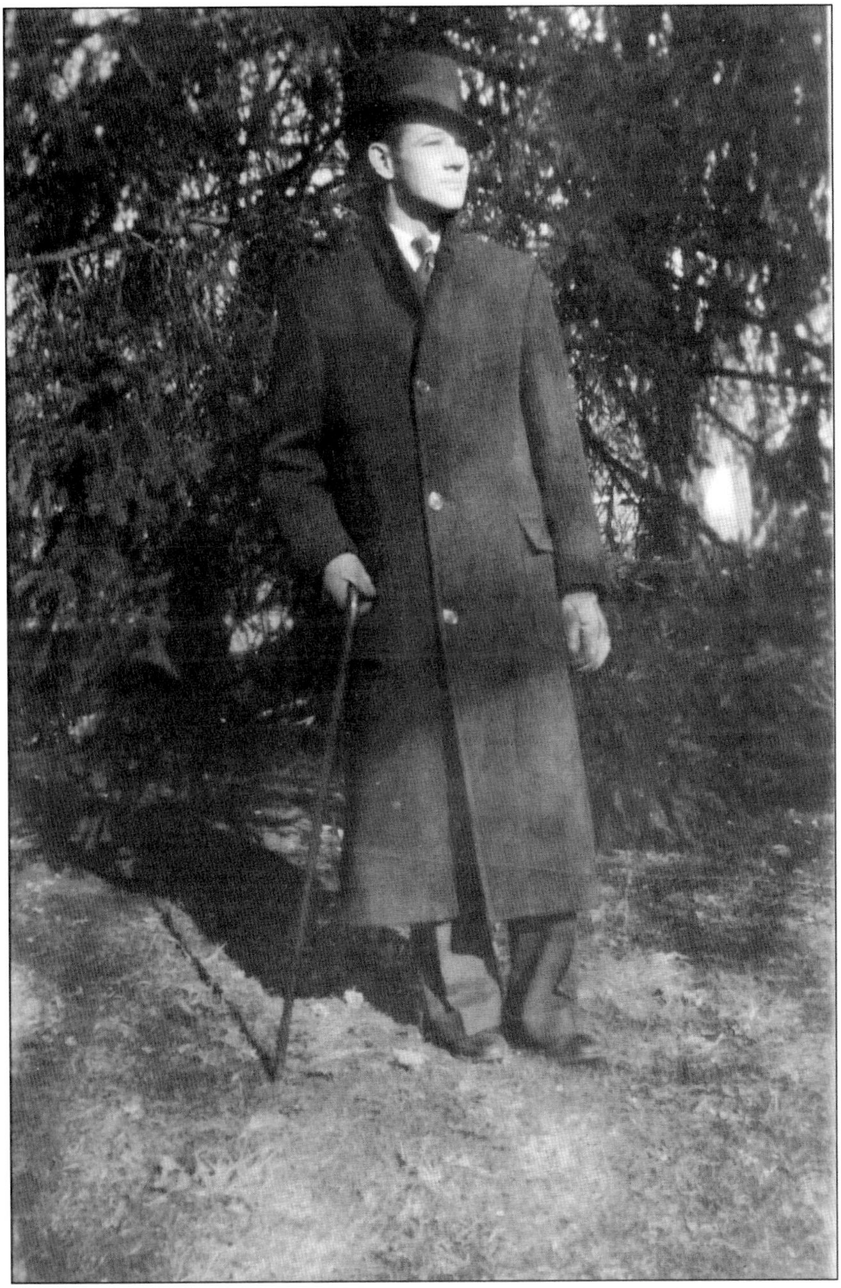

Frederick W. Moehlmann (1908–1990) was born in Conover. He was a dedicated horseman and trainer of five-gaited horses and harness trotters. He would also judge at local show events. He also owned a small print shop on Main Street. He served briefly as a chief of the Conover Fire Department. Moehlmann had an amazing talent for woodworking. He was an accomplished organist, having served Concordia Lutheran Church in this position for over 50 years. He was in sales, service, and installation for the Wicks Pipe Organ Company of Highland, Illinois. He attended Concordia High School in Conover and Concordia College in Bronxville, New York. He was married to Pauline Cline, of Hickory, now deceased. Together, they had daughter Shirley (Canrobert) and son John.

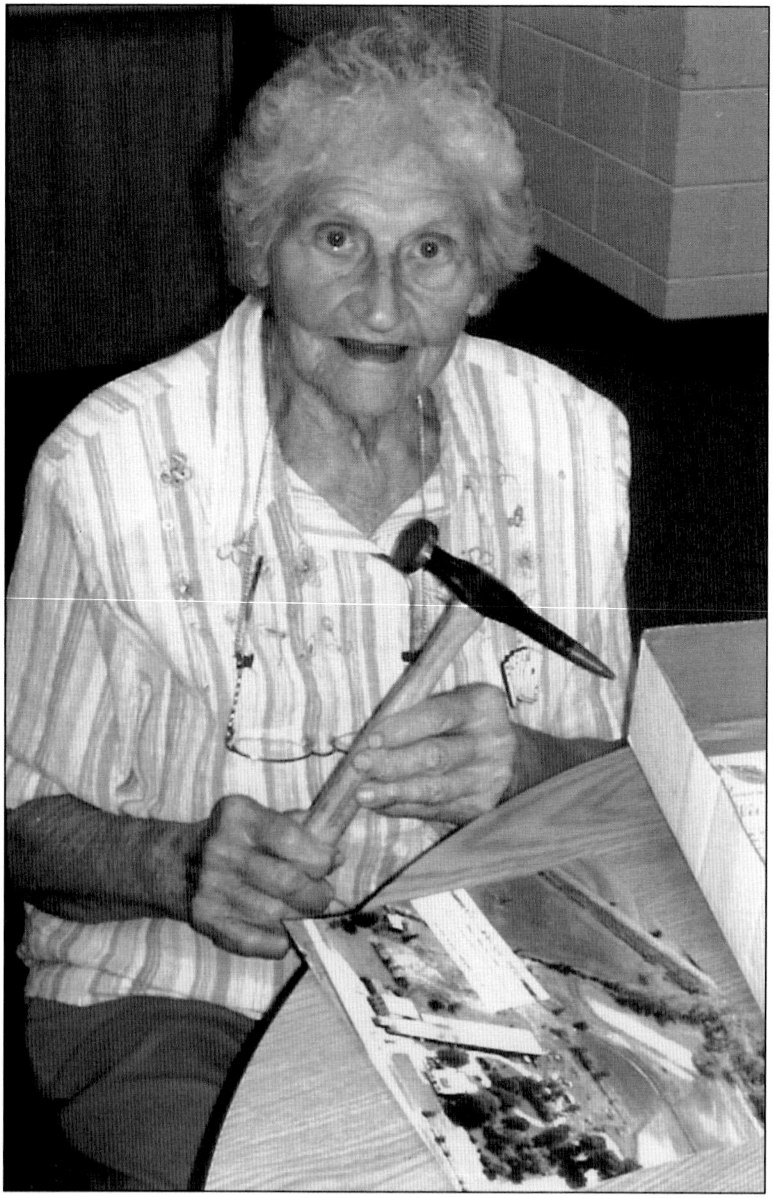

This photograph is of Margaret Sparkman, a most lovable lady of Conover. This popular person is also well known from her television appearances on the Jay Leno show (clunk!) and the annual Christmas show in Charlotte as the Gourd Lady of Conover. She is holding the hallmark product of the Streamline Tool Company, a once thriving business in Conover. It was the largest of its type in the United States. The company originated the body and fender repair tools and floor creepers used by mechanics. This business actually began in the late 1930s in St. Louis, Missouri. It was there that Margaret Henry met Clyde Sparkman. In 1946, the couple moved the business back to Conover. Involved in the business along with Sparkman were Eugene Henry, Percy Henry, George Smith, Floyd Hollar, Boyce Hollar, and Edith Wyke. The company had a lifespan of 63 years. Margaret Sparkman still resides next door to the plant site. She is a lifelong member of Concordia Lutheran Church. The new community building at the YMCA in Conover has been dedicated and renamed the Sparkman Community Building.

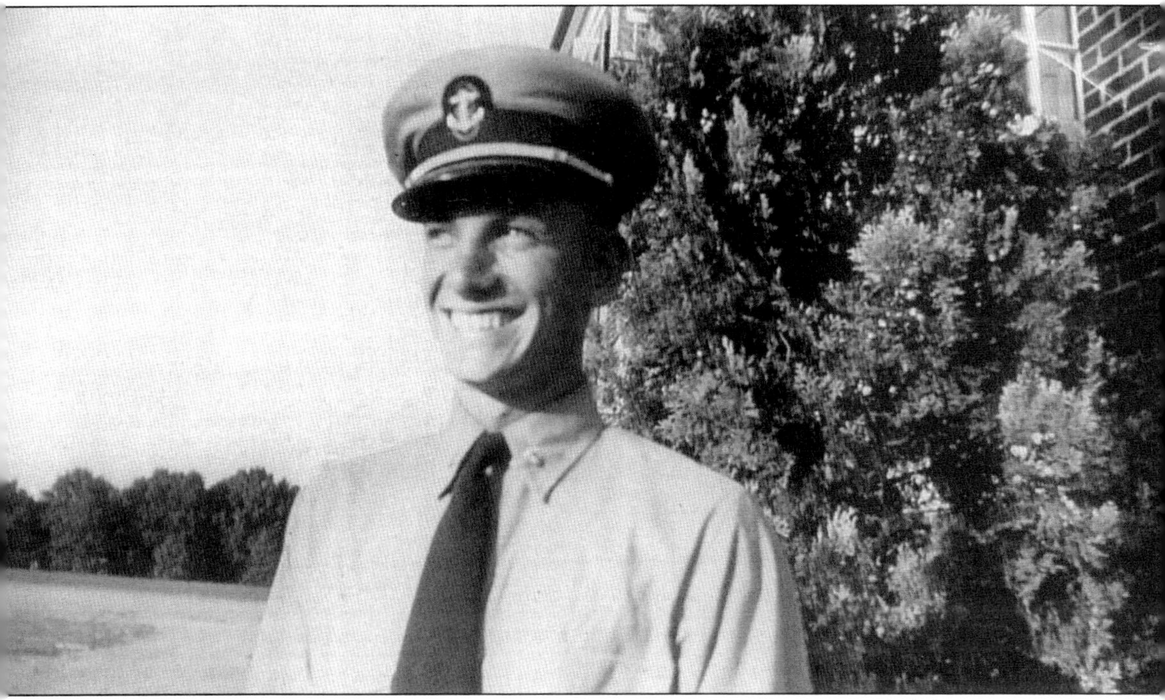

After high school in the early 1940s, Lt. Percy E. Deveney, of Conover, attended the US Navy flight training school in Florida. Earning his golden wings, Deveney was assigned to the Jolly Rogers, a more prestigious squadron of the Navy. He would fly his new Corsair with the VF-17 Squadron out of San Diego, California. While awaiting orders for the Pacific, the young ensign met up with Leannah Power, of Conover, now working for American Airlines. She rented out her apartment to Deveney and four other pilots in training. This was his last meeting with her, for in February 1944, the Japanese shot him down over Rabual, New Britain, during the battle of the Solomon Sea. He was 20 years old. A memorial service was held at Trinity United Reformed Church in Conover.

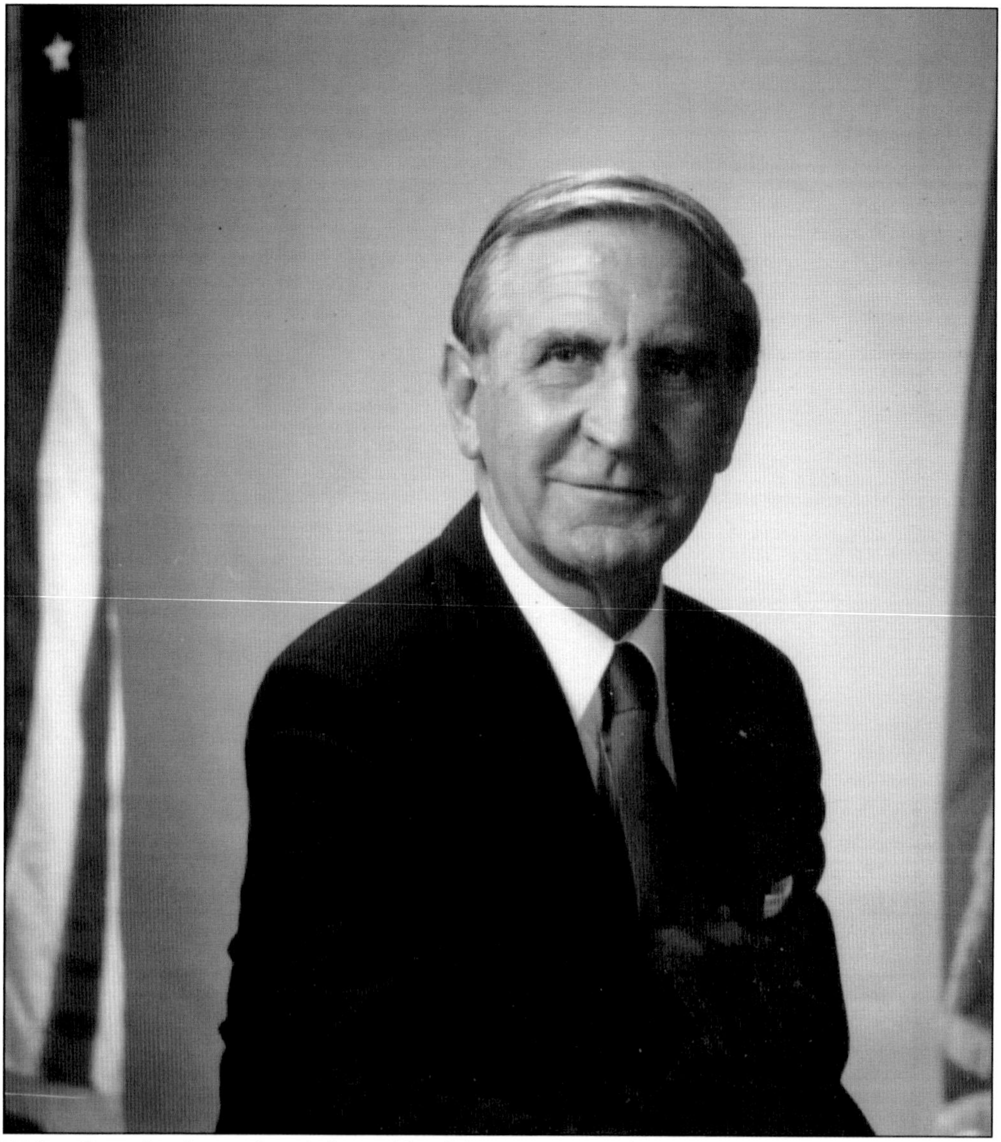

Walter Stine Isenhower has dedicated his life to service to his community, his church, family, and his fellow man. He served in the North Carolina House of Representatives from 1986 to 1992. He is better known in Conover as "Mr. Catawba County." He is also a veteran of the US Army. He and his wife, Carolyn, reside in Conover. They are of the Lutheran faith and are members of Concordia Lutheran Church. He has served as a Catawba County commissioner and volunteered his services to many organizations, including the Catawba County Chamber of Commerce, Conover Lions Club, Conover Volunteer Fire Department, Catawba County YMCA, the Boy Scouts, American Red Cross, March of Dimes, and other professional associations. He was associated with the Owen United Insurance business in Newton until his retirement. In 2006, Isenhower was awarded the Daughters of the Confederacy Medal of Honor for his longtime service and leadership to his community, state, and nation. His memories of growing up in Conover are put in his own words, "Memories are a tribute to special people, who with faith, love, vision and forethought, created the area we call home today. Their names are forever intertwined with the heritage of our community and will be carved into the stones that mark their footprints."

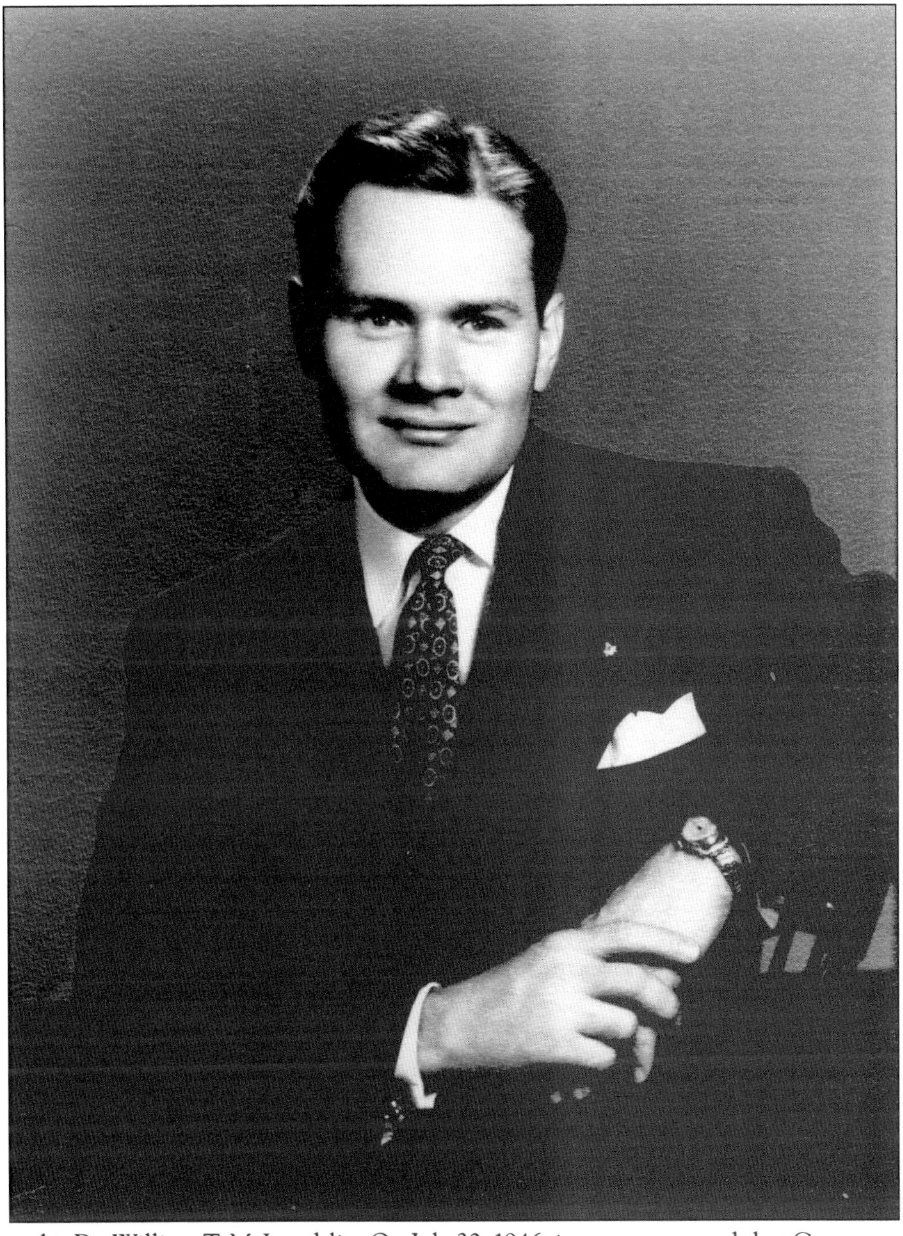

Pictured is Dr. William T. McLauchlin. On July 30, 1946, it was announced that Conover would get a new medical clinic, to be located about one block east of the main intersection in downtown Conover. This was a request made to the Civilian Production Administration by Dr. Charles E. Cloninger and his associate Dr. William T. McLauchlin, of Chester, South Carolina. Cloninger is a popular longtime resident of Newton and a licensed pilot. McLauchlin attended the Medical College of South Carolina and interned at Garfield Memorial in Washington, DC. McLauchlin was a highly decorated US Army veteran, having joined in July 1942 for medical surgeon duties with the 2nd Battalion, 47th Infantry, Ninth division. Reaching the rank of major, his decorations include the Silver Star with Cluster, the Bronze Star, the Purple Heart, and the ETO Ribbon with nine battle stars. He was discharged in September 1945. His sister was Charlotte McLauchlin, of Conover.

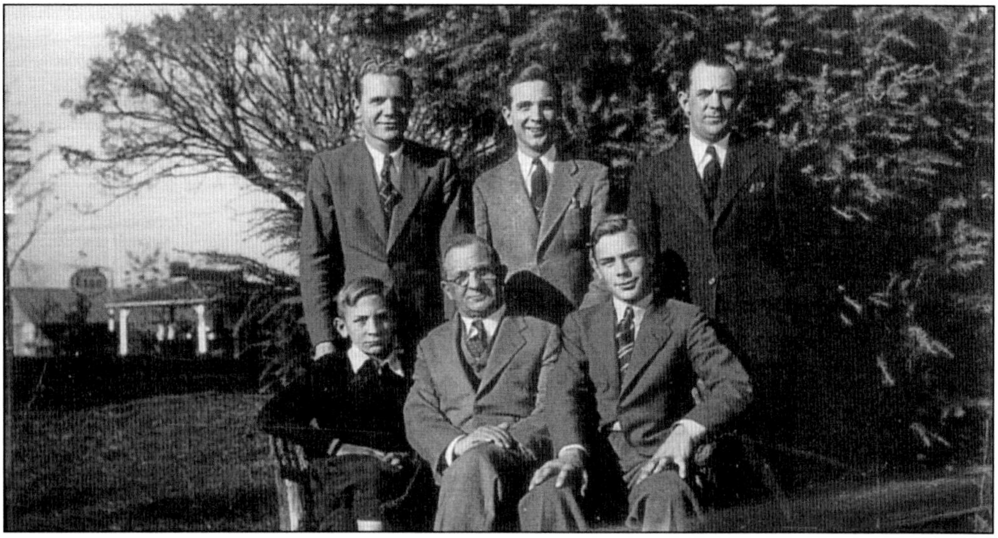

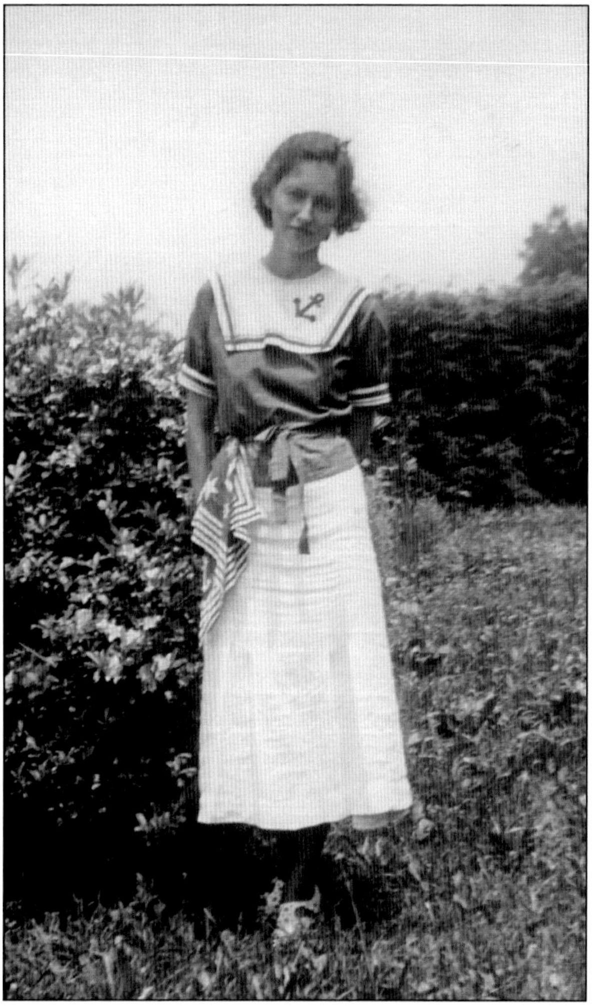

Shown in front of their Conover home are the men of the J.A. Isenhower family. From left to right are (first row) Stine, John Abel, and Joe Andy; (second row) James, Sam, and Horace. The Isenhower men were noted businessmen with a devotion to the community and their family. J.A. Isenhower is credited with constructing many of the buildings on Main Street in Conover. He was also engaged in the banking industry.

This 1934 photograph shows Conover sweetheart Lucile Love. She was a 1940 graduate of Lenoir-Rhyne College, and in 1945, she received her master's degree in education from the University of North Carolina at Chapel Hill. She was the daughter of Henry and Carrie Herman Love. Lucile Love was a former Sunday school teacher and lifelong member of Concordia Lutheran Church. She retired after 35 years as an elementary school teacher at both Startown and Conover schools. In April 2003, Love, while looking for her cat, was tragically killed in front of her home by an automobile. She touched many lives and will always be missed.

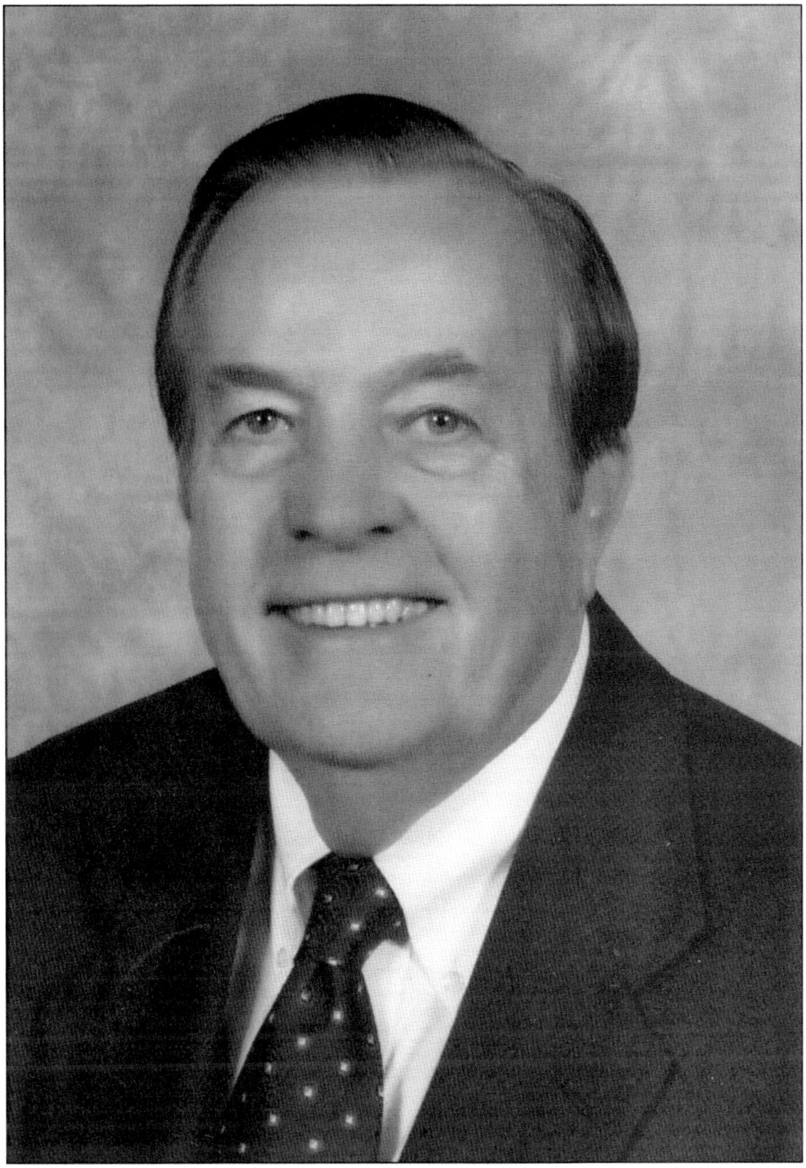

Shown is Jerome W. Bolick of Conover. In 1884, when Jerome Bolick and Sons Company opened its doors as a wholesaler of "High Grade" buggies, no one could have known that 120 years later, Southern Furniture Company would be one of the South's largest family-held furniture manufacturing operations. The company houses the world's finest artisans, master craftsmen, master cutters, and sewers, all combining their talents to bring to their customers the finest quality bench-crafted furniture made today. The founder of the company, Oscar W. Bolick Sr., began in 1926 by transitioning from upholstery of buggy seats to furniture upholstery. His son Jerome W. Bolick maintains ownership of Southern Furniture Company as president and CEO. He was born and raised in Conover. He was also a US Navy veteran, holding the rank of lieutenant (junior grade), having served on the USS *Taluga* during the Korean conflict. In 1954, he served as president of the American Furniture Manufacturer's Association. His daughter Judith will soon join the family business. Jerome and his wife, Linda, and Judith reside in Conover and attend Concordia Lutheran Church.

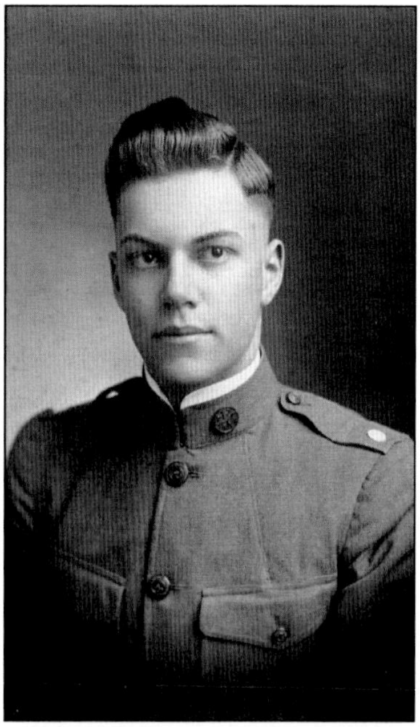

This is Conover native Carroll M. Barringer. He was Conover's first car dealer, a farmer, and lumberman, and he served in World War I with a rank of second lieutenant. He was also elected Catawba County commissioner. He was president of Superior Oil and Fuel Company and a captain in the Newton National Guard. Barringer also served with the Catawba County Sheriff's Department as a sword deputy. While single-handedly attempting to apprehend some bootleggers one evening, he was ambushed and nearly beaten to death before being rescued by fellow officers. He was a cofounder of Faith Lutheran Church in Conover and a Christian gentleman.

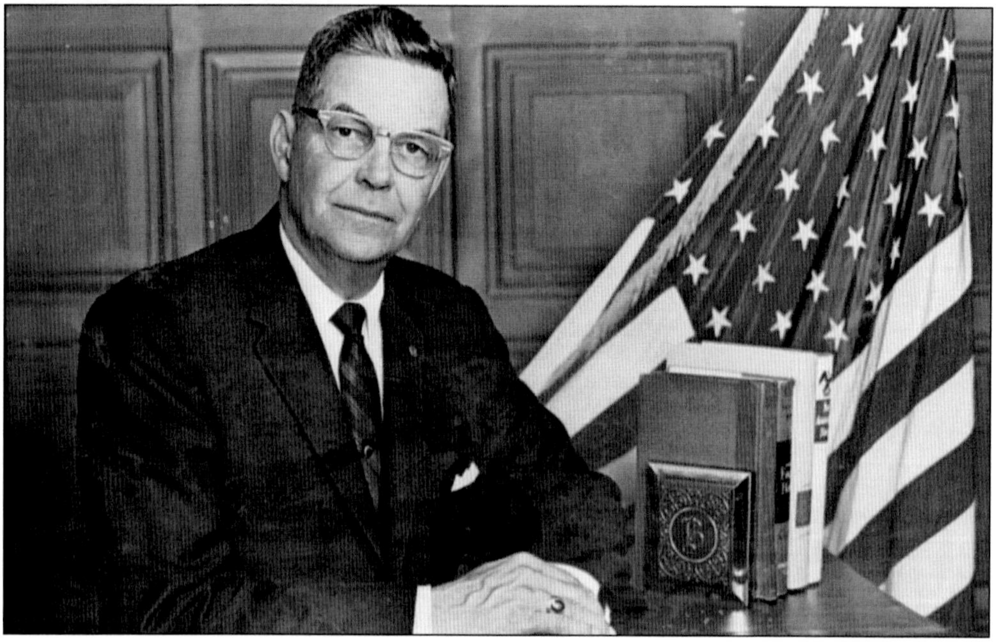

Carroll M. Barringer was a graduate of Kansas State College with degrees in animal husbandry, agriculture, economics, and education. He took meticulous care of his animals and practiced sheep shearing and horsemanship. Extraordinarily good-looking with a melodious, distinct actor's voice, he is said to have broken the heart of every eligible woman when he married the beautiful Artimesa from eastern North Carolina. Not all of his ventures were successful, such as a run for Congress in 1962. His next venture was buying geese to rent out to farmers to eat the weeds in their cotton fields, but he forgot that geese have to be fenced in; after that, there was a failed radio station in Florida. He never drew back from life and was, as stated on his gravestone, a "Man in the Arena."

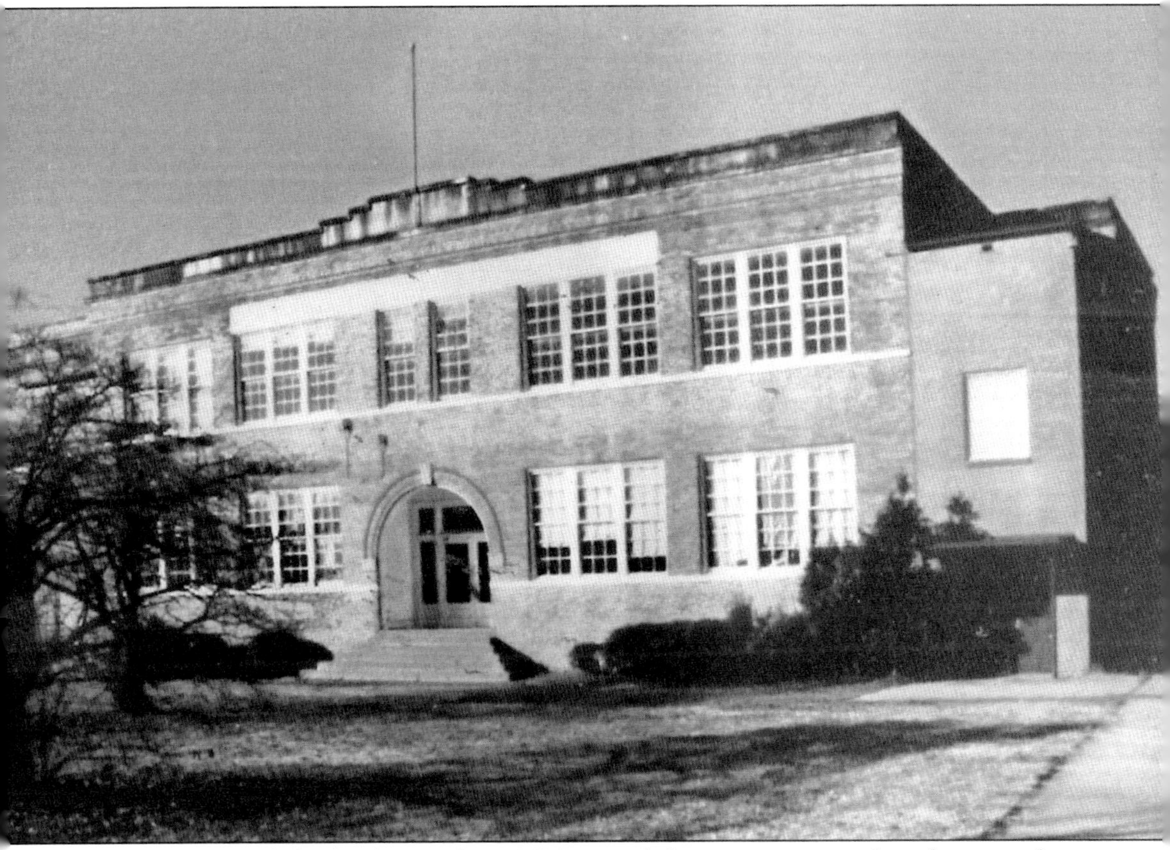

The Conover Graded School opened in 1917. It served the community until its closing in the 1970s. The first movie in Conover was shown here. Pageants, concerts, and Halloween festivals were also held here. Some of the teachers of the school were Elizabeth Herman, Mildred Sox, Eula Young, Mildred Greene, Neil Smyre, Essie Hodson, Addie Campbell, Onnie Smith, Lucile Love, Ms. Davis, and Ms. Wray. Ethel Brown was the first principal, followed by W.F. Warlick, Fred Barkley, and William Gore. The bus driven by Yates Heavner that took students to the high school in Newton would leave from here. The couple who gave the land for the school are said to be buried beneath where the apple trees once graced the property. Children still run and play on the grounds of the school, now renamed the Conover School.

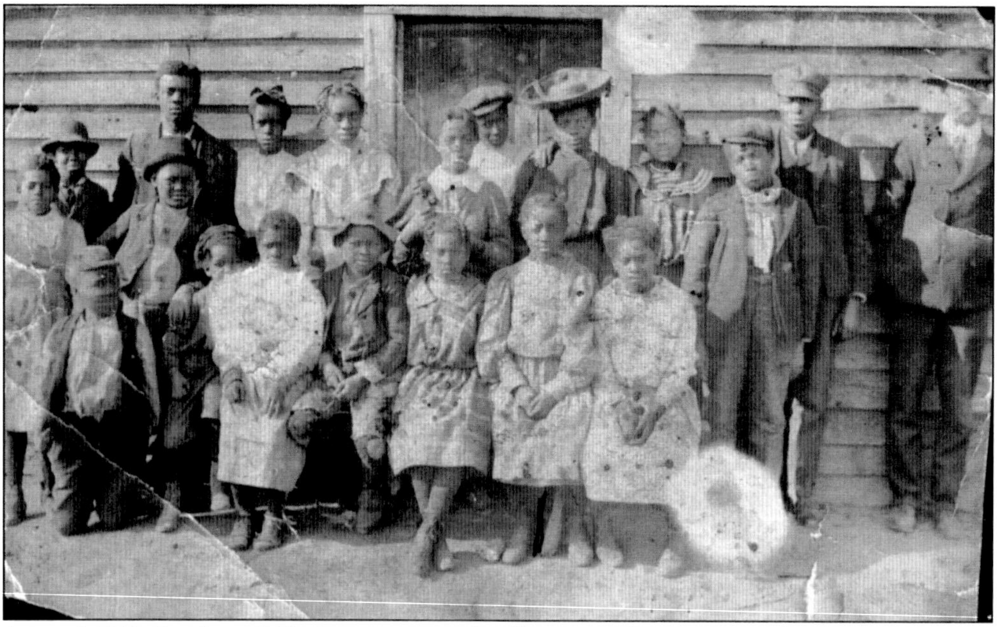

Around 1919, the first all-black, one-room schoolhouse in the Newton School District was in Conover. It was located at Washington Park in Conover near the cemetery and the ball field. This small schoolhouse was torn down for the construction of a new four-room school building in 1920 on the site of the old school. Professor Jasper Cherry Jr. was the principal and teacher. He was from Lawndale. Cherry also served in the Spanish-American War.

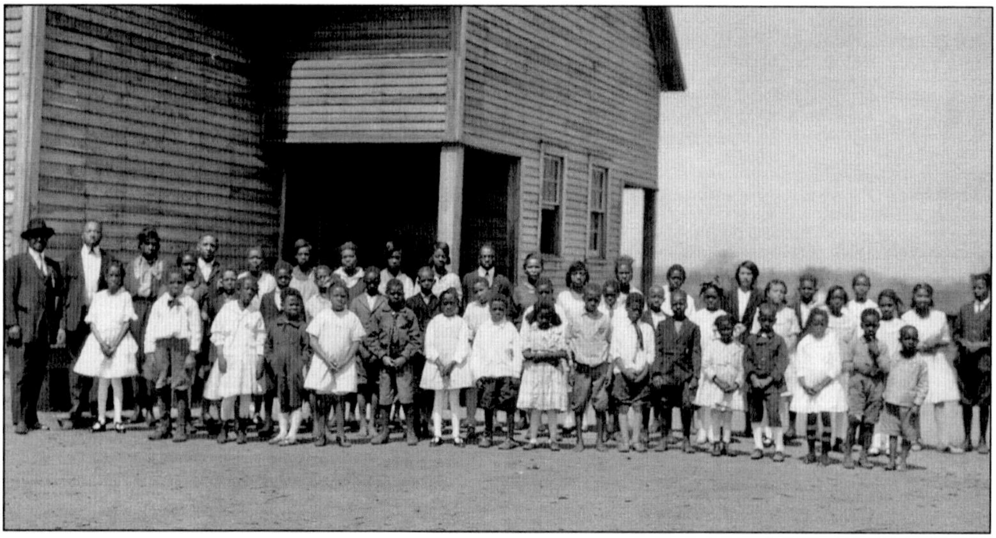

Located at the Washington Park is the early Conover Colored School, as it was called in 1920. Names include, from left to right, (first row) Frances Baker, Crawford Lorittz, Vosilene Baker, unidentified, Connie Lorittz, Marshall Cline, Frankie Baker, J. Reinhardt, Frieda Kincaid, and the other students are unidentified; (second row) Osborne Reinhardt, Marvin Reinhardt, Azalee Kincaid, unidentified, and Raymond Reinhardt; (third row) Professor Jasper Cherry Jr., Ruth Cherry, Holland Reinhardt, Vera Loritts, Rosie Reinhardt, Dora Bergans, Bernice Cline, Mary Cline, unidentified, Recie Baker, Enola Reinhardt, Elmada Baker, two unidentified, Mrs. Jasper Cherry, A. (Baker) Mayfield, Clara Cherry, Lillian Cherry, and unidentified.

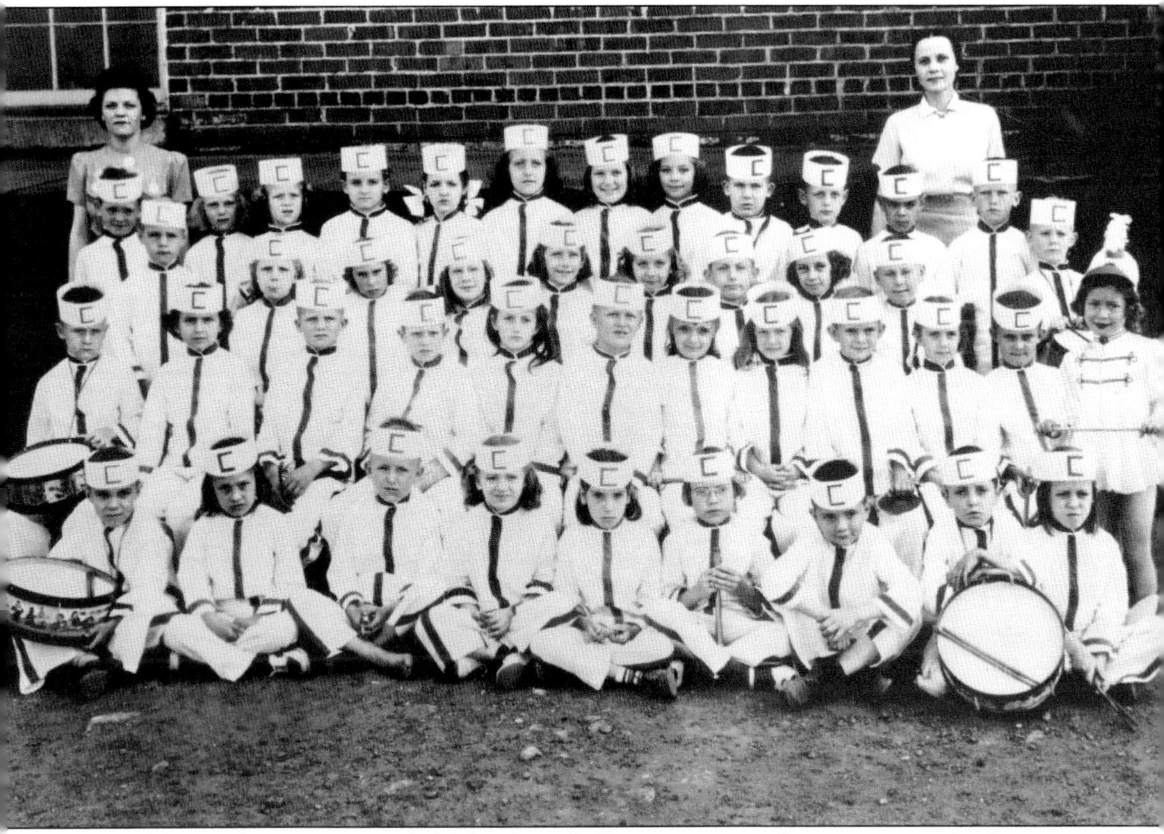

Pictured here is the Conover Graded School Band. This picture was taken just prior to the Canova Theater grand opening parade in 1941. From left to right are (first row) Hugh Yount, Merida Bell, Bill Clarke, Shirley Moehlmann, Betty Power, Joyce Herman, Fred Isenhower, Charles Parkhurst, and Barbara Thayer; (second row) Jimmy Gilbert, Mary Sigmon, Bob Keller, A.C. Yount, Mabel Brittain, Terry Settlemyer, Dorothy Marlow, Joyce Curlee, Hugo Leim, Kay Cline, Joe Kaylor, and majorette Ann (Holt) Brady; (third row) Don Gilbert, Betty Saunders, Alice Lou Hefner, Shirley Lail, Patricia Heavner, Mary Catherian Drum, Bernard Smith, Katherine Wallace, Charles Simmons, and Dickie Cheek, (fourth row) Donnie Barker, Dot Brady, Janice Brady, Frankie Herman, Sally Drum, Millie Deal, Bobbie Bolick, Betty Brown, Grady Hamrick, Jack Smith, Bobby Spencer, and Kenneth Freeman; (fifth row) teachers Mildred Greene and Ms. Davis.

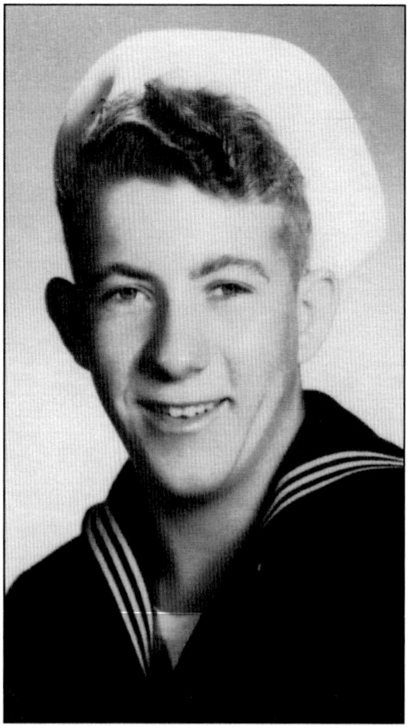

Pictured is the popular Conover-born Joe Dale Bolick. He was a graduate of Startown High School. He was employed at the Canova Theater, often riding a pony to and from work. The pony was relieved of its duties in 1951, when Joe Dale joined the US Navy. He served as a coxswain aboard the USS *Winston* AKA-94, an amphibious attack ship, during the Korean War. After service, he was employed in sales for various furniture supply and manufacturing companies. He and his wife, Rowena, reside in Newton.

Pictured is Olin Winters, of Conover. Olin was a driver for Queen City Bus Company. Clyde Bost, of Newton, and his brothers had the first jitney service in Newton with routes to Lenoir, Charlotte, and Spartanburg, South Carolina. They would sell the business to L.A. Love, the founder of the Queen City bus line, which was later purchased by the Holiday Inn and renamed Continental Trailways. Olin would manage the Cities Service Station at five points in downtown Conover. Later, he would operate the Winter's Men's Store. Assisting him at the store was Richard "Dickie" Power. Olin and his wife, Frances, were members of Concordia Lutheran Church.

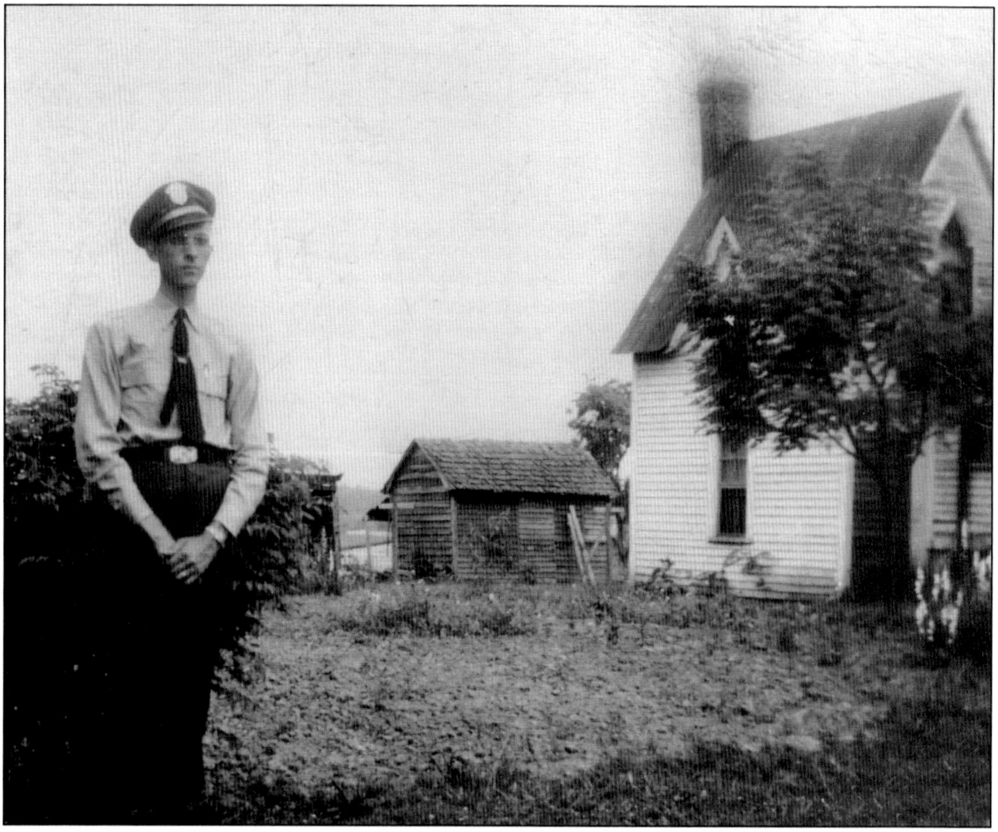

Shown are Lycurgus and Ava Hunsucker, of Conover. They had children Clyde, Helen, and Elma. This couple was known for their kindness to children and family and for devotion to their faith. Lycurgus had a grand garden, growing corn and raspberries alongside a barn. Every evening, he could be seen milking his cow, much to the delight of the local felines who gathered for their tasty portion. Ava's pastime was sitting on the spacious porch in the afternoons along Third Street Southeast. Clyde, a veteran of the US Army, was married to Ruby Love. Together, they had daughters Clydie, Rita, and Jane. Clyde was a longtime employee of Ridgeview Hosiery mill in Newton.

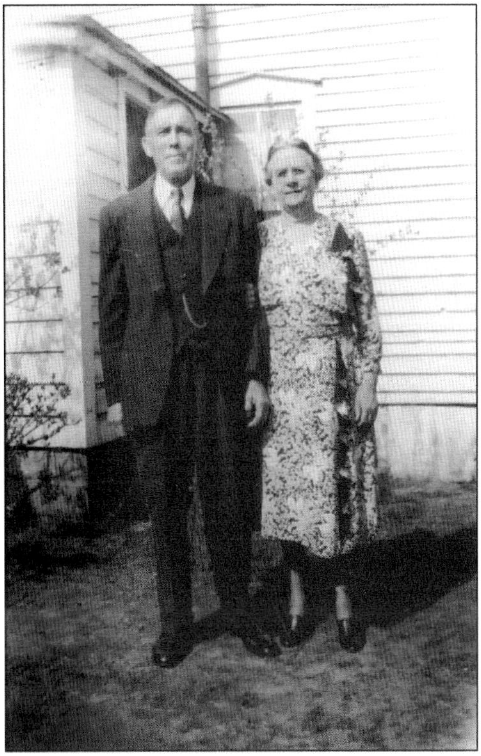

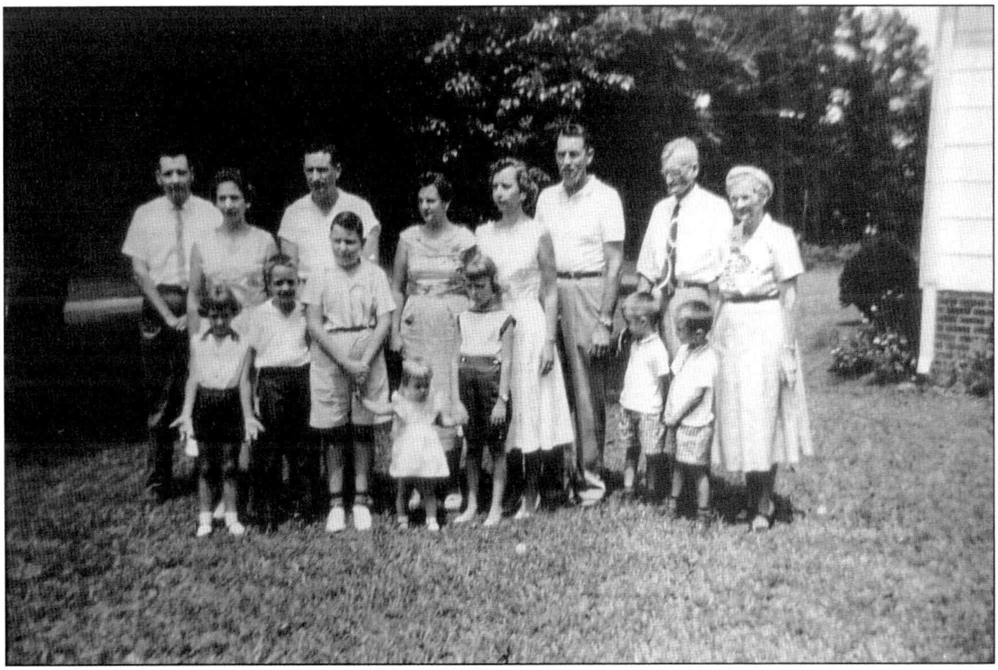

Pictured in this 1959 photograph is the C.A. Smith family reunion gathering. From left to right are (first row) Janice Smith, Alvin Smith, Mike Smith, Jane Sigmon, Sandra Smith, and David and Donald Smith; (second row) Herman Smith, Ellen Smith, Merritt Smith, Nelma Smith, Bertie Smith, Darvin Smith, Clarence Smith, and Mrs. Willie Smith.

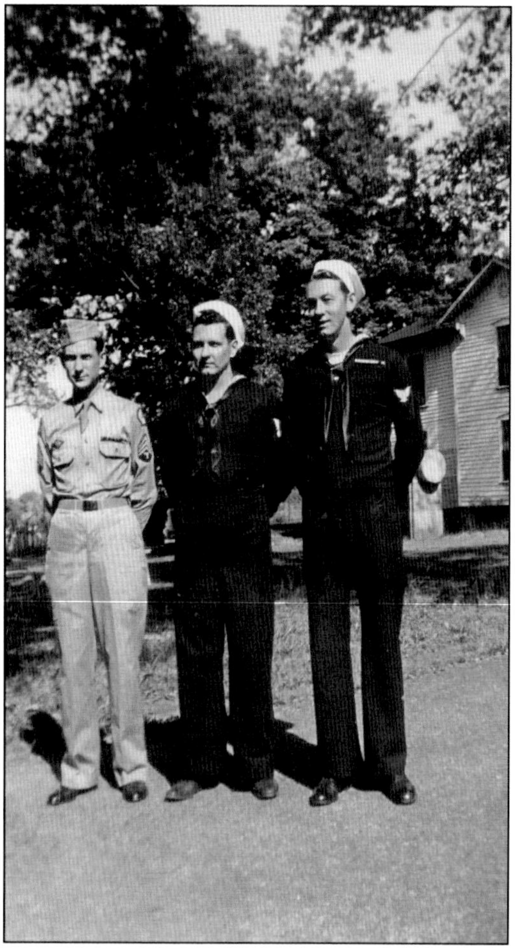

This photograph is of the Clarence Smith boys, of Conover, home on leave from military service. They are, from left to right, Merritt Smith, US Army; Herman Smith, US Navy; and Darvin Smith, US Navy.

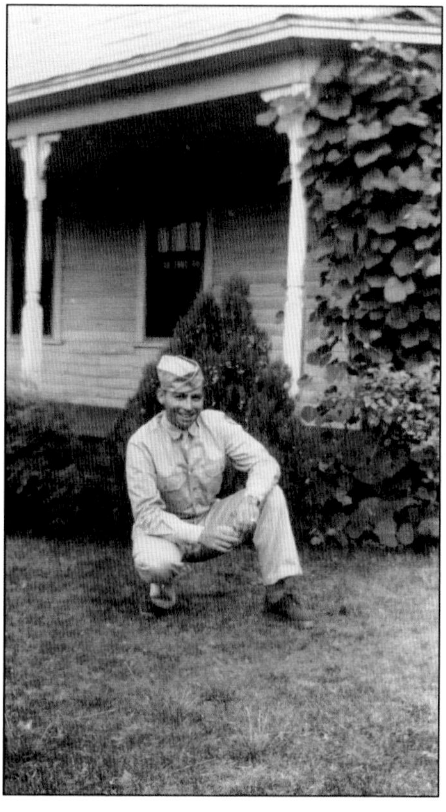

While home on leave from the US Army, Conover native Blair "Scorchy" Deal is having his picture taken in front of the Deal home. Deal served with Charles Brady, another local, in the North African Campaign and was stationed in Casablanca.

This is the Conover home of James "Jim" and Mary Deal (pictured). Here, they raised their sons Franklin, Henry, Blair, and Gerald "Fat" Deal. Jim was a lifelong employee of Conover Furniture Company. The home was the first public schoolhouse in Conover. It is located across from the soccer field of Concordia Lutheran School on First Street East.

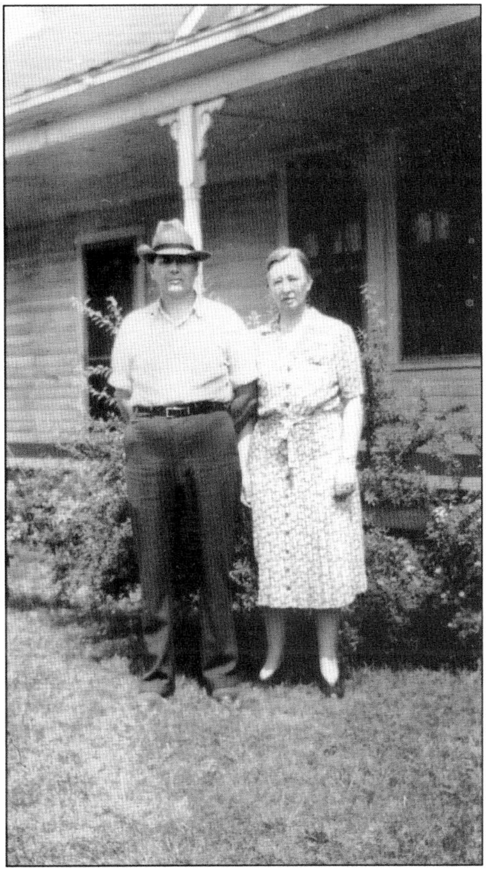

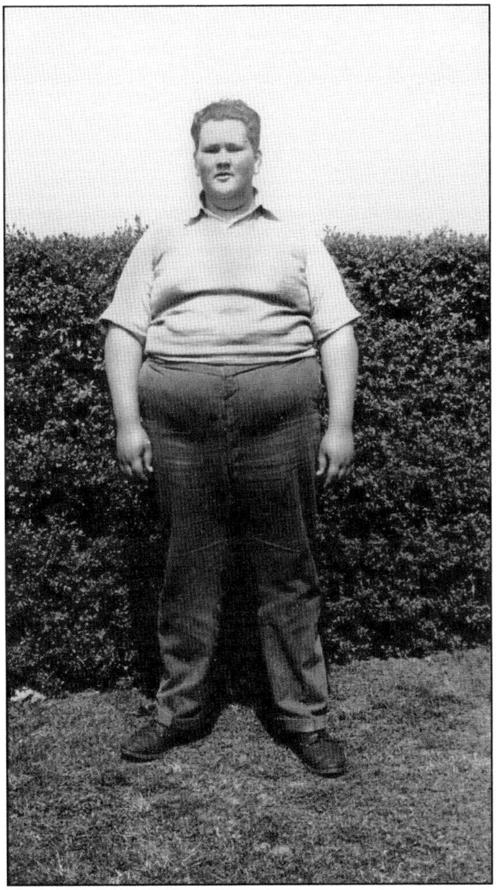

Shown is Gerald "Fat" Deal, of Conover. Big and lovable was just his manner. A splendid softball player for the Concordia Church team, he could literally hold down his position at first base. He was funny and a joy to be around. He enjoyed the days spent at Camp Linn Haven, the Lutheran Church camp. In the camp dining hall, it was most important to get to the table first. He liked to hang out with his many buddies and go to the Silver Moon or Clinker Brick for a late-night dinner. He loved the chicken gizzard plates and usually had two.

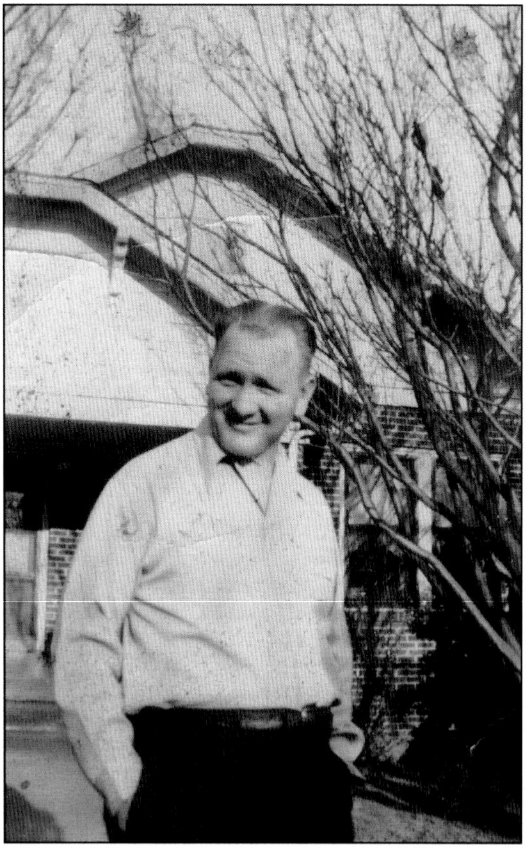

Businessman James Council "Lefty" Lingle is shown at his home in Conover. He was married to Christine Warlick, the daughter of Farell Warlick, the principal of Conover Graded School. Lingle was a business partner with Bill Barker, with a store in Conover and a distribution wholesale business on South Boulevard in Charlotte. His son Jim and family reside in Conover.

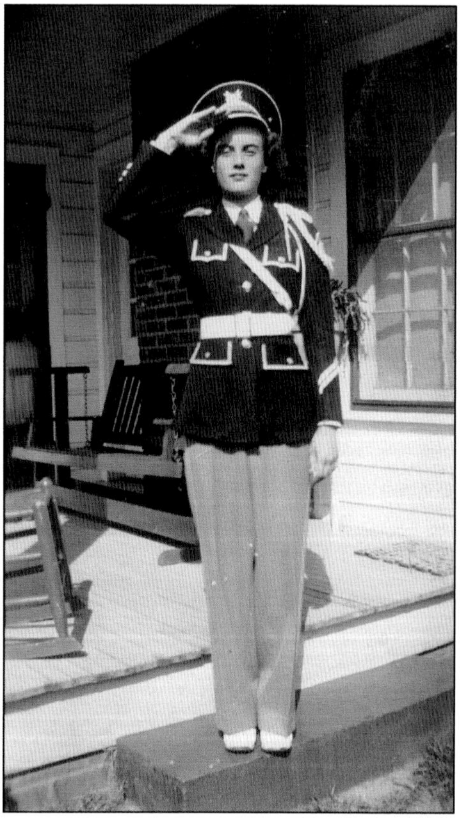

"Strike up the band!" says a young Phillis Lail, of Conover. She is dressed out in her Newton-Conover High School band uniform, most likely for a Friday-night football game at the old baseball stadium. In 1945, the uniforms cost $25 and were passed down to the next-year band student.

"NO LOUD TALKING," is the reminder upstairs at the projection room at Conover's Canova Theater. This picture shows projectionist Jim Bogle at work, at the age of 17. The projectionist was the "Captain" of the operation. Taking care of two 35-millimeter film projectors with the correct changeover was no simple task. Jim later enlisted in the US Army, and upon his discharge, worked at Charlie's Bait and Gun business uptown in Conover. Jim was married to Edith Deal.

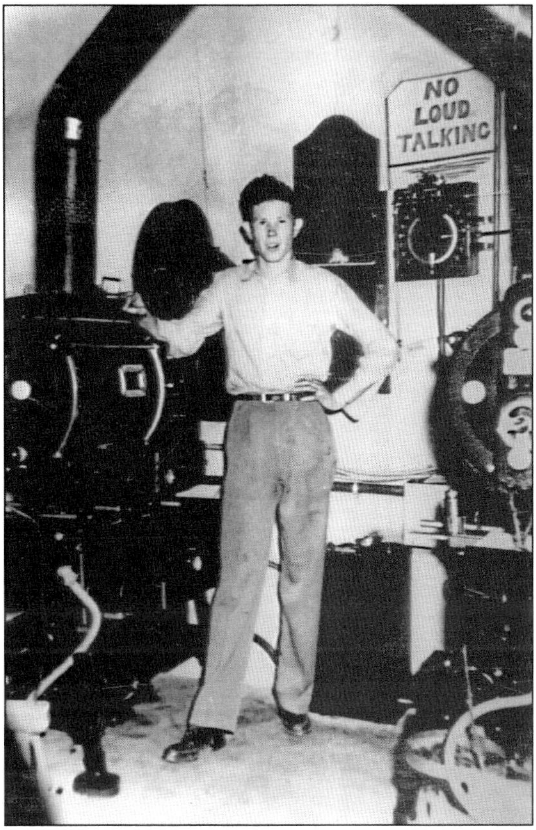

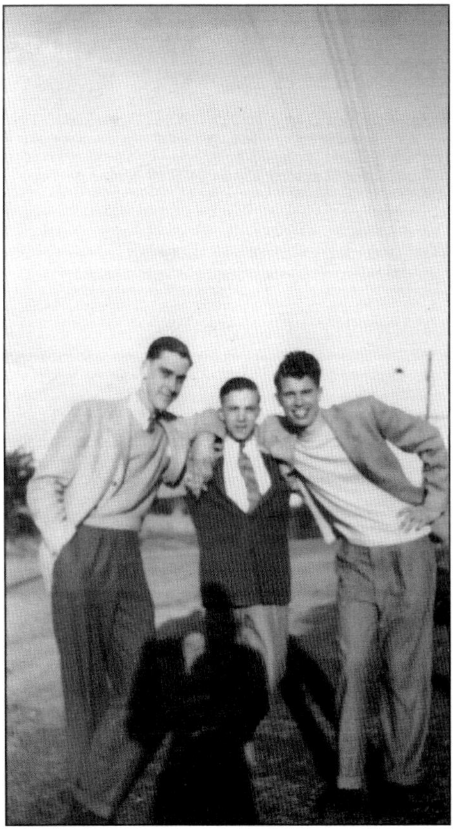

Having their photograph taken around 1945 in Conover are, from left to right, Joe Power, Bobby Matthews, and Floyd "Brownie" Brown Jr. These buddies are trying to get some girls and go to a movie or just ride around for the evening. There was never a dull moment when around these three guys.

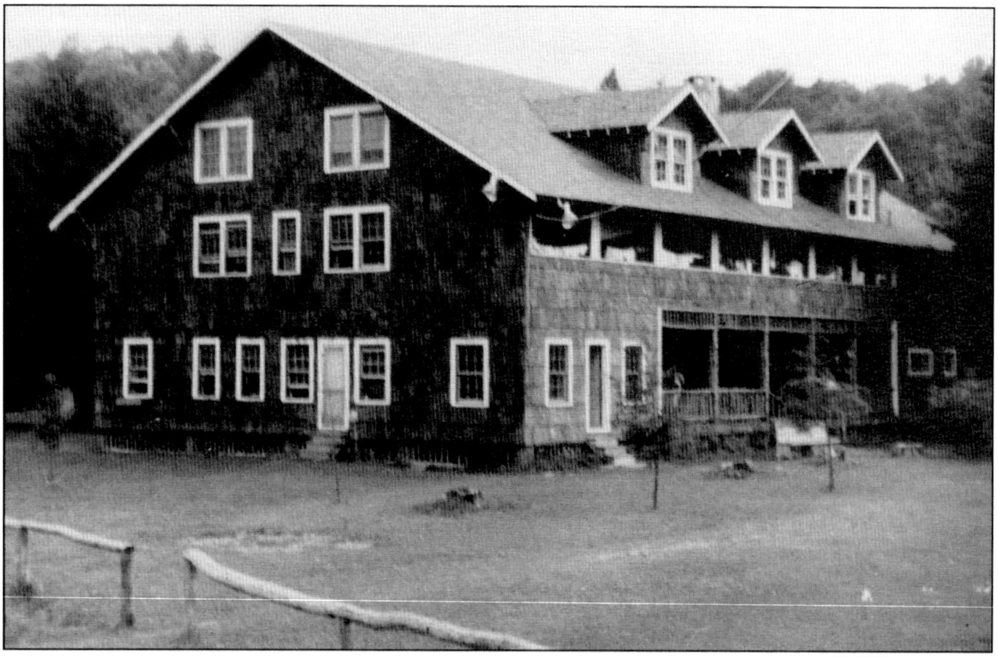

For boys and girls looking for fun and a place to escape the heat of summer, no place was more enjoyable than the Lutheran Camp Linn Haven at Linville, North Carolina. The place meant great food in the dining hall, plenty of games, mountain climbing, and late-night gatherings by the campfire. It was coed, with boys on one side and girls on the other when bunking down. Did some Lutheran boys really keep their private stock of beer in the nearby Linville River? "Surely not," said one pastor.

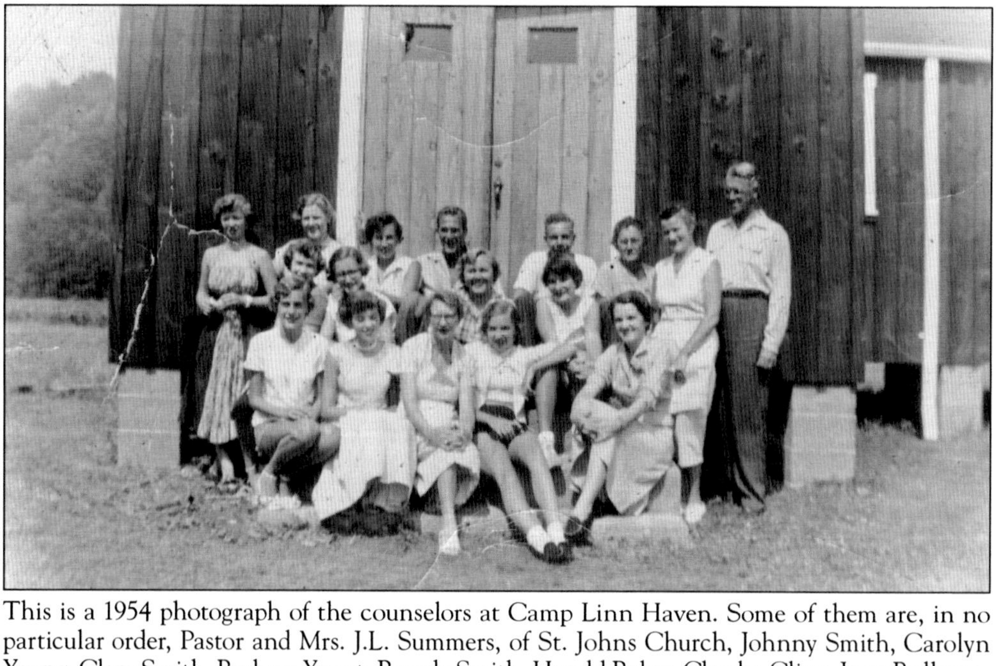

This is a 1954 photograph of the counselors at Camp Linn Haven. Some of them are, in no particular order, Pastor and Mrs. J.L. Summers, of St. Johns Church, Johnny Smith, Carolyn Young, Clara Smith, Barbara Yount, Brenda Smith, Harold Baker, Charles Cline, Jetty Rullman, Betty McRee, and the others are unidentified.

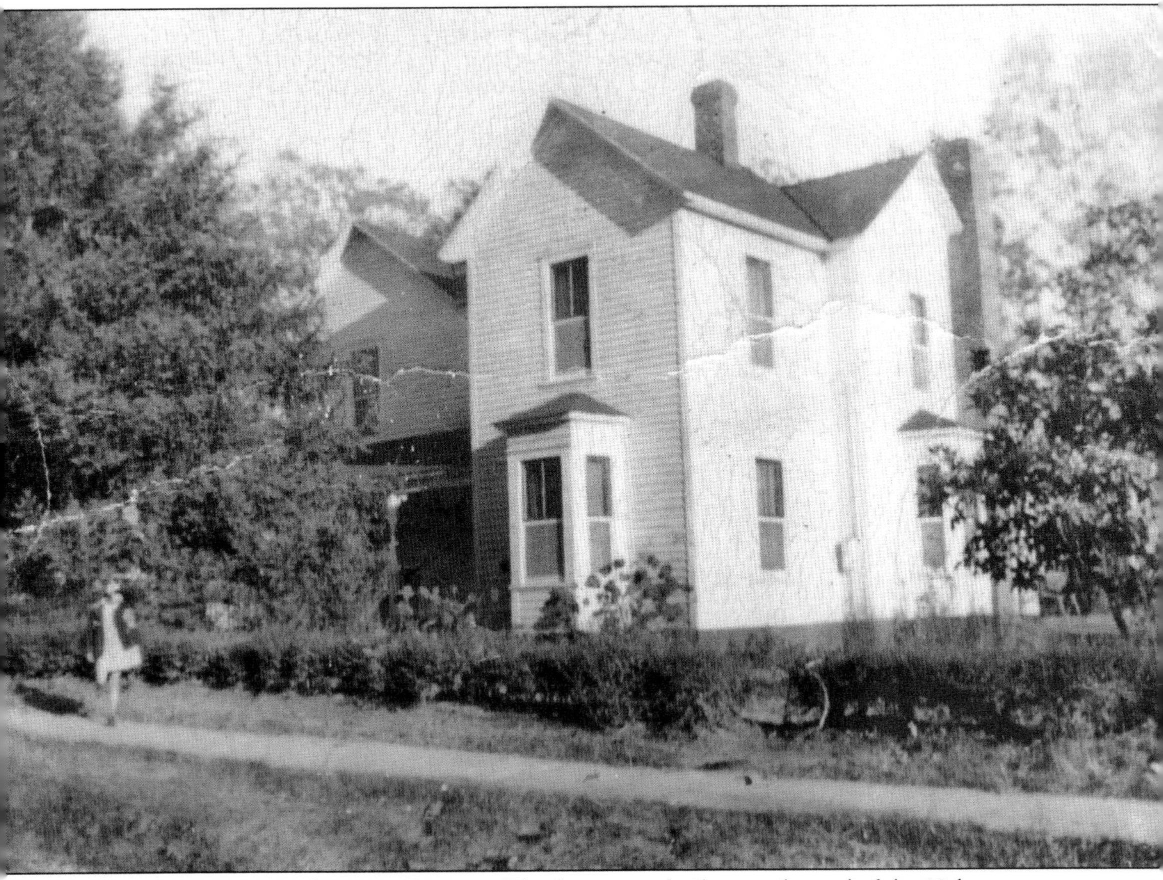

This is the M.L. Power home in Conover. This home was built near the end of the 19th century. Power was a rural mail carrier for the city of Conover. His wife was a wonderful cook, and after school, a peach custard pie could often be found under a cloth on the kitchen table. The children who lived here were Leanna Power, American Airlines; Capt. Nancy Power, US Army Air Corps, Nurse Corps, 1945, World War II; Morris Power, US Army, Korea and FBI, Washington, DC; Joe Power, US Navy, Korea; Jack Power, US Navy, Korea; and Richard Power, US Army, Vietnam. The house was the home of professor Reverend Lindenmeyer before the Concordia College burned. Reverend Lindenmeyer became pastor of Mt. Olive Lutheran Church in Newton.

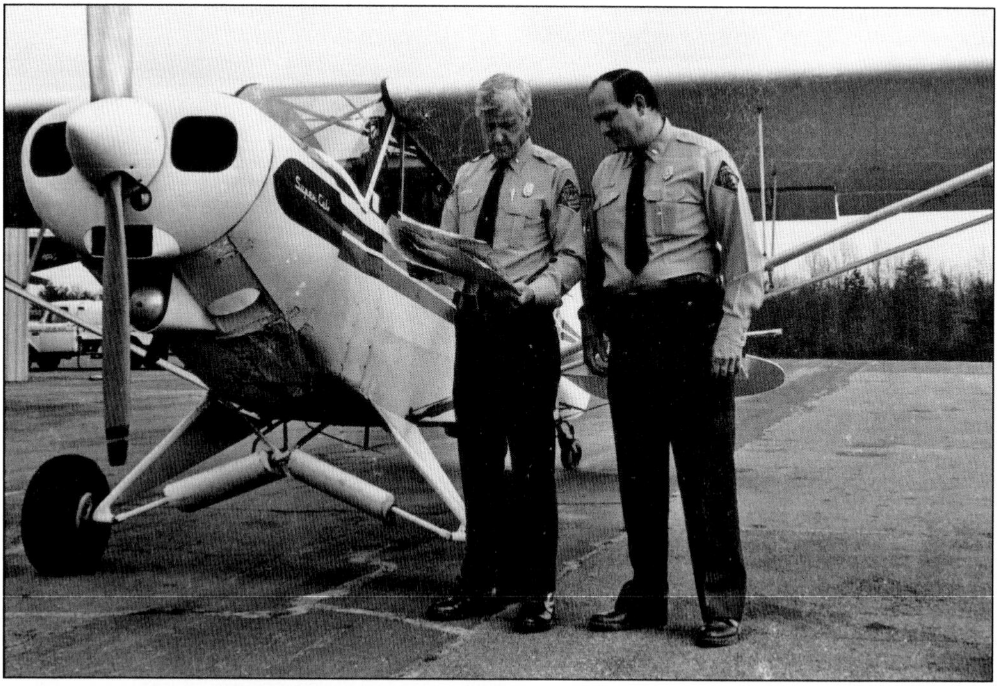

Checking their flight maps at Cannon Aviation in Hickory are North Carolina Wildlife Aviation Unit lieutenants Joe James (left), of Conover, and Tony Lewis, of Caldwell County. They are preparing for a night flight over the streams around Wilson Creek and Upper Creeks, looking for poachers and illegal activity. This dangerous flying is in the dark of night with only the moon to light the way and the ever-present downdrafts and wind currents within the canyons. These two officers have over 15,000 hours logged in flight service.

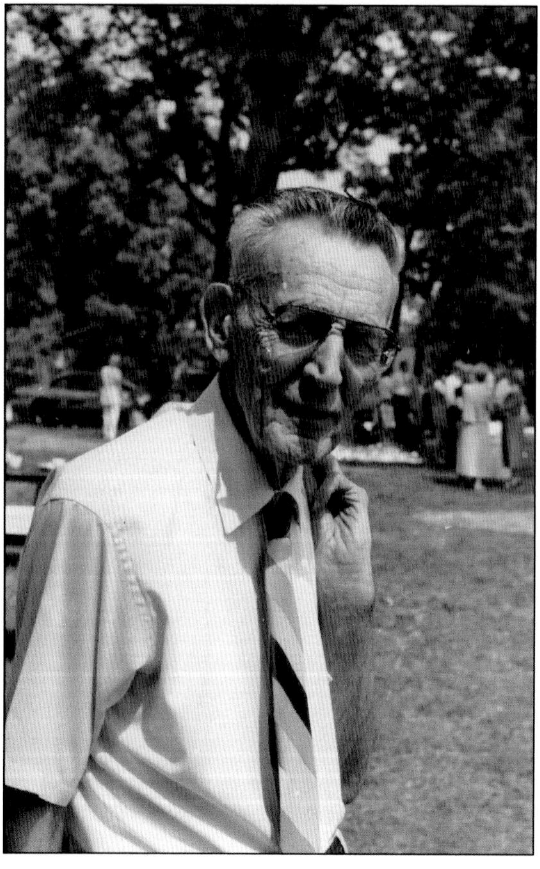

The favorite science teacher at Newton-Conover High School was Yates Heavner, of Conover. He is pictured here at a dinner on the lawn at Concordia Church. He and his wife Alma had one son, Steve. Their home still stands in Conover. Yates Heavner was also the bus driver who took the Conover pupils from the Conover Graded School to the high school in Newton.

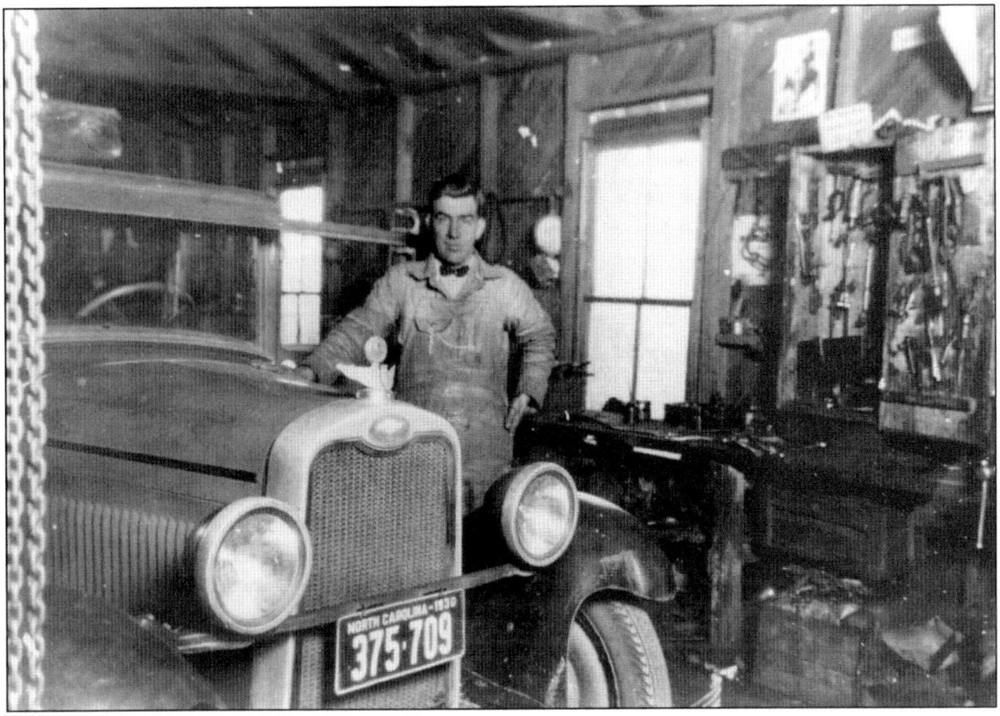

Shown at his garage in Conover is Lynwood Gantt. A professional mechanic, he once worked for Ted Smyre at his garage in uptown Conover. He even repaired a Norfolk-Southern Railroad diesel engine that had broken down in Conover one afternoon. He also helped a Trailways bus driver to get the engine started one morning. Gantt was an accomplished piano player and loved to entertain by playing gospel hymns.

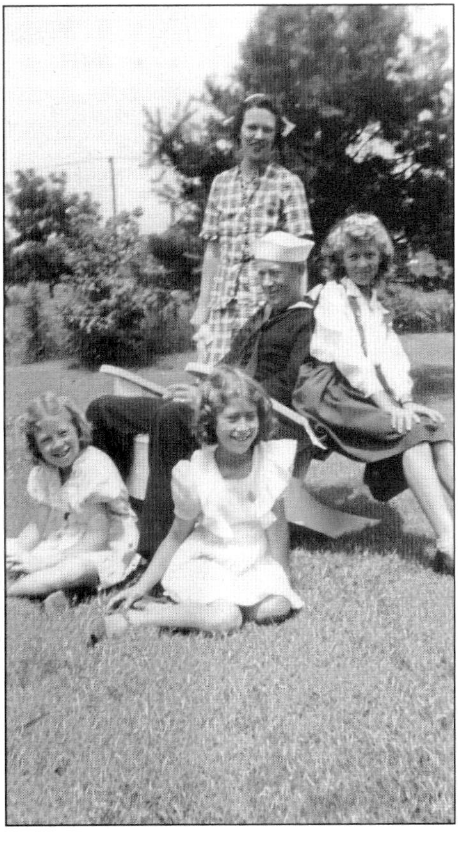

Enjoying the summer sun is the Harvey Brady family. Standing is Harvey's wife, Pauline "Polly" Brady. Seated is US Navy seaman Harvey Brady with daughter Janice at his side. On the ground are daughters Glenda (left) and Ann. All three of the young girls would become nurses. Harvey worked as a shipping clerk at Conover Furniture Company, American Drew in Wilkesboro, and later with Johnson Brothers Trucking of Hickory. During his entire Navy service, he would be assigned duties as a beachmaster on the island of American Samoa, checking supplies in and out to naval vessels.

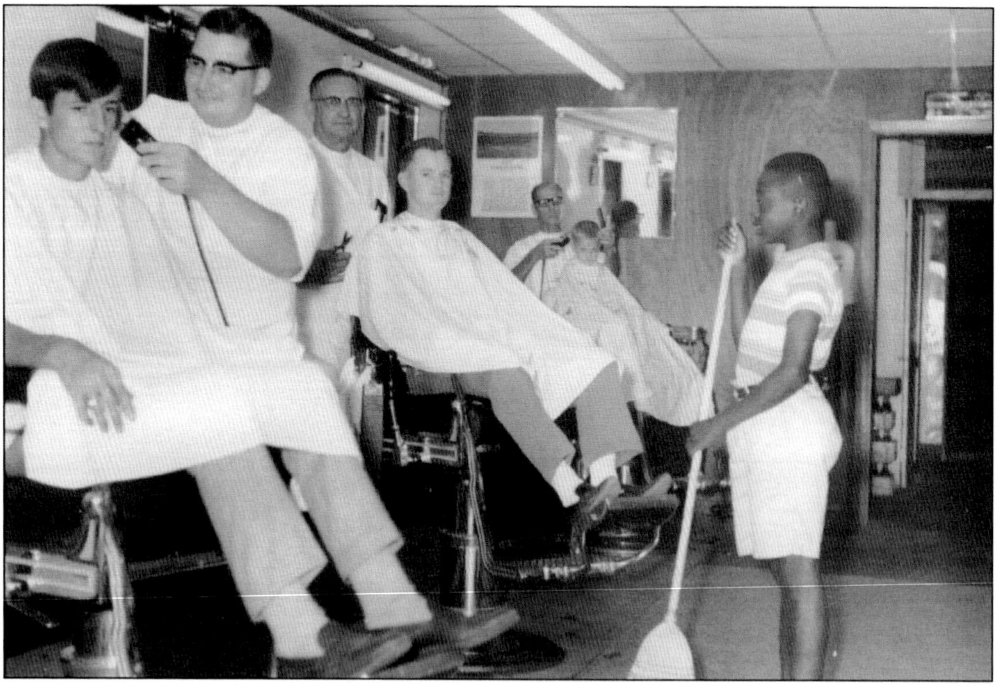

This picture was taken in the barbershop of George Smith in Conover in the late 1960s. The barbers are Ellis Cline, first chair; George Smith, second chair; and Johnny Shelton, third chair. The young cleanup boy with the broom is Steve Powell, of Conover.

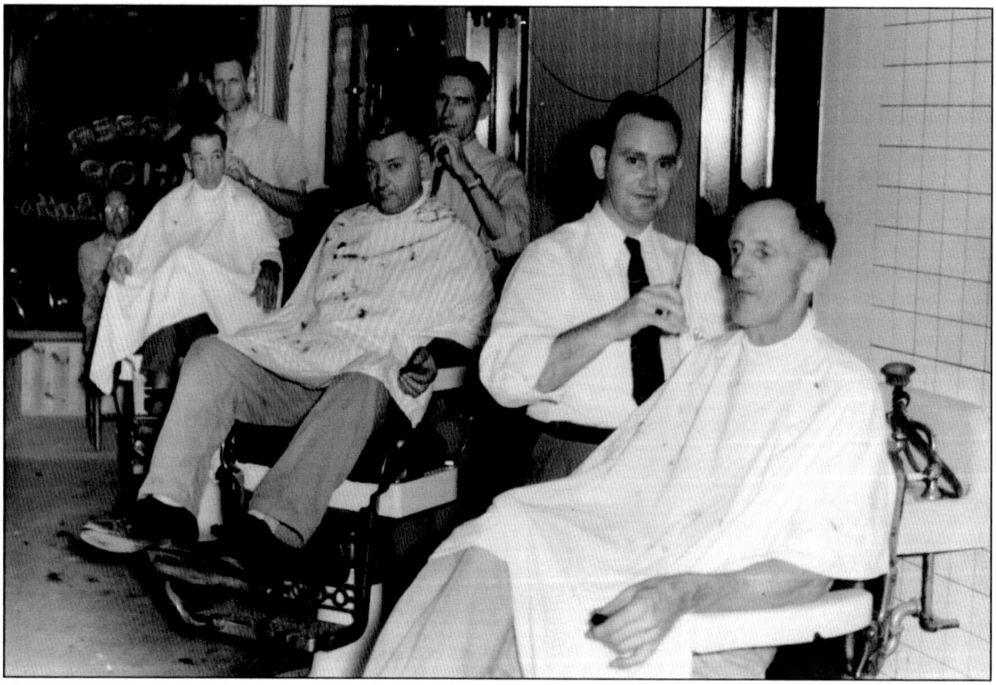

This is another priceless photograph taken prior to 1958 at the George Smith Barbershop in downtown Conover. Pictured from front to back are Russell Sigmon Sr., Charles Presswood, Claude Smith, Loy Punch, George Smith, Coley Yoder, and Ken Herman.

On Main Street in downtown Conover, just hanging out, are Zula Mae Spencer (left) and Edith Deal. Zula would marry Norris Rockett, and Edith was later married to Jim "Bud" Bogle. At the Royal Crown Cola sign is the L.E. Hunsucker Hardware Store. Next to it was a gasoline station owned by Joe A. Isenhower and later leased to the Shook family for a cafe.

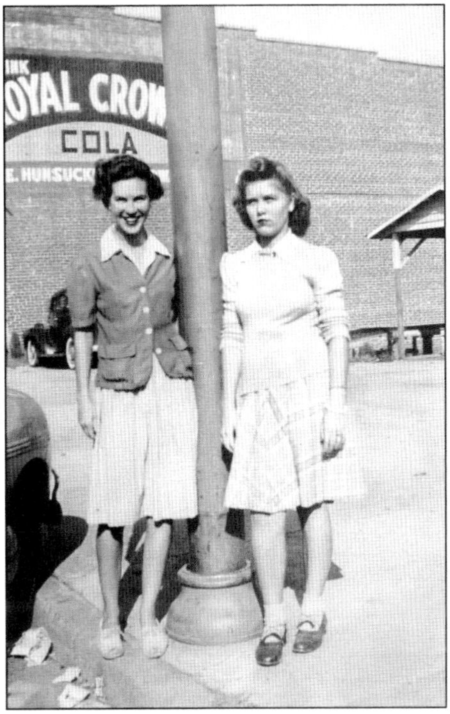

Pictured is the one-time home of Professor Hemmeter, president of Concordia College. Hemmeter built a smaller home across the street. This large home then was purchased by G.W. Moehlmann. Later, he would build a brick home just east of the White Pine Club. Carroll Barringer purchased the house and converted it into apartments. Rev. George Mennen retired here. Also living here was the Cashion family and wildlife officer John Fairchild and family.

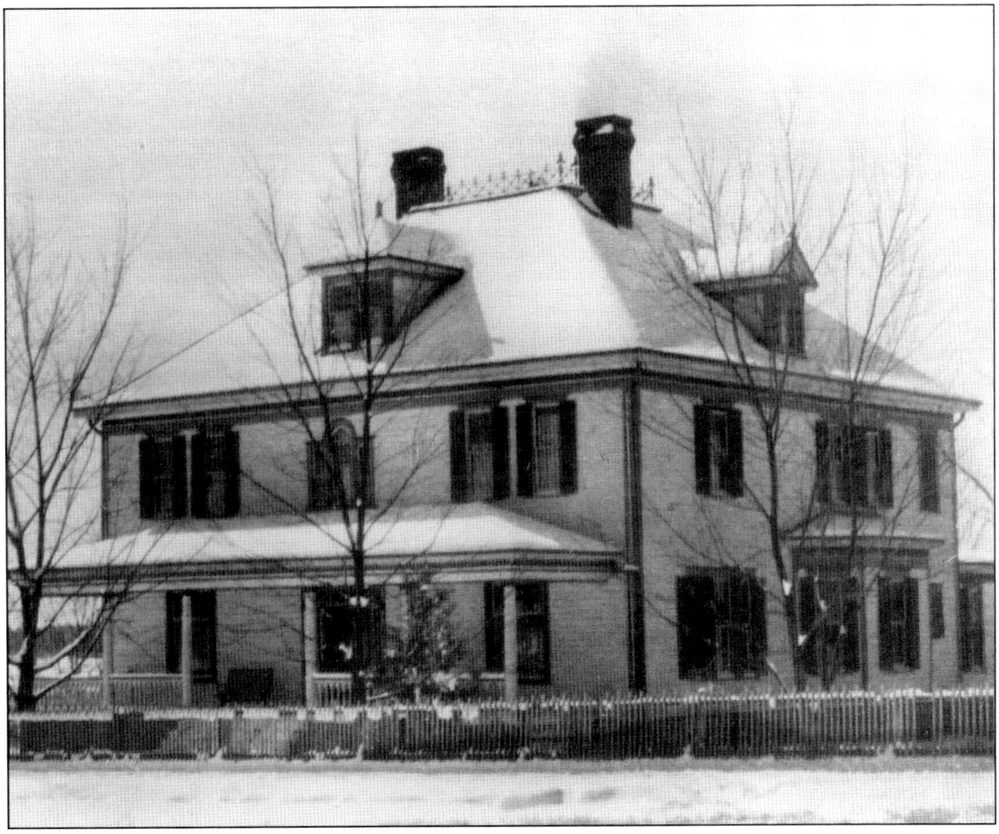

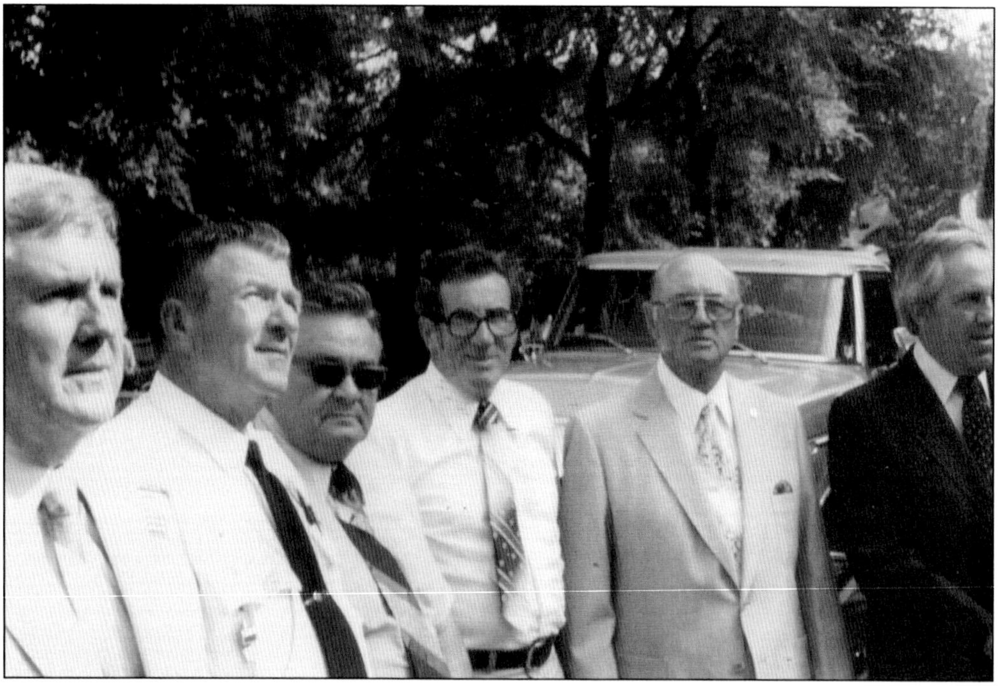

Gathered for the 1976 Old Soldier's Reunion parade in Newton is this group of Conover notables. From left to right are chief of Conover Police Franklin "Sonny" Herman, Franklin Travis, Harvey Hawn, Hal Kaylor, Floyd Brown, and Hugh Eckard.

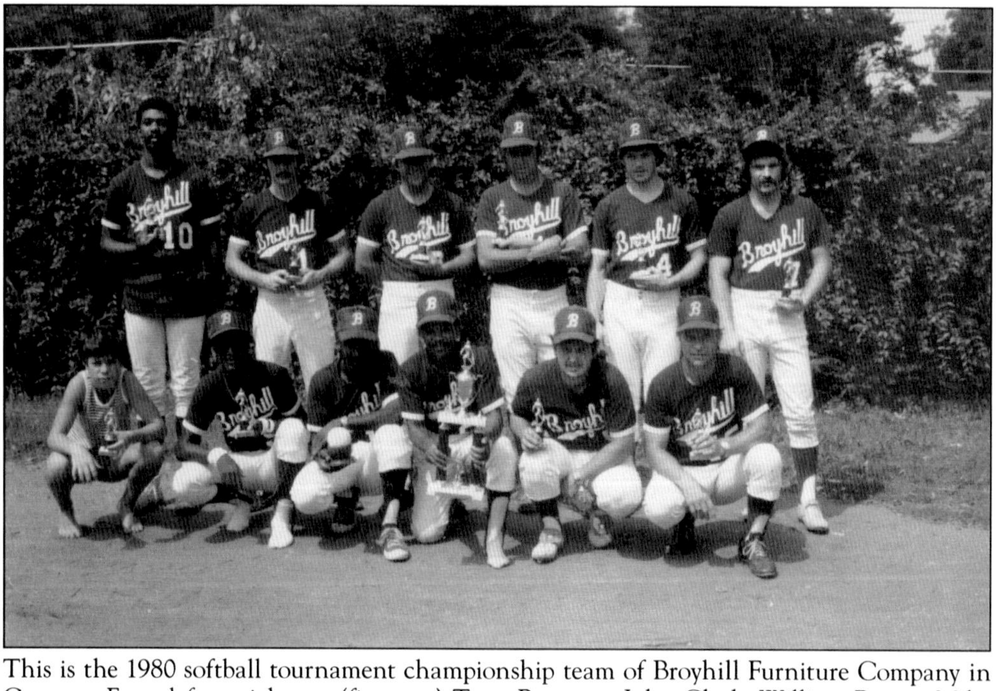

This is the 1980 softball tournament championship team of Broyhill Furniture Company in Conover. From left to right are (first row) Terry Ramsuer, John Clark, William Beatty, Mike Sigmon, Larry Heavner, and unidentified; (second row) Benny Clemmons, Brett Jerone, Ronnie Tolbert, Jerry Benfield, Ray Blackburn, and player-coach Wess Hass.

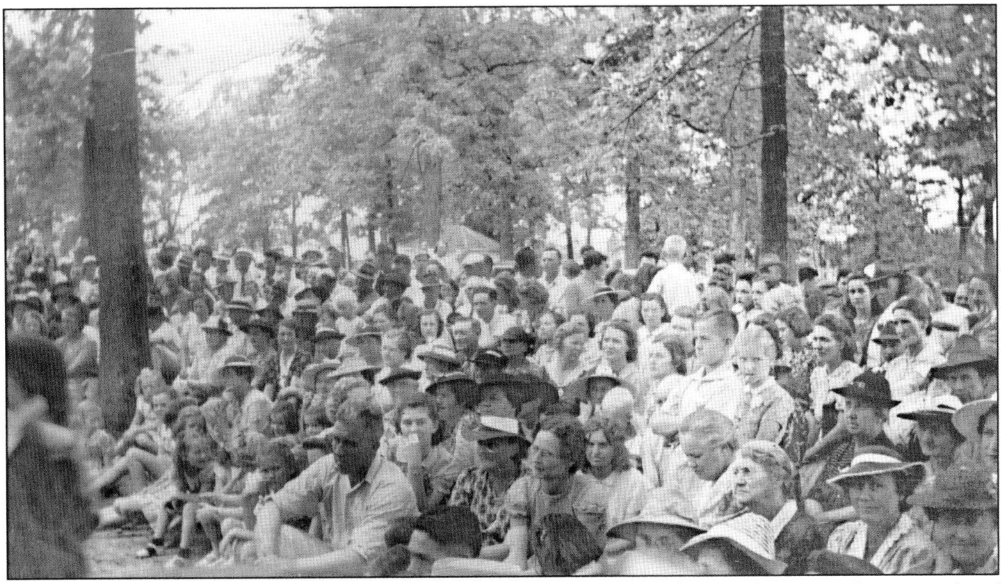

Pictured is an early gathering to hear Governor Hoey, of North Carolina, on the grounds of Concordia Park. The US Army band played for the event. So grateful was the crowd that they let the band members eat first, only to discover that the musicians had eaten all the fried chicken.

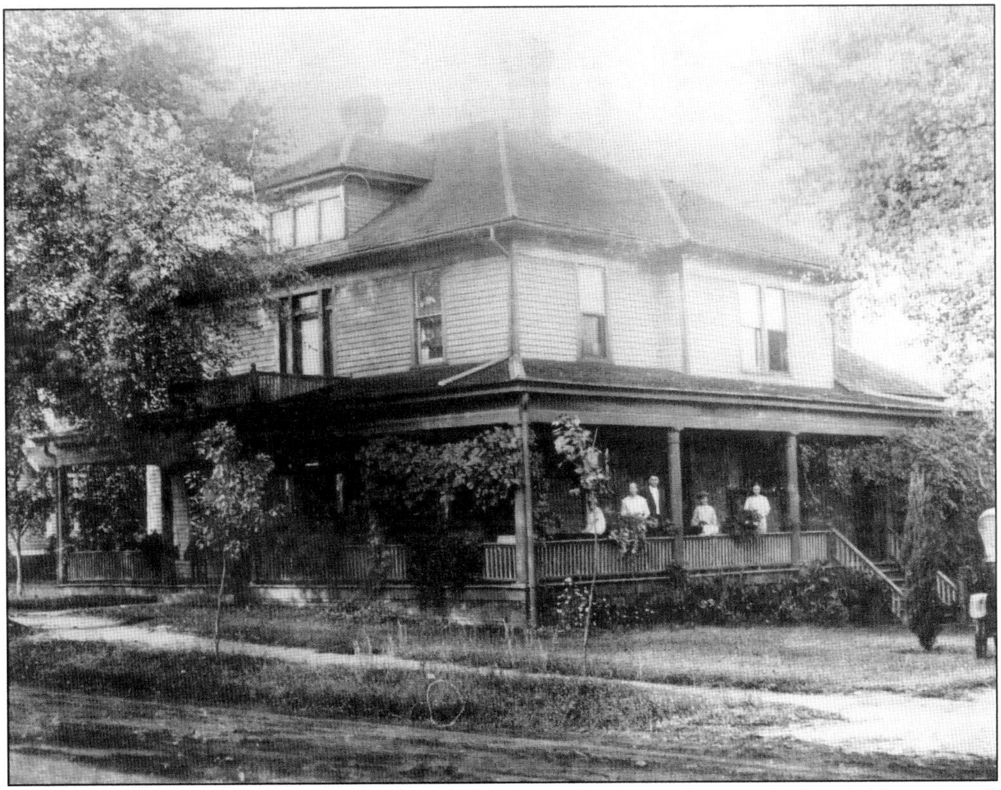

This photograph shows the stately Ed Little home in Conover, along with the children. It still stands today and was once the business home of Dellinger's Interiors at 410 First Avenue South. Little was employed at the Conover Post Office.

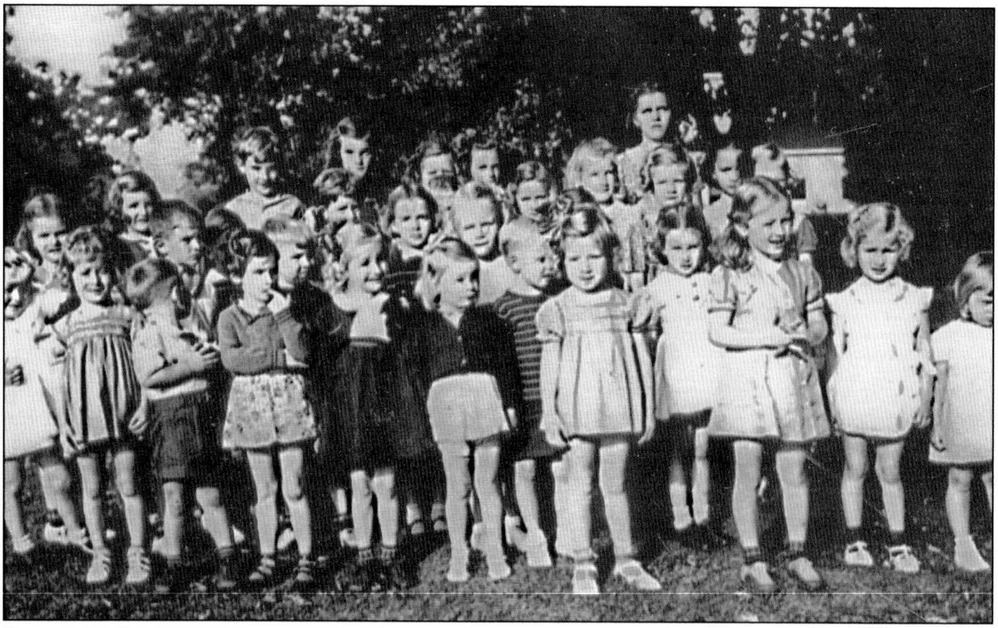

One of the largest gatherings of children in Conover was the sixth birthday party at the home of Shirley Moehlmann. A story is that during the polio quarantine, each child had to stay in their own yard. Living across the street from Shirley was Patricia Bowman. An ingenious idea was to attach a note to her dog's collar. Young Patricia would call the dog, retrieve the note, answer with another message, and Shirley would call her dog back across the street.

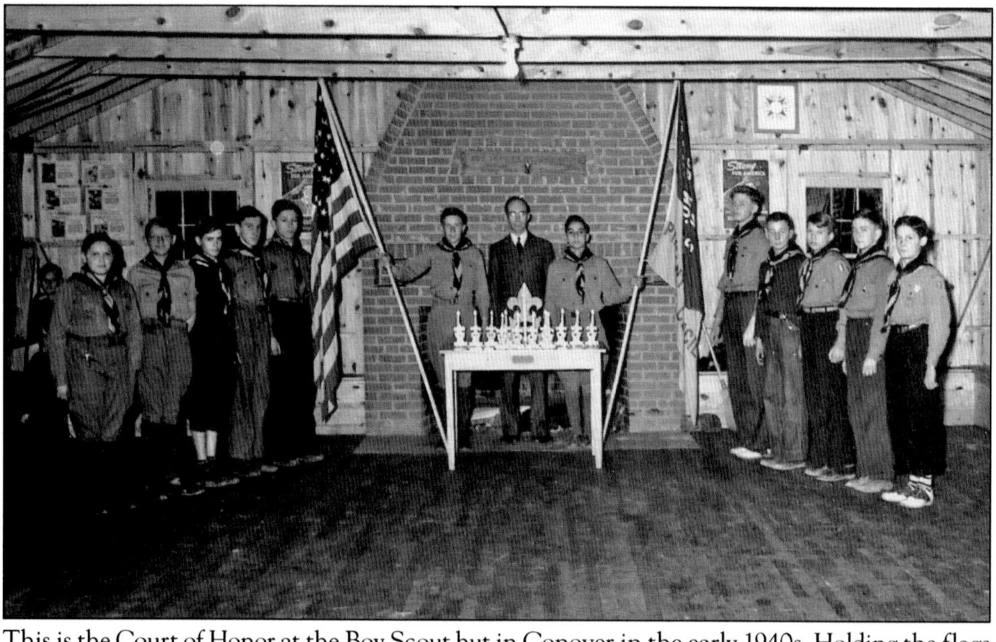

This is the Court of Honor at the Boy Scout hut in Conover in the early 1940s. Holding the flags are Ewin Rockett (left) and Jack Abernathy with Scoutmaster Walter Brady in the center. On the left are, from left to right, Walter Drum, Jasper Smith, Rudy McRee, Morris Power, and Robert Holland. On the right are, from left to right, Kenneth Coyner, Eddie Simmons, Floyd "Brownie" Brown Jr., Walter Holland, and Junior Lofland.

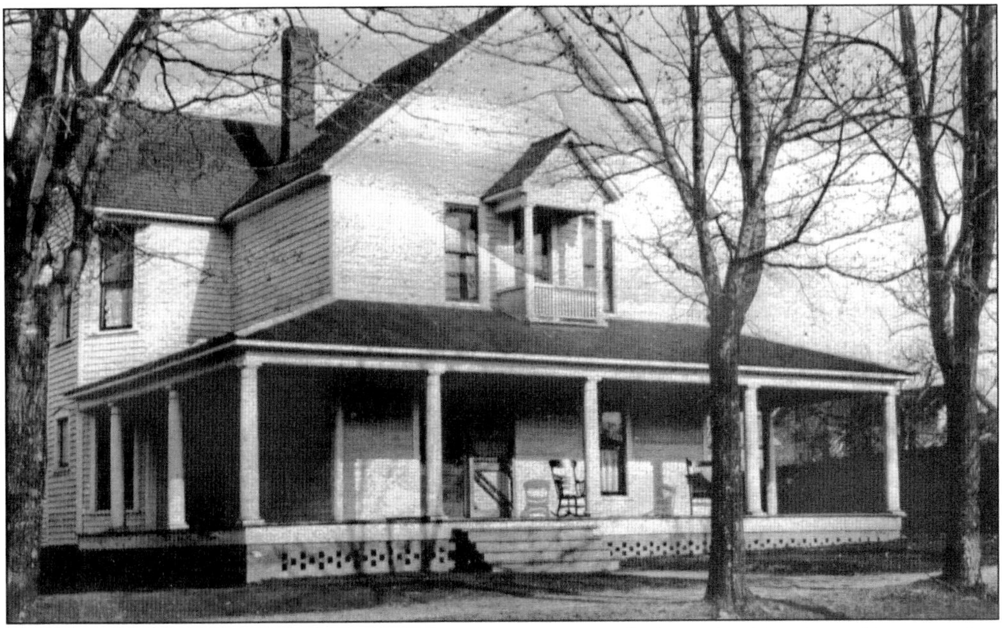

Shown is the first John A. Isenhower home that once stood where the Matthews Construction Company building is now located. John Isenhower needed a new home, and Colonial Theaters of Valdese needed a lot to build the new Canova Theater. A deal was made with builder V.O. Sipe and the Isenhowers, to trade this house and lot for a new home built across from Charlie's Bait Shop.

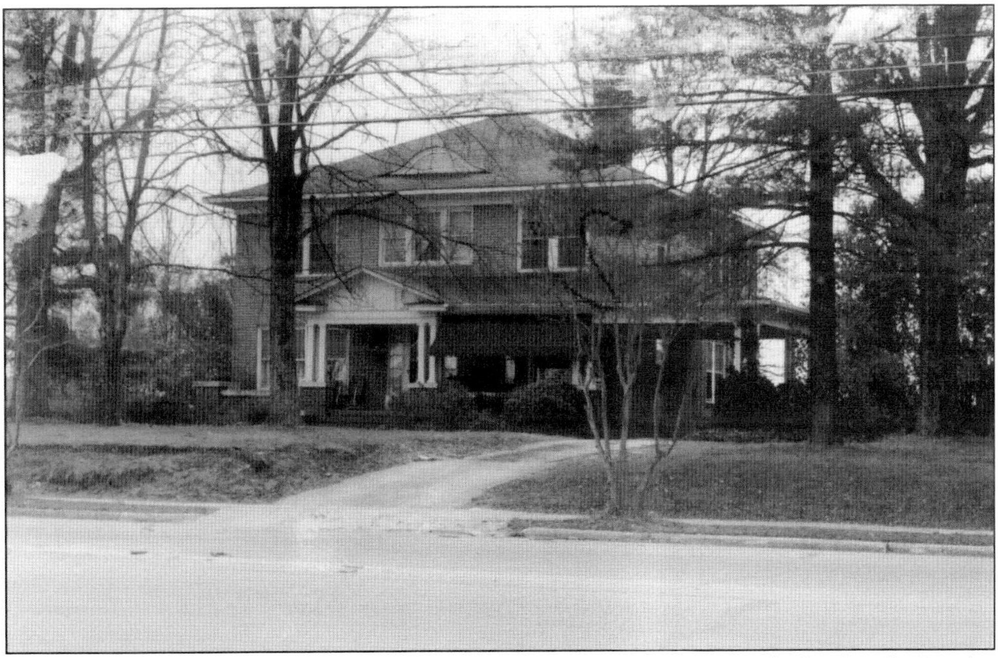

Shown is the new home of the J.A. Isenhower family in Conover. It was on the lot that the Peoples Bank now occupies. This stately home built of rock was well suited for the growing Isenhower family. This was in the trade with V.O. Sipe for the lot space that would be the location of the new theater. The previous home was demolished.

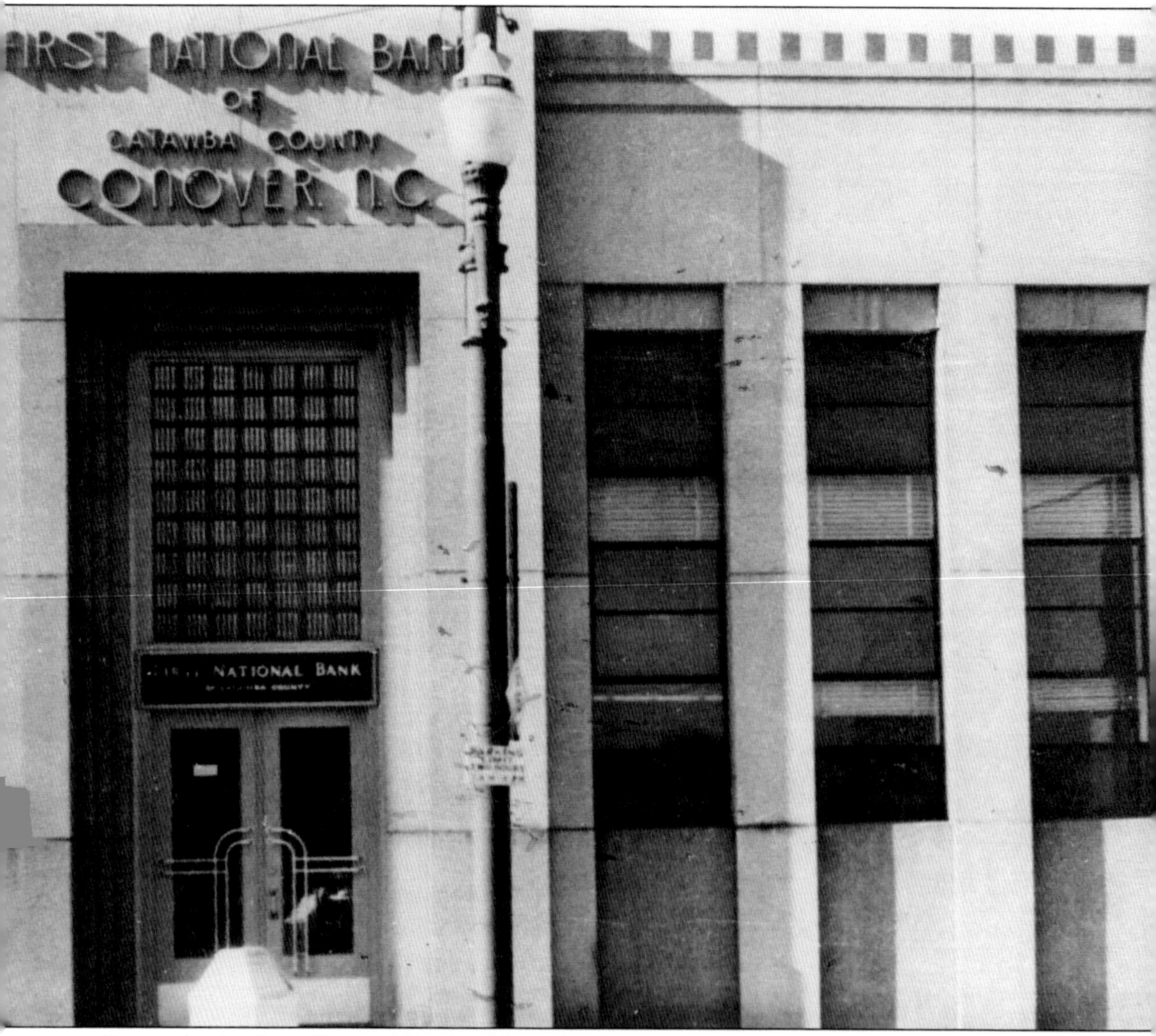

Pictured is the First National Bank of Catawba County in Conover. Prior to this, it was named the Citizens Bank. The Citizens Bank officers and employees were J.A. Isenhower, president; L.E. (Squire) Hunsucker, vice president; Adrian L. Shuford Jr., cashier; Robert Boatright, assistant cashier; C.L. Sigmon, teller; and Betty Shuford, bookkeeper. The directors were R.K. Bolick, L.E. Hunsucker, John A. Isenhower, S.S. Rowe, T.W. Saunders, A.L. Huford, and P.E. Yount. Changes were about to take place downtown. Aldrian Shuford became a director with the First National Bank of Catawba County in Hickory and the First Union Bank. It was in the late 1940s that the First National Bank and Citizens Bank merged. This beautiful structure was demolished to make space for a newer First Union Bank. The lot is now occupied by the Wachovia Bank.

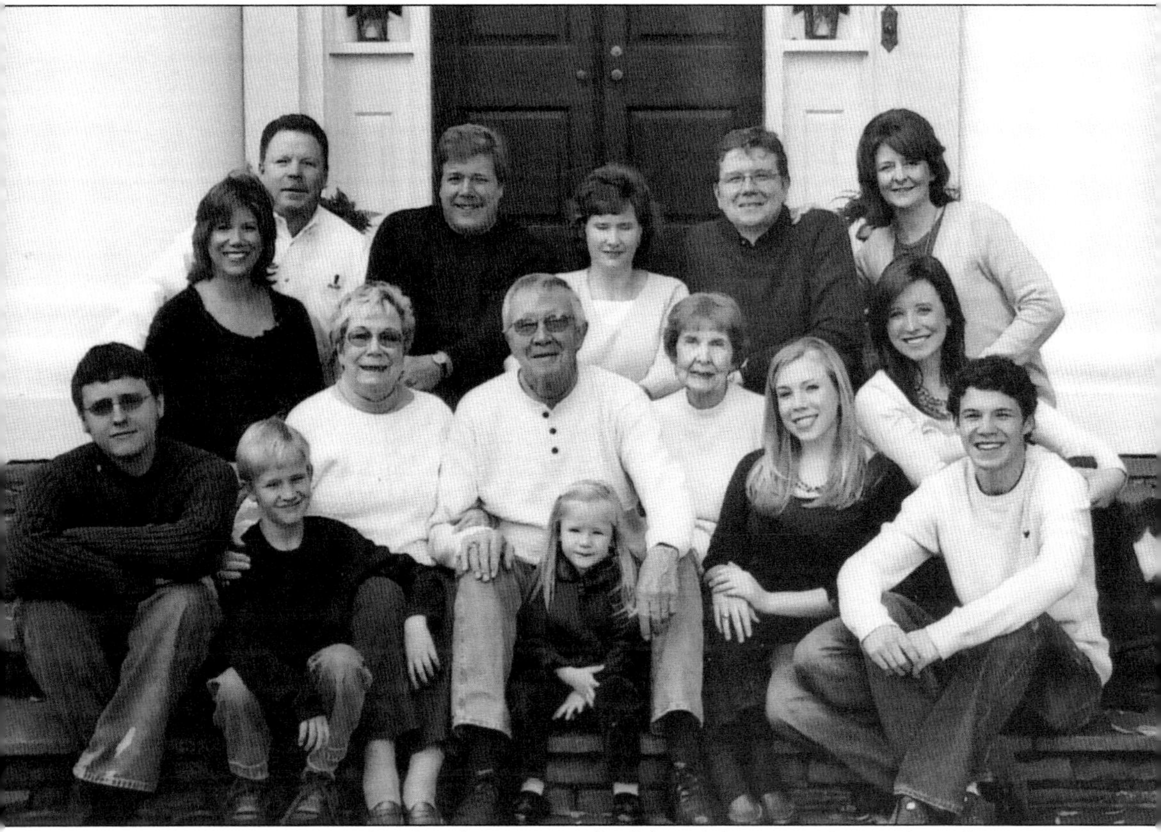

Shown is the Lee Moritz Sr. family, of Conover. All of the adults are professionals in their own field of work. They are from the Moritz-Saunders generation of prominent businessmen of the town of Conover. T.W. Saunders was the founder of Saunders Furniture Company. His son Walter would join the firm in 1934 to continue the operation of the business in downtown. He was the first chief of the Conover Volunteer Fire Department, and during World War II, he was appointed the official Conover air raid warden. Pictured from left to right are (first row) Lee Moritz III, Kyle Moritz, and Erin Moritz; (second row) Betty (Saunders) Moritz, Lee Moritz Sr., Betty (Moritz) Bula, Jordan Bolick, Lindsay Moritz, and Jonathan Bolick; (third row) Elaine (Moritz) Bolick, Tim Bolick, Michael Moritz, Debbie Moritz, Lee Moritz Jr., and Michele Moritz.

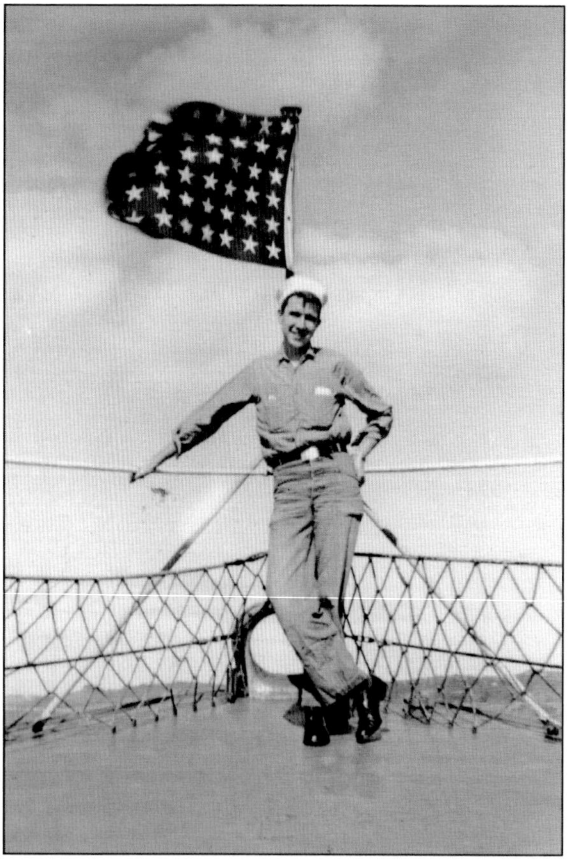

Anchors aweigh! This handsome US Navy "Tin Can" seaman is Lee Moritz Sr., of Conover. He served onboard the USS *Hanna* (DE449) during the Korean War. In 1952, while on maneuvers off the coast of Korea, she was hit broadside by enemy shore batteries. Moritz was reassigned to the USS *Epperson* (DE/DD719) to continue hunter-killer missions off the Korean coast. The Epperson was awarded five battle stars for her seagoing operations. Lee is now retired from Conover Chair Company. He and his wife, Betty, attend the First Methodist Church.

Dinner on the grounds is the setting for this Isenhower family photograph. Pictured from left to right are (first row) Ashley Isenhower, Stine Isenhower, Dr. Sam Isenhower, Suzie I. Hambright, and Celia Saunders; (second row) James P. Isenhower, Carolyn Isenhower, Mary Lillian Isenhower, Frank Mauney, John Hambright, Brian Isenhower, and Mary Louis Mauney.

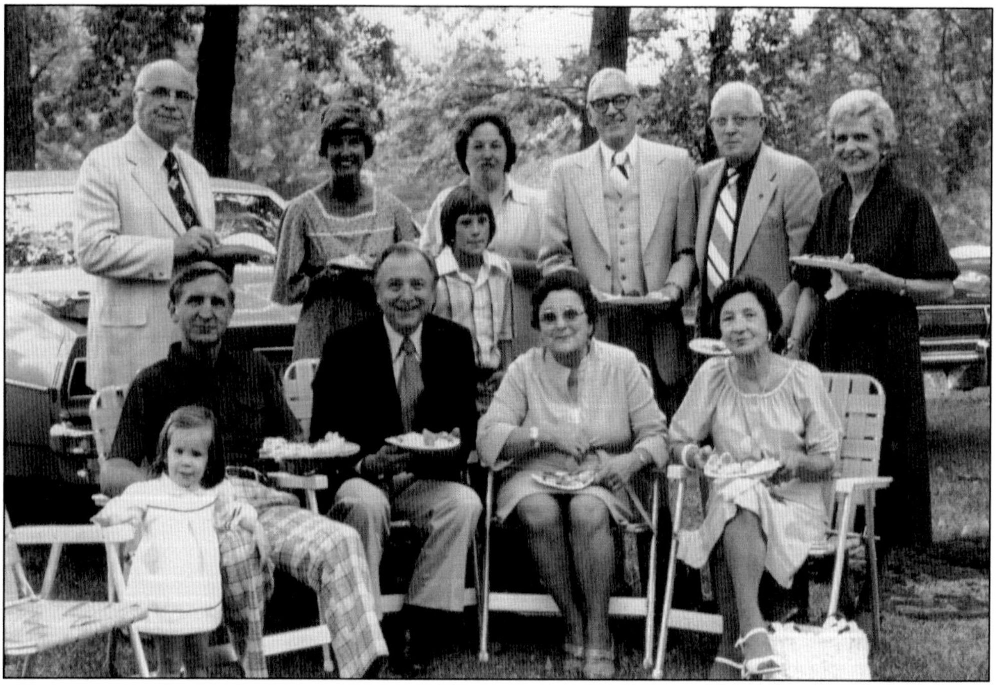

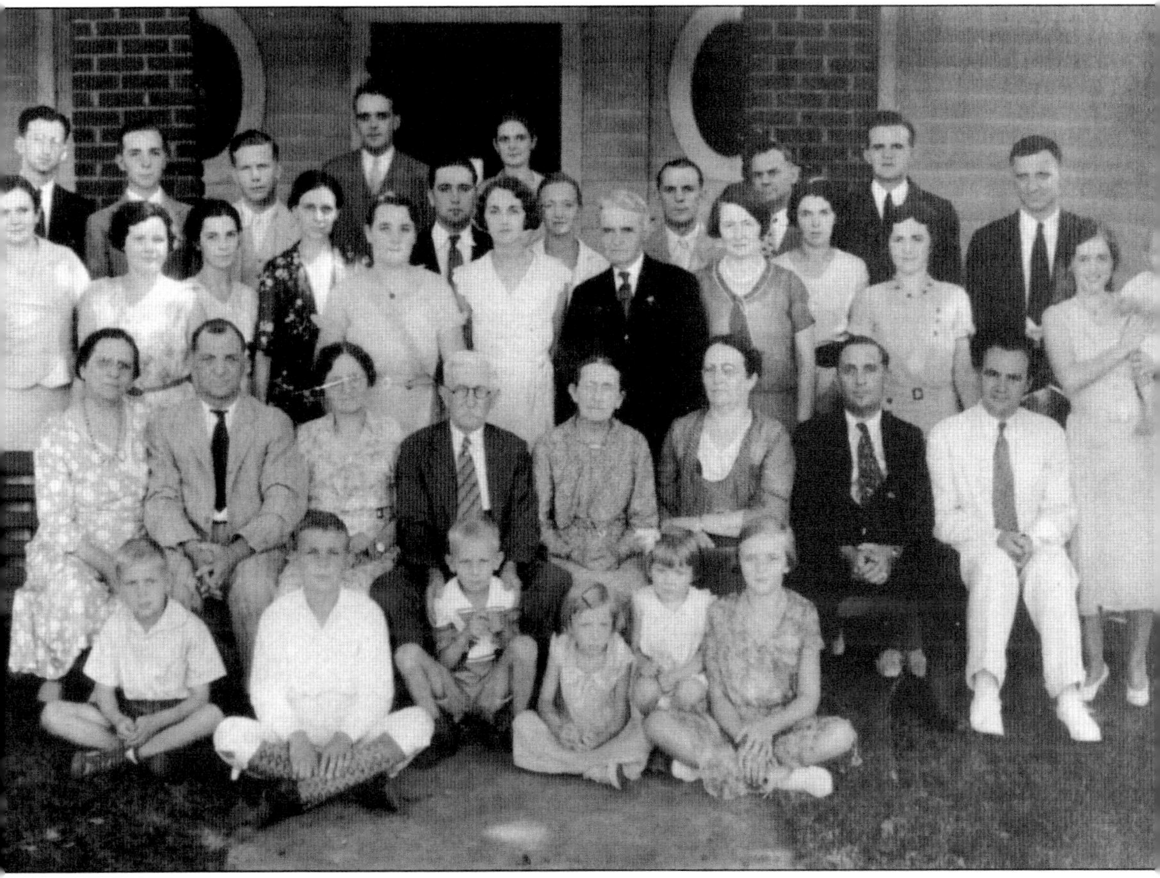

This is a scene from the Philo Isenhower family reunion. From left to right are (first row) Joseph Andrew Isenhower, James Isenhower, Stine Isenhower, two unidentified Wolfe daughters, and Martha Lee Mauney; (second row) Mattie Little, John A. Isenhower, Sarah Cline, Philo Isenhower, Frances H. Isenhower, Anna Mauney, Berman Isenhower, and Auburn Mauney; (third row) E.V. Little, Margaret Setzer, Alberta Isenhower, Celia Saunders Isenhower, Susie Isenhower, Suzie Hambright, Francis Mauney, Gus Mauney, Lottie Isenhower, Christine Isenhower, Juanita Wolfe, and Kathryn Mauney; (fourth row) Ray Setzer, Sam Isenhower, Walter Saunders, Howard Little, Mary Louise Mauney, Harold Isenhower, Mildred Isenhower, Horace J. Isenhower, Austin Cline, Jake Mauney, and Herman Wolfe.

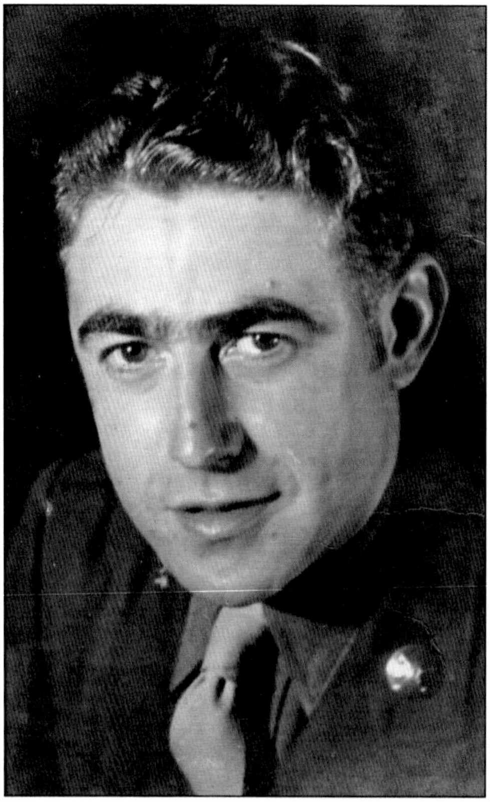

Pictured is Pfc. Adrian Hefner, of Conover. He was in the US Army during World War II from 1943 to 1945, serving with the 6th Armored Division in Patton's Third Army Group, Battery C, 231st Armored Field Artillery, and later with a military police unit. His battle campaigns were at Normandy, Northern France, Ardennes, Rhineland, and Central Europe. His medals included the Good Conduct Ribbon, American Campaign Ribbon, World War II Victory Medal, and the European Theater of Operations Ribbon with six battle stars.

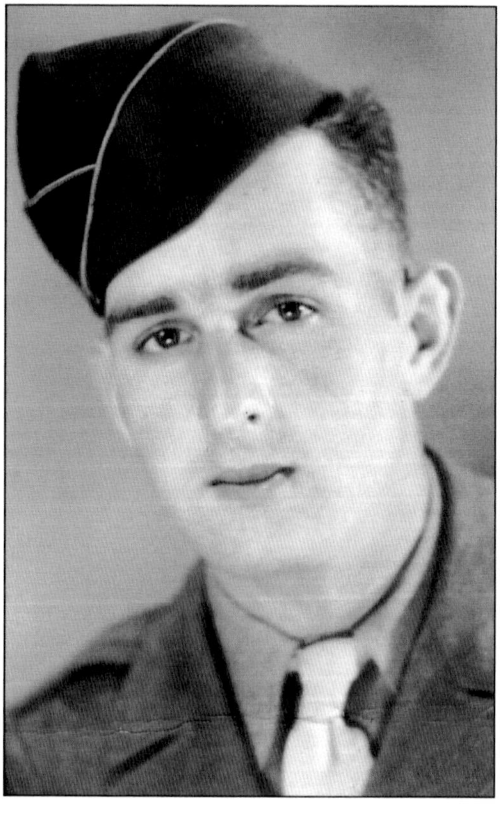

This well-known, likable young man is Otto Lambert, of Conover. Lambert served in the European Theater of Operations during World War II. He served in the 106th Infantry, 3rd Armored Division. While trapped in the Ardennes in winter, he gathered firewood and set it ablaze with gasoline traded from a tank unit for two quarts of French wine. Seeing the forest on fire, a general drove up and asked, "Who the h—l set this fire?" Otto spoke up and said, "I did sir, we're about to freeze to death!" The general replied, "You'll have every German pilot in the sky down on us." Otto replied, "Sir, it would take one dumb German to bomb something already on fire." With that said, the general departed.

Pictured is the popular Conover dentist Dr. Borden Caldwell Drum. He was married to Catherine Scott, of West Jefferson. His father was Commodore Drum, of Newton. He began his practice in Conover in 1936. This was interrupted in 1941 when he enlisted in the US Army with the rank of second lieutenant serving with a dentist medical unit and EVAC unit. He opened a new office upstairs in the Canova Theater building in 1945, while still in the military reserves. He served in Korea in 1950 and 1951, after which he returned to his practice in Conover. His daughter Sally Black resides in Conover.

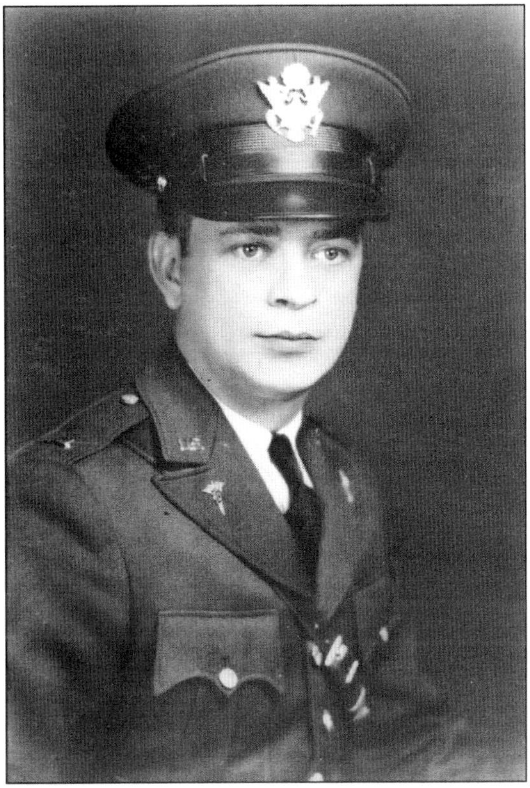

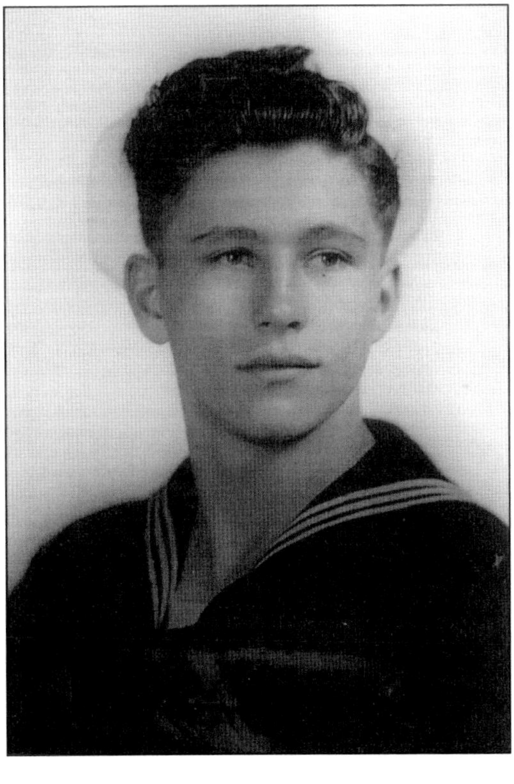

This young navy seaman is Robert E. "Bob" Holland, of Conover. His parents were Millard and Olive Brady Holland. Bob enlisted in the US Navy in December of 1945 and was discharged in 1947. He took boot camp in San Diego and was sent to storekeepers' school at the Great Lakes Training School. He was then stationed in Cleveland, Ohio. He held the rank of storekeeper third class at his discharge. He then attended North Carolina State College and graduated with a bachelors of science in textiles. He was employed with Shuford Mills for 43 years. He retired in 1993 as vice president. He is an accomplished photographer.

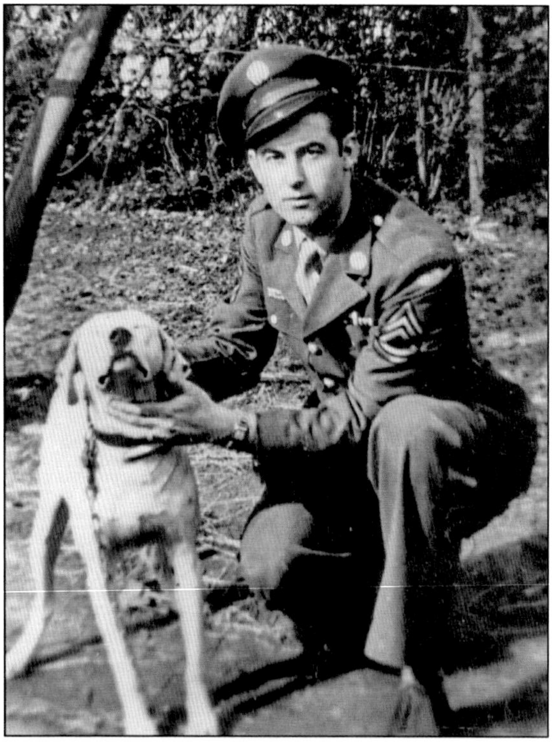

Pictured with his favorite pal, Sally, is Mack Brady Melchor, of Conover. He was an ardent fisherman, birddog trainer, and hunter. After graduation from Newton Conover High School, he enlisted in the US Army Air Corps. He served on a B-17G as top turret gunner and flight engineer with the Mighty Eighth Air Force, 2nd Battle Wing, 381st Bomb Group (H), L Group, with the 532nd and 533rd Squadrons at Ridgewell Station, England. He flew more than 35 missions over Germany. Tech Sergeant Melchor received numerous medals: two Presidential Unit Citations, the Distinguished Flying Cross, the Air Medal with five clusters, the European Theater of Operations Medal with five battle stars, the American Campaign Medal, the World War II Victory Medal, the Army Good Conduct Medal, and the UDC World War II Cross of Honor. His son Gary survives and lives in Conover.

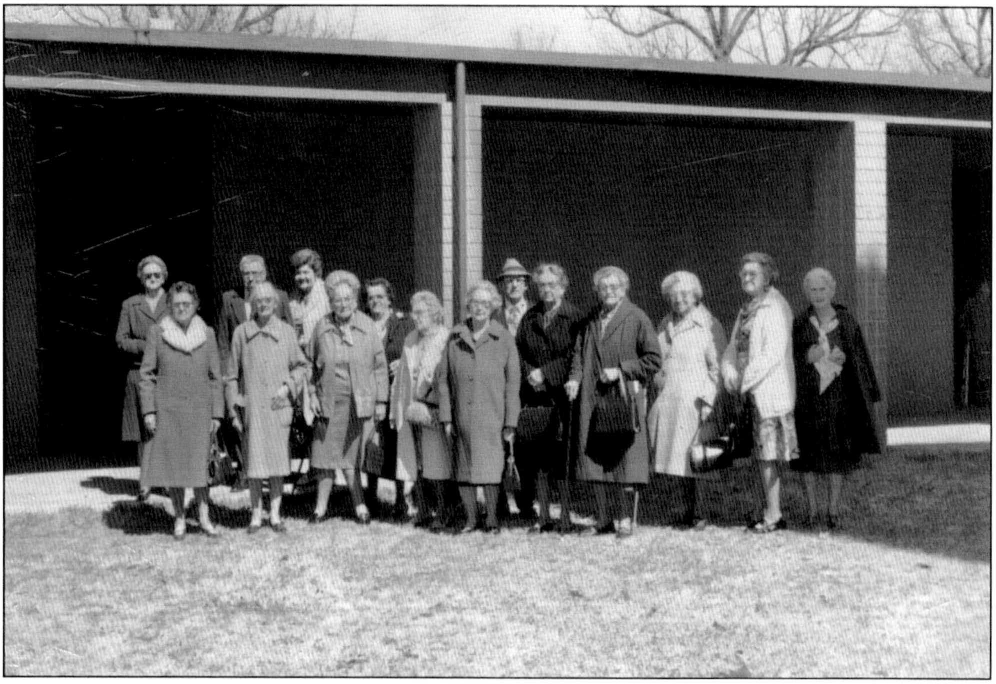

This photograph was taken at a senior citizens dinner at Concordia Lutheran Church in the early 1970s. Pictured from left to right are Hattie McRee, Thelma Hollar, Rev. Fred Graff, Bessie Parker, Mary Graff, E.C. (Claudia) Seitz, Lena Kaylor, Ola Matthews, Berta Bolick, Walter Mathews, Mrs. L.C. Hunsucker, Mrs. Edward Simmons, Mrs. Pinkey Henry, Leno Spencer, and Susie Stearms.

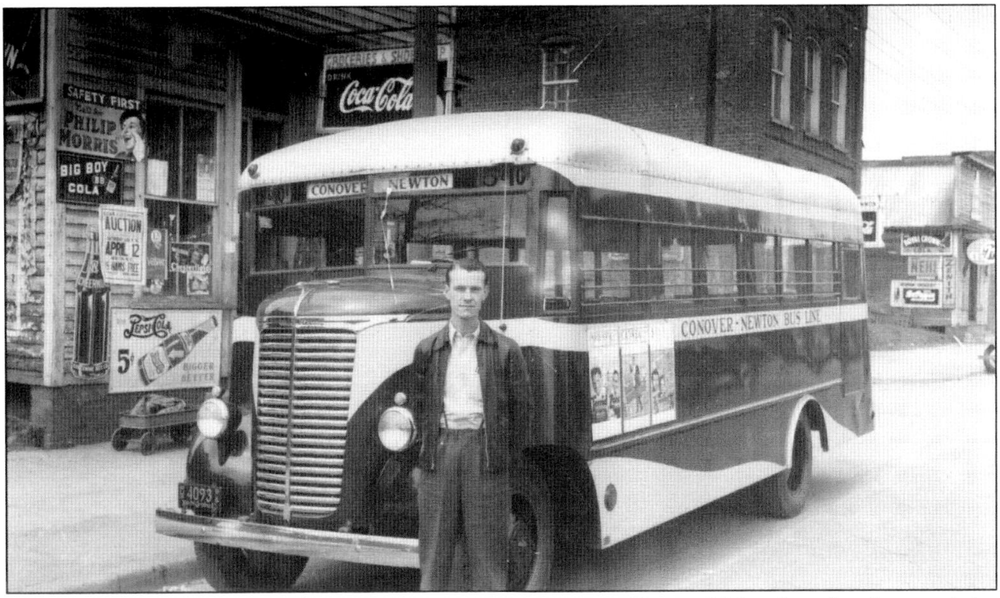

Standing in front of the Ed Herman store in Conover is Howard Murphy, the driver of the Conover-Newton bus. The transportation company was owned by Allen Arndt, of Newton. During the weekends, it was called the "Showbus," as it would transport moviegoers to the Canova Theater in downtown Conover from outlying areas such as Catfish, Maiden, Catawba, Claremont, and Newton.

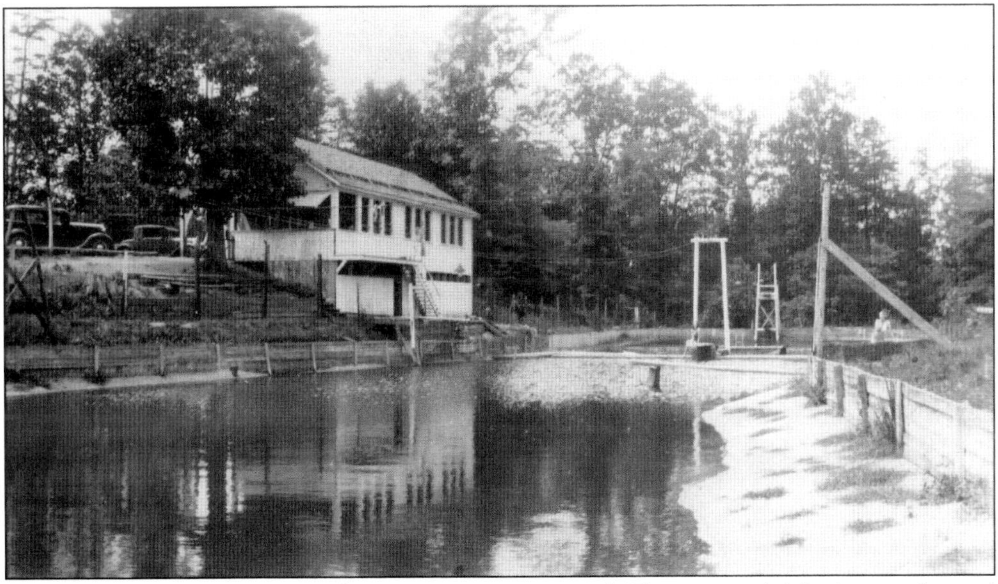

Shown is the first and renowned Conover swimming pool. This stream-fed facility was located just outside the city limits. It was built in the mid-1920s by Marion M. Hunsucker. It had a much deeper upper pool with a very high diving board. The lower pool was right in front of the main building and dressing rooms. The grounds were used by church groups and for family reunions. Joe and Juanita Isenhower once operated the pool, which was later sold to Horace J. Isenhower in 1947. Isenhower used it to store hay and other equipment. The building caught fire around midnight one night in June 1952, thus bringing to a close this popular gathering place.

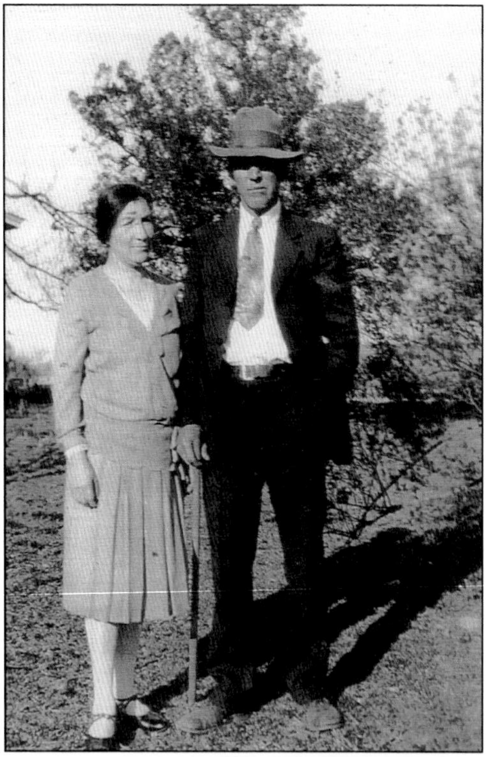

Pictured here are Marion Hunsucker and his wife, Anna Cline Hunsucker, the grandparents of Joyce (Curlee) Shaw, in a picture taken around 1931. Marion Hunsucker was the builder of the Conover swimming pool in the 1920s. This was long before Kool Park, another swimming pool in the St. Stephens area, was built. Here at the Conover pool, it was important to watch carefully at the upper and deeper pool because of the snakes, frogs, and other marine life. This was a fun place to cool off on hot summer days.

Seen here at an awards ceremony at the Conover Furniture plant, Fay "Cookie" Black is recognizing Woodrow Burris for his 18 years of employment at the Broyhill plant in the shipping department. It was not unusual for men and women to spend their entire employment years at the Conover plant. It offered fair wages, good working conditions, and steady work.

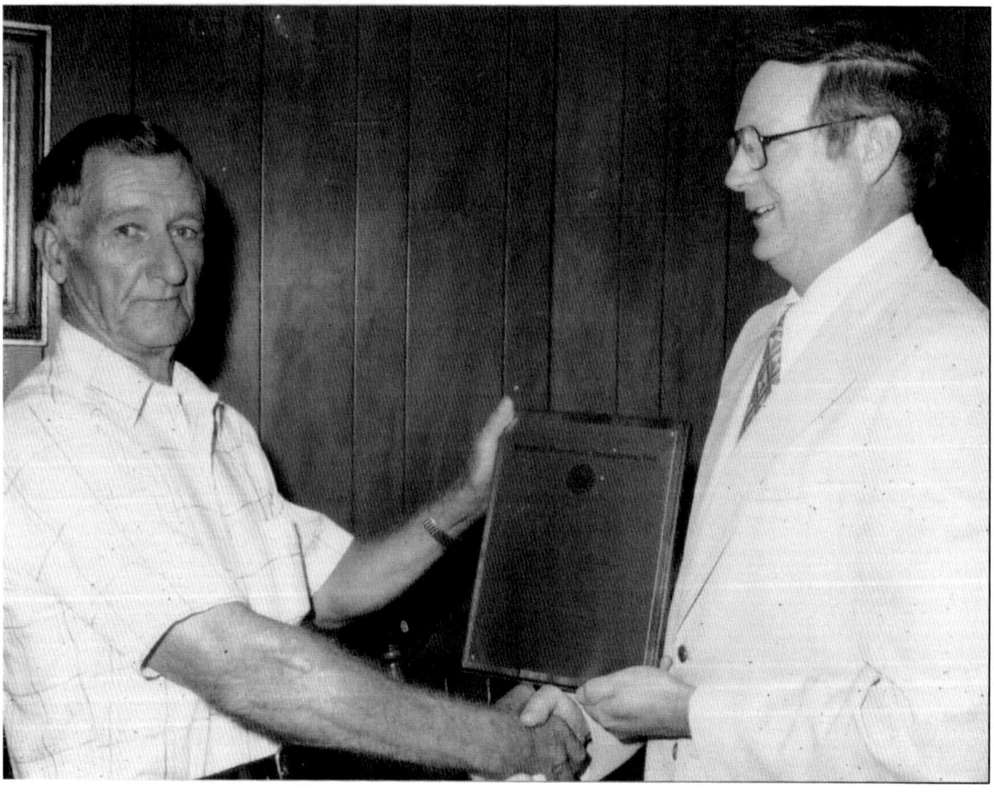

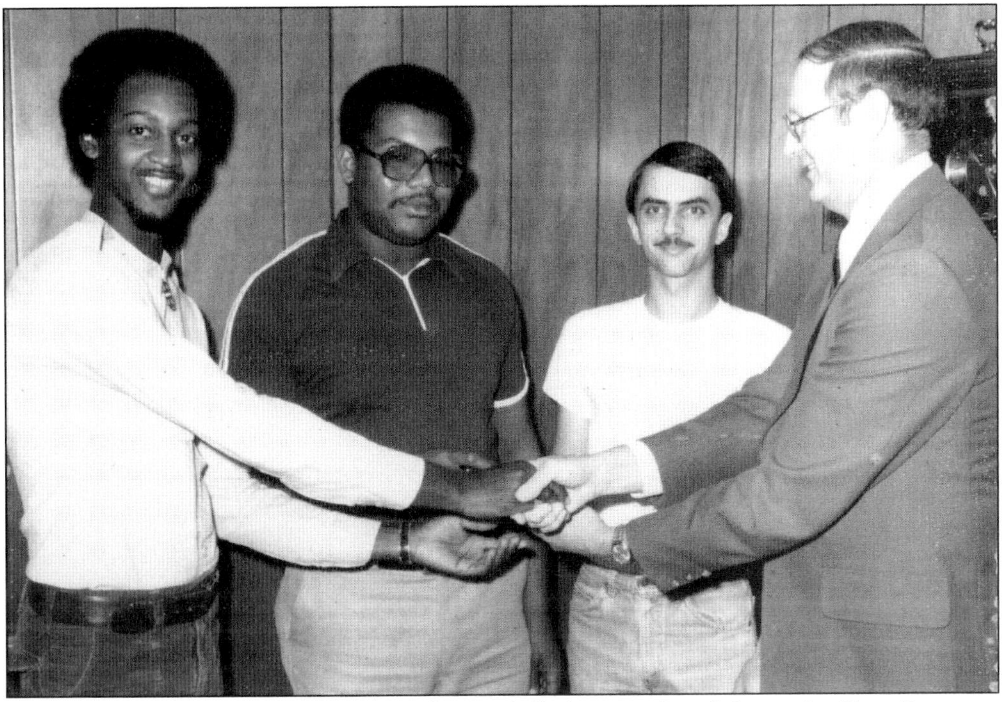

Pictured at another awards ceremony at the Broyhill plant are, from left to right, Terry Ramseur, Clarence Curt, David Schronce, and plant manager Fay "Cookie" Black. This recognition in 1980 was for five years of perfect attendance.

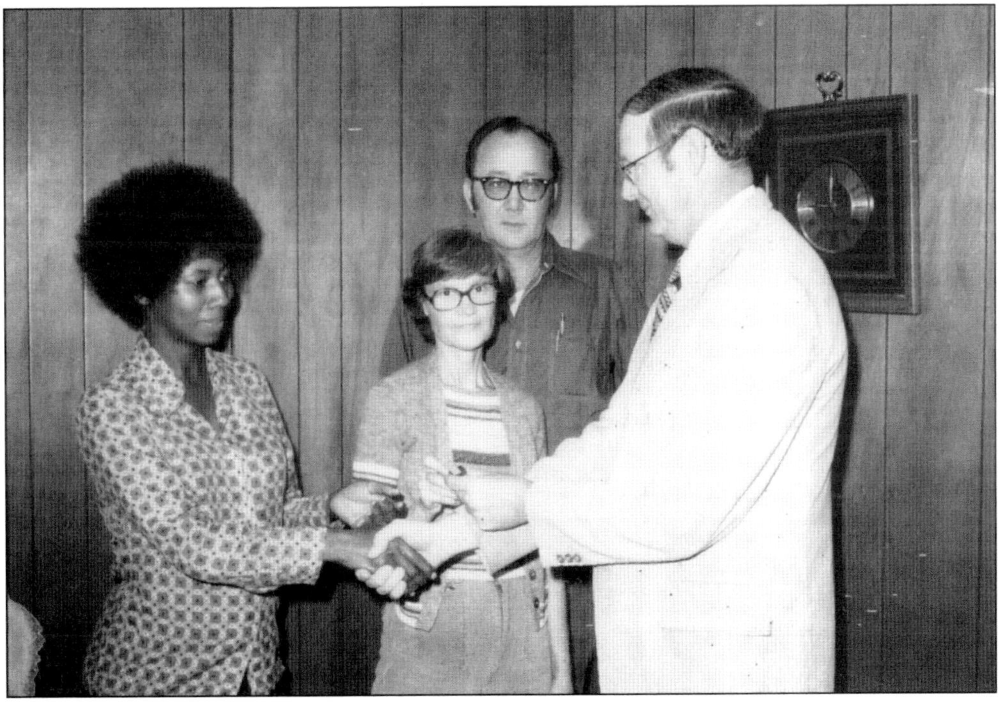

Shown is Fay "Cookie" Black (far right), manager of the Conover Broyhill plant, giving service award pins to Dixie Anthony (left), Lena Hedrick (second from left), and Floyd Pennell.

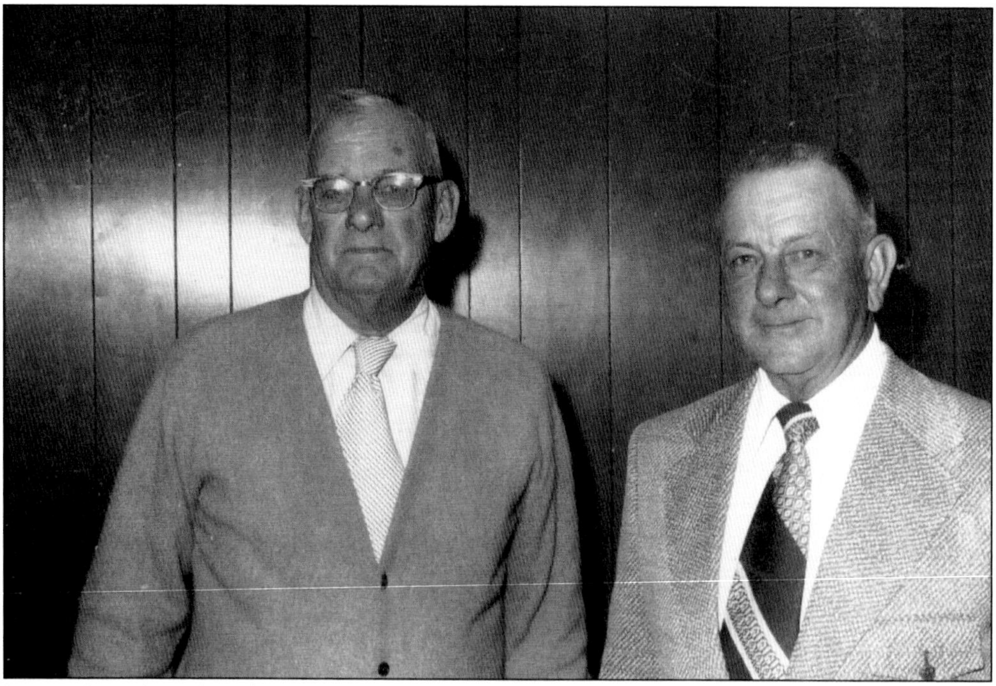

Pictured on their day of retirement from the Conover Furniture Company are John Dellinger (left) and Bob Carpenter. Dellinger served as the chief of police for the city of Conover from 1947 to 1953.

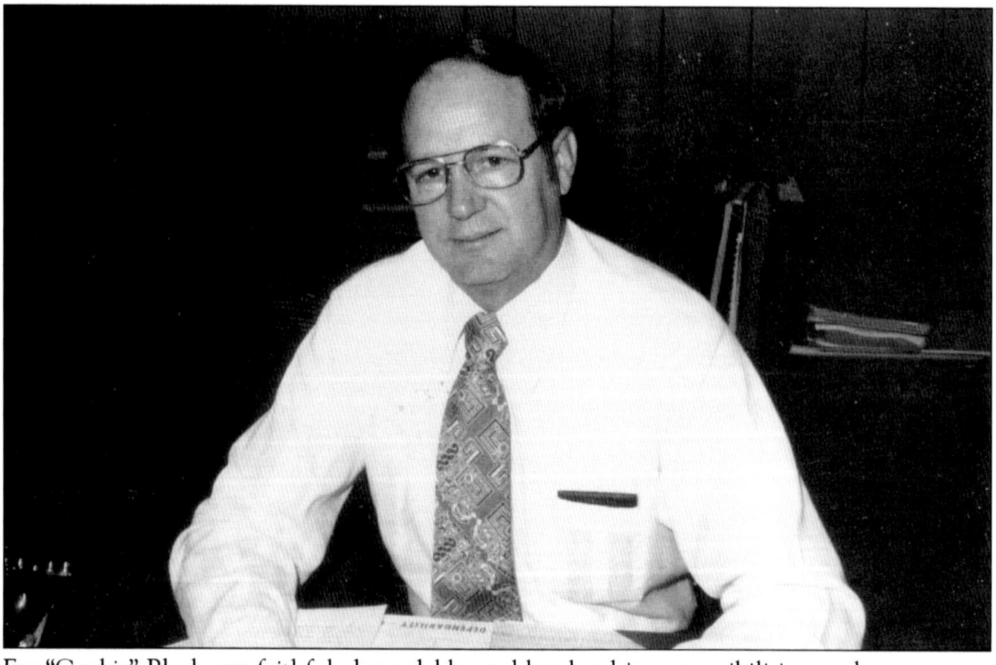

Fay "Cookie" Black was faithful, dependable, and loyal at his responsibilities as plant manager of the Conover Broyhill plant. He always presented himself with neatness and business-like appearances. He was fair and just to all in having the ability to work out any problems with personnel. He is now retired and lives in Conover.

This is an aerial view of downtown Conover in the late 1940s. It was most likely taken from the aircraft of George Smith, as the Canova Theater is in existence at the time of the photograph. The small, wooden shack in the center on Main Street is the barbershop of Preston Baker.

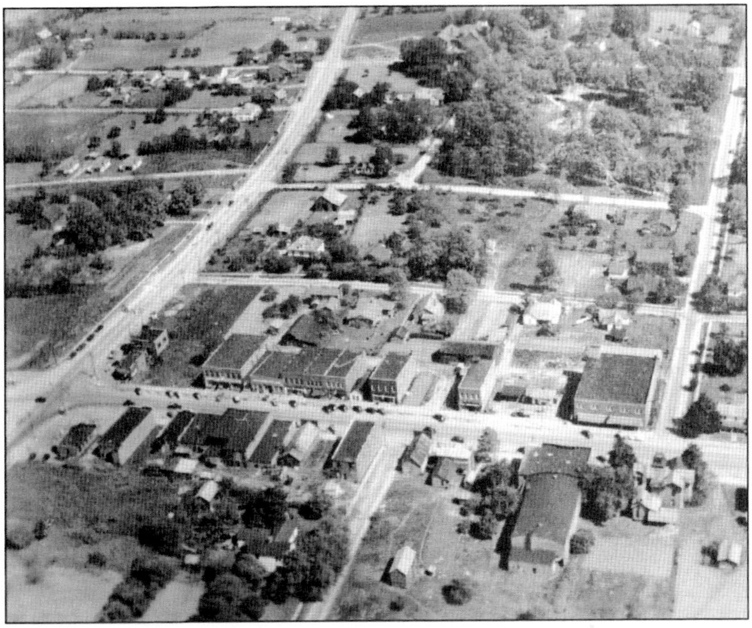

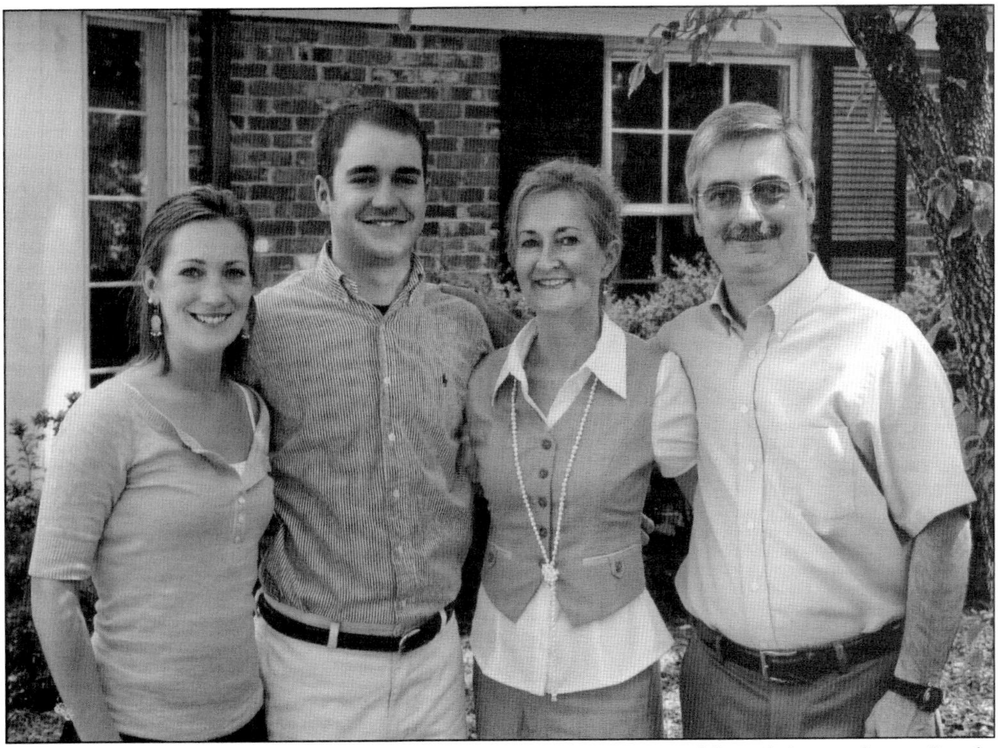

This is the Mark and Mary Canrobert family, of Conover. Pictured from left to right are Sarah, Chris, Mary, and Mark. Mark is the business unit manager for the Neptco Company based in Lenoir. Mary (Stearns) Canrobert is a former elementary and middle school teacher and currently works as a freelance writer and editor. Mark and Mary lived in China in 2006–2009, where he supervised the building of a new Neptco facility. Daughter Sarah Dorrier lives in Charlotte, and son Chris, an accountant, lives in Raleigh. Mark and Mary attend Concordia Lutheran Church.

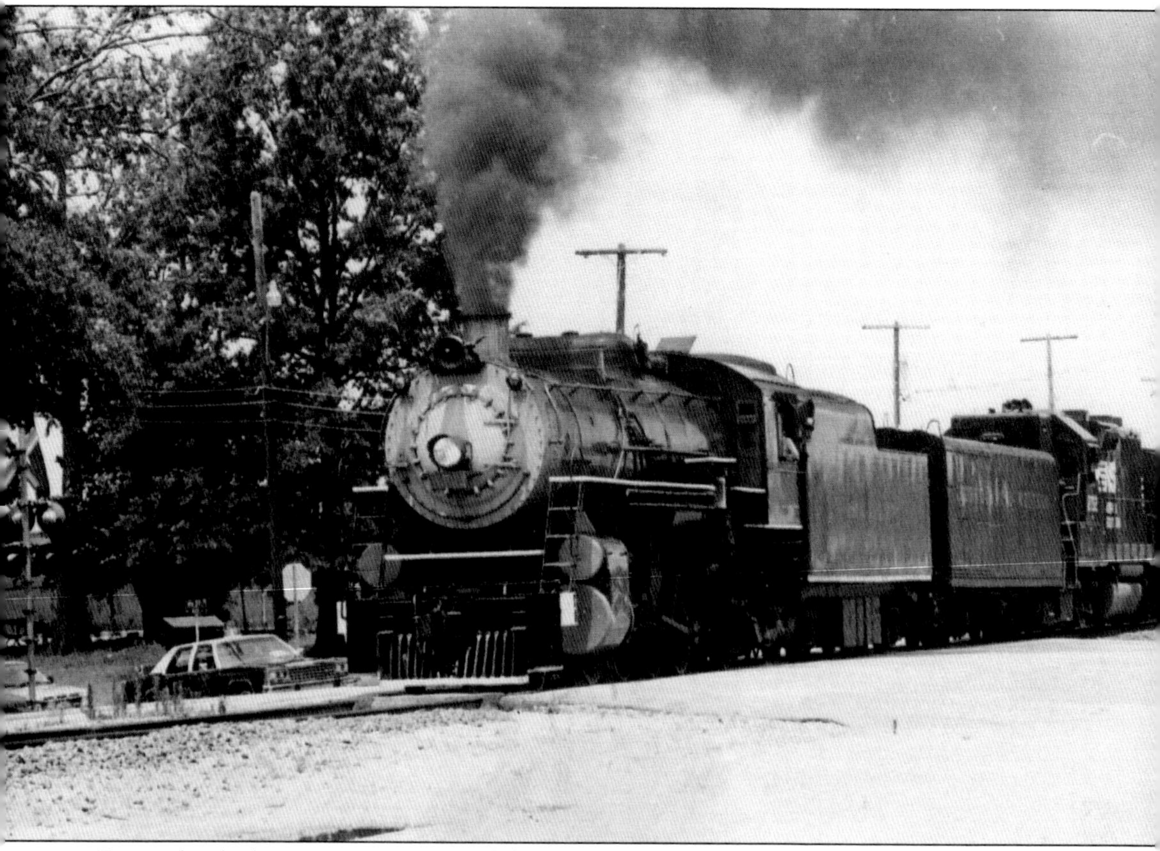

Pictured is the last steam train to travel the rails through Conover. The photograph was taken at the crossing at Conover Motors in 1974. It was the decision of the president of Norfolk-Southern Railroad that steam engines would no longer be used for excursion events on Norfolk-Southern rails. This engine No. 4501 would soon be retired from the system.

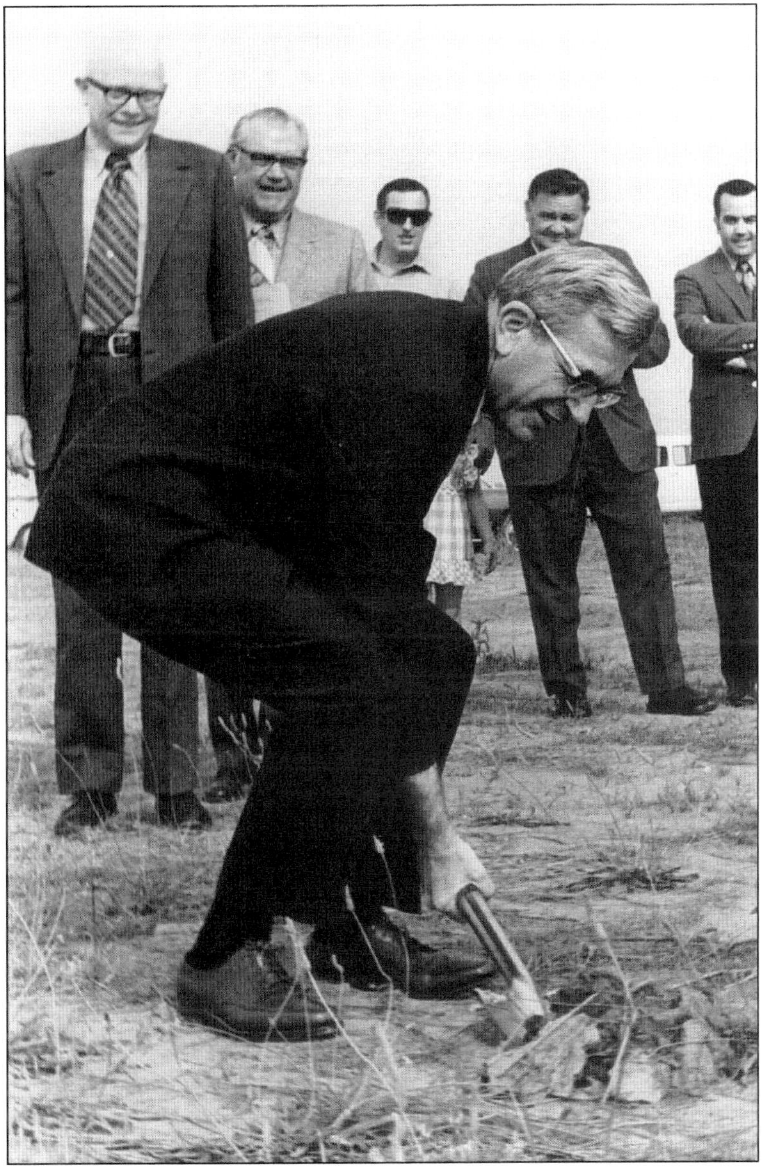

On June 28, 1972, Adrian L. Shuford Jr. turned the first spade of earth in the groundbreaking ceremonies for the new $1.2 million YMCA in Conover. Each of the other officers took turns with the spade. Rev. Stanley Stiver concluded the programs with the benediction. Standing behind Shuford are, from left to right, O. Leonard Moretz, vice president and co-chair of the fundraising; Martin Keisler, treasurer; David Smith and daughter Shelly; Harvey Hawn, mayor of Conover; and co-chair member Jerome Bolick. Moretz singled out Shuford for his time, effort, substance, and meritorious leadership. Shuford later reminded the crowd that we have come a long way but have a long way to go. Introducing Shuford was Bob Mize, YMCA executive director. Present too was Dr. Andrew Holt, president emeritus of the University of Tennessee, who commended those who had the foresight to go forward with such a task. He called the occasion "momentous" and said their motivation was "your love for the children." Also present for the occasion were the Reverend Edward Meyer, secretary; building committee chairman Billy G. Beason; Jack Kincaid, architect; and Grover Herman, contractor.

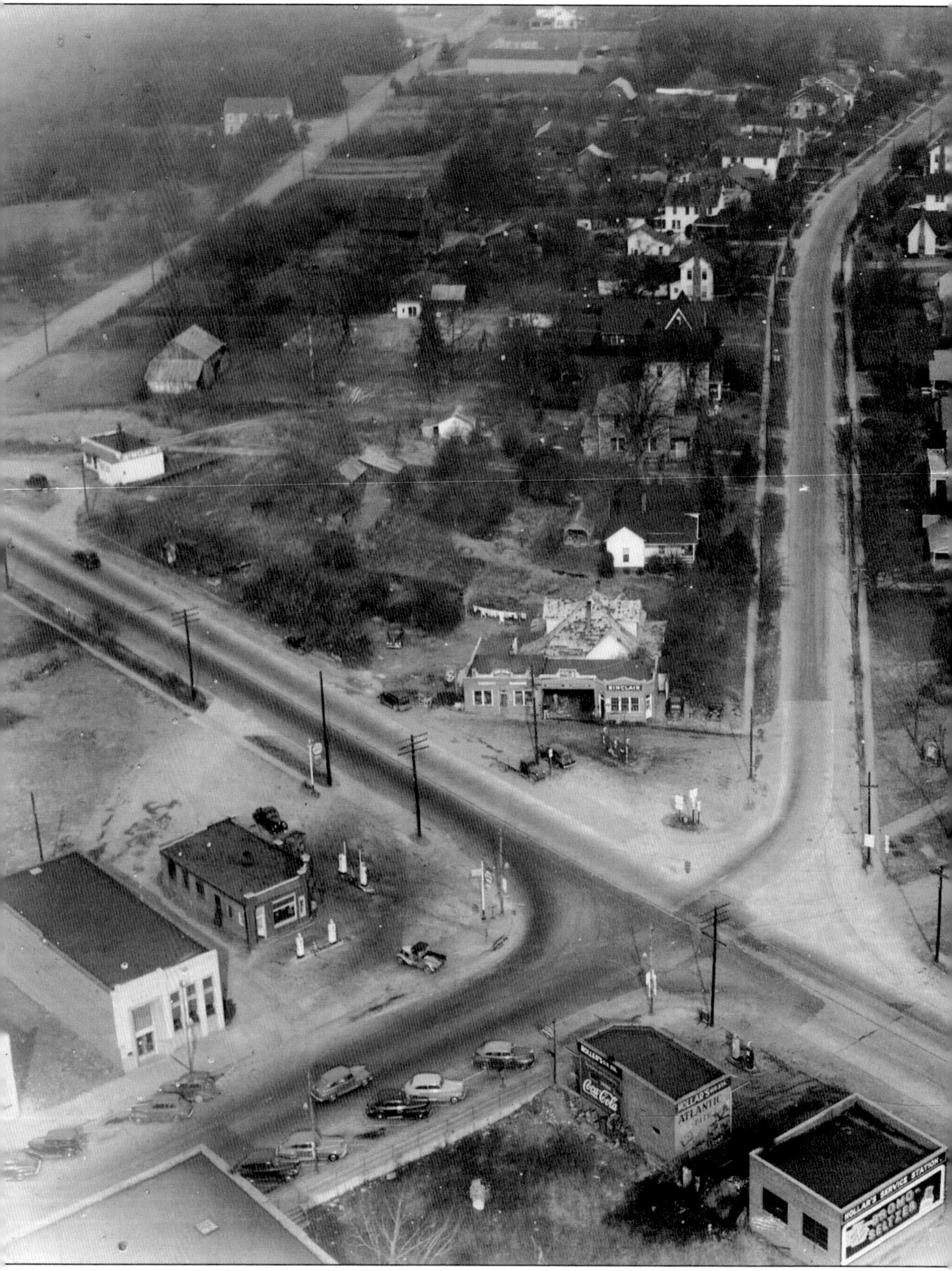
SINCLAIR
Coca-Cola
HOLLAR'S
ATLANTIC
HOLLAR'S SERVICE STATION
BROMO-SELTZER

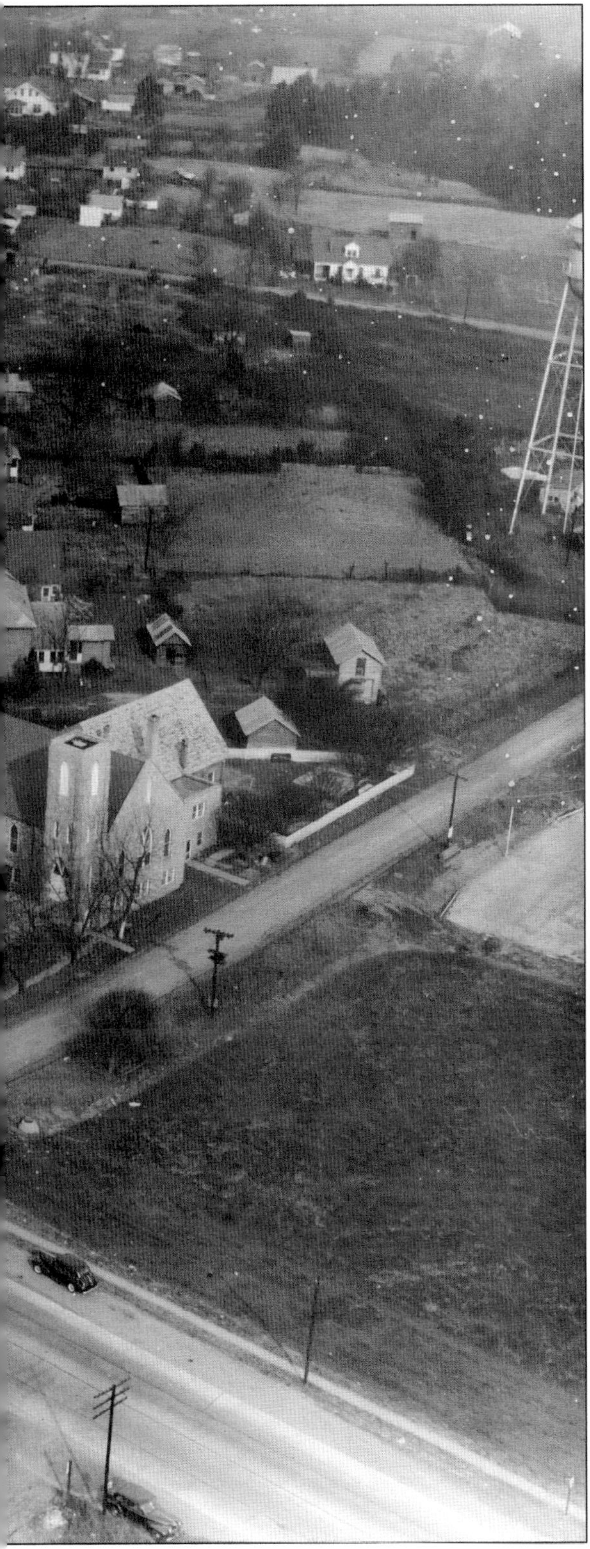

This is a rare aerial view of Conover at five points. In the center is the Sinclair station of Jonas Hunsucker, and to the right is Trinity Reformed Church, better known as the Rock Church. In the foreground are the Hollar Gas and Taxi Service, and to the left is the Cities Service, managed by Olin Winters. The highway in the direct center is NC16.

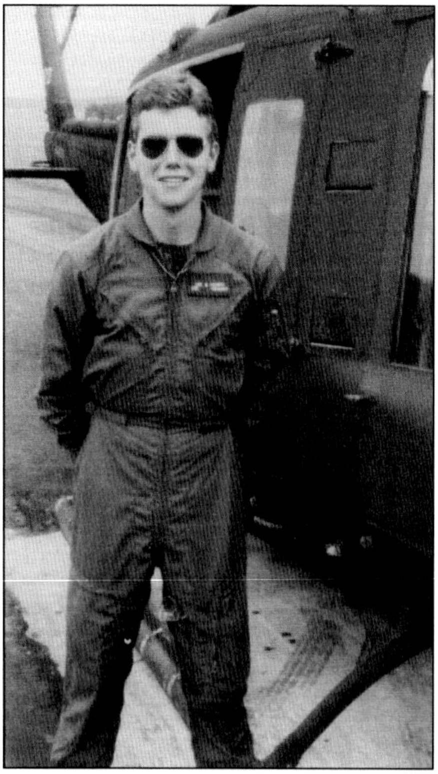

This young warrior served in the 2nd Armored Cavalry Regiment, 7th Corps. A graduate of Newton-Conover High School, he was in military duty from 1975 until 1979 with the US Army. He was stationed in the European Theater of Operations in Germany. He was a proficient aviator, flying the UH1 and UH60 Blackhawk helicopters. This airman retired with the rank of lieutenant colonel. He is associated with Moretz Mills sales division in Newton. He and his family reside in Conover. Lee Moritz Jr. is the present mayor of Conover.

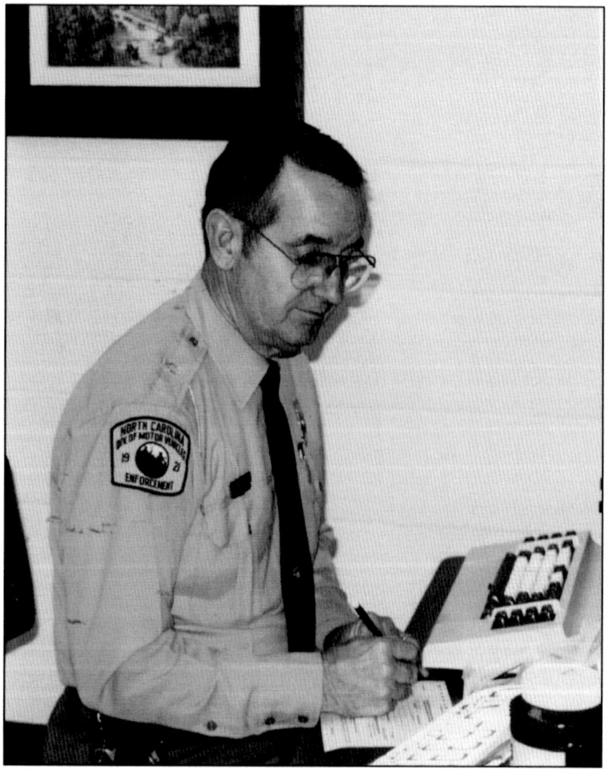

Robert Carcey of Catawba County served with the North Carolina Highway Patrol maintenance division in Newton from 1976 to 1980. In 1983, he transferred to the North Carolina Department of Motor Vehicles Enforcement Division and was stationed in Catawba County until his retirement in 1993. He and his wife, Judy, reside in Newton.

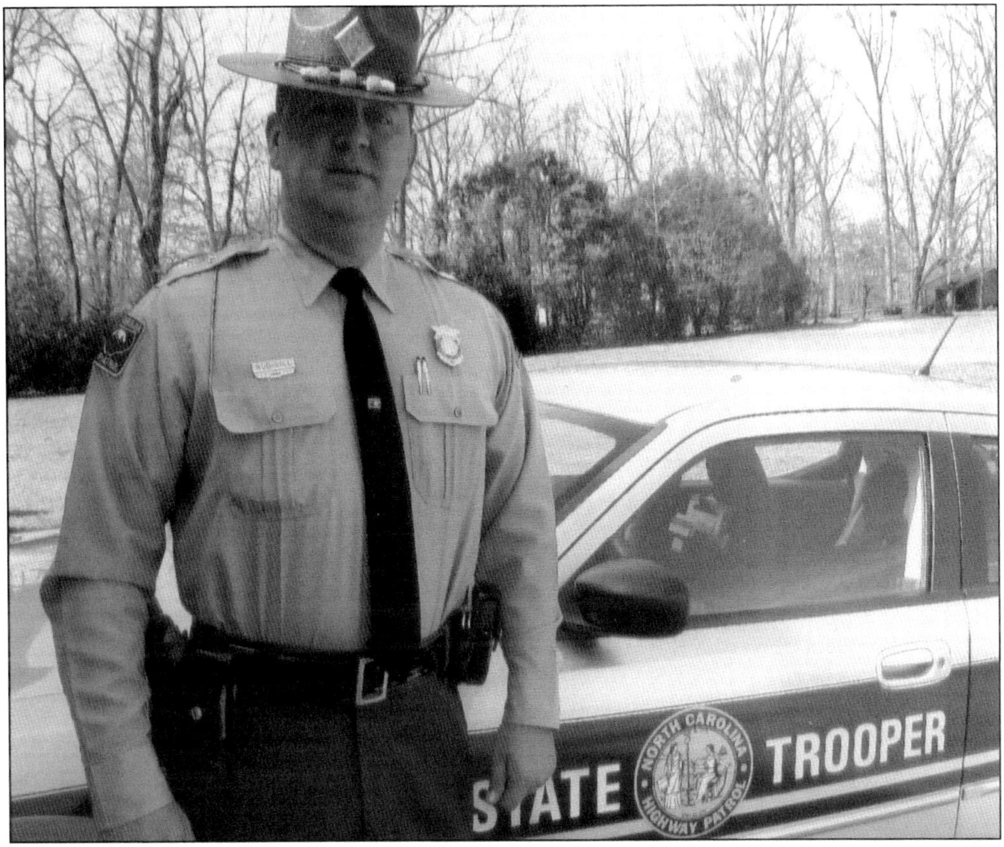

Patrolling the roads and highways of Conover and the county is one of the newest officers with the North Carolina Highway Patrol, trooper Ryan Rudisill. This officer attended patrol school and graduated in 2000. He then was assigned to Mecklenburg County from 2000 to 2001, at which time he was reassigned to District Five Headquarters in Catawba County, with Troop F. He and his wife and young son reside in Newton. They attend Concordia Lutheran Church in Conover.

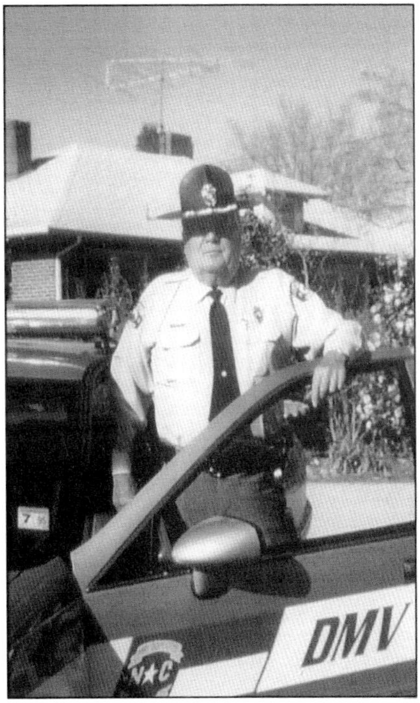

Pictured is a popular lawman from Conover, patrol officer N. (Norman) Dean Sigmon. Sigmon served with the Bureau of Alcohol, Tobacco, and Firearms enforcement division, the state highway patrol Department of Motor Vehicles enforcement division, and was a veteran of the US Army. Sigmon was also a reserve officer with the Conover Police Department. He was an avid fisherman, hunter, and gardener. After retirement, he received from the state of North Carolina the coveted Order of the Long Leaf Pine for his outstanding years of service in law enforcement. He was a member of Concordia Lutheran Church in Conover.

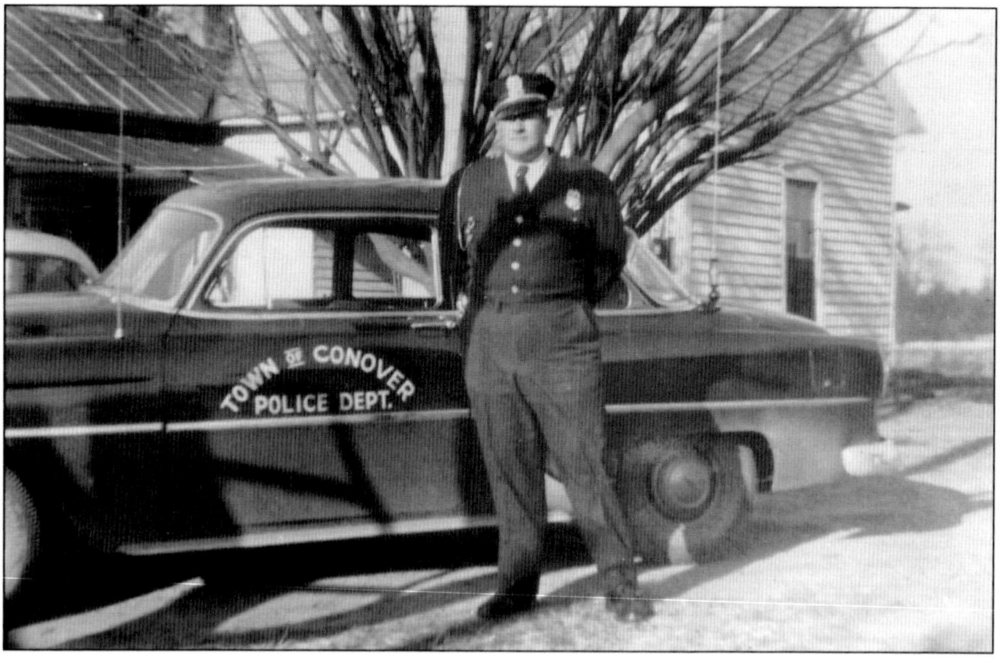

Standing next to his personally owned patrol car is officer James A. Fairchild, of Conover. He would work long shifts patrolling the streets and roads of Conover from the morning hours until past midnight. Once, while inside his car practicing the art of quick draw from his new holster, a bullet discharged and destroyed the red light atop the patrol car! Fairchild was the police chief of Conover from July 6, 1953, until June 5, 1962.

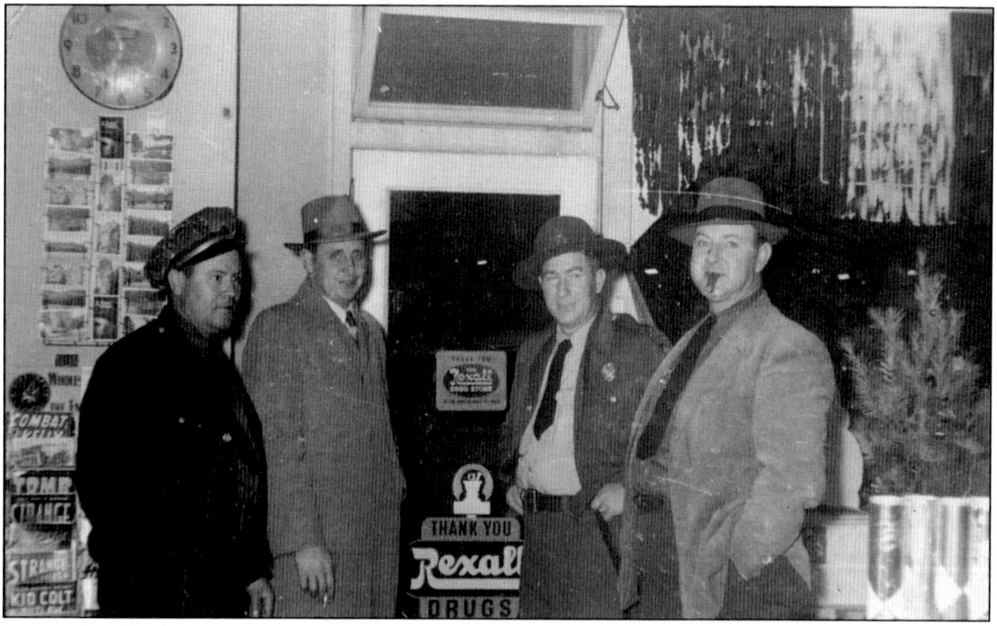

Pictured in the doorway at Bowman Drug Company in Conover is a rare gathering of lawmen from four different agencies. They are, from left to right, officer J.C. Bryant (Conover night patrolman under Chief John Dellinger), Carroll Sigmon (Deputy US Marshal), John Fairchild (North Carolina wildlife officer), and alcohol beverage control officer George Gilbert (of Catawba County).

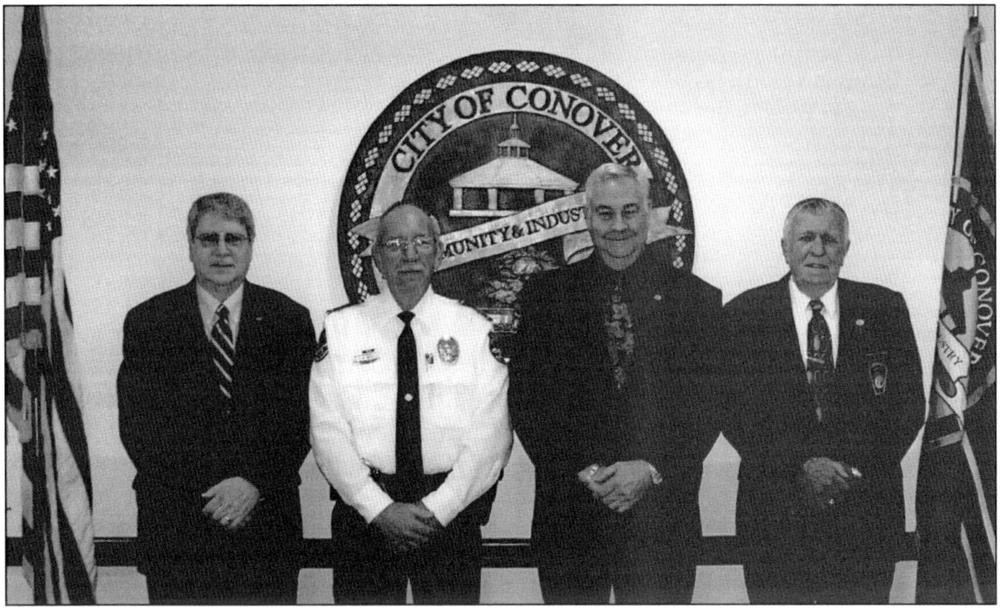

Pictured in this 2009 photograph taken at city hall in Conover are some Conover police chiefs. Shown from left to right and listed with their service dates are Gary W. Lafone, 1996–2009; Steve W. Brewer, 2009–present; Dale C. Stewart, 1987–1996; and Franklin L. Travis, 1962–1987. Other chiefs were Harlan L. Sigmon, 1931–1947; John F. Dellinger, 1947–1953; and James A. Fairchild, 1953–1962.

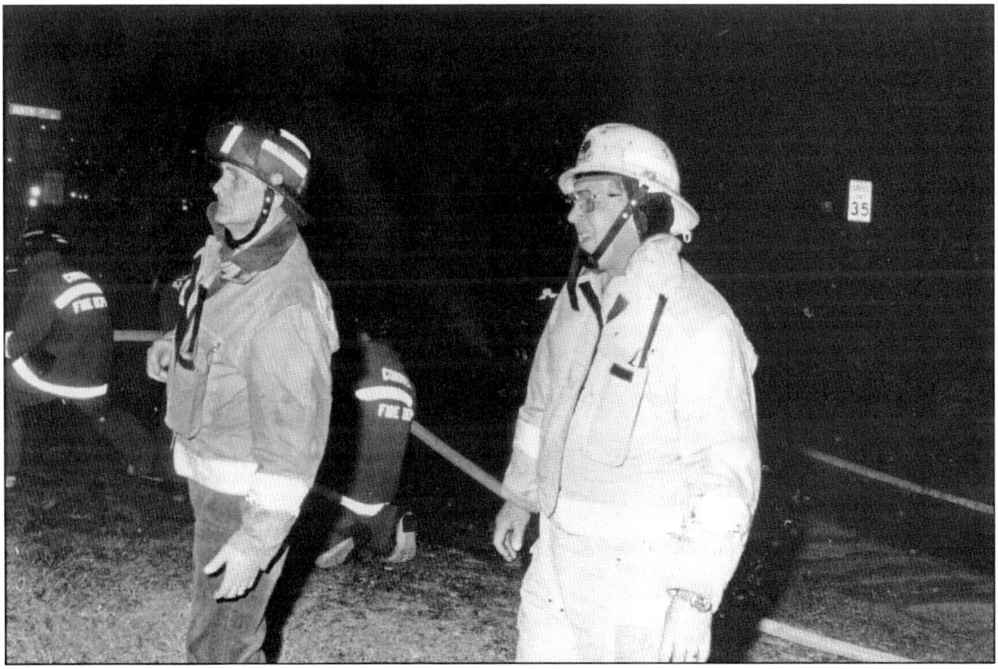

Pictured on the left is Conover assistant fire chief Ronald Kaylor with Chief Reid Poovey, as they observe operations on this fire call. They have over 100 combined years of continuous service with the Conover Fire Department. As of 2011, Kaylor will have 55 years of service with the Conover Fire Department.

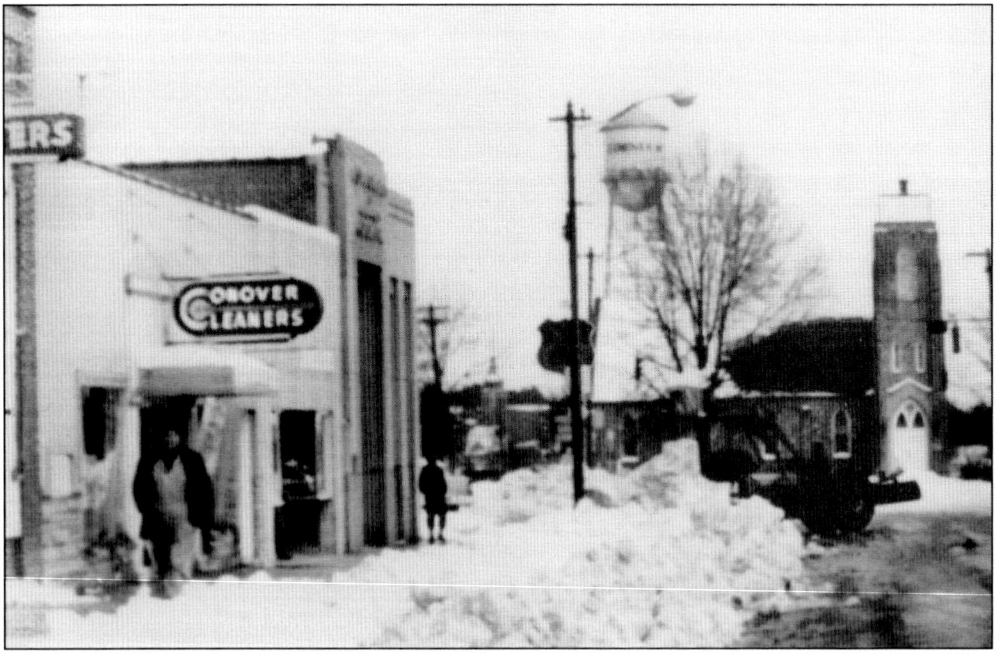

This image of an early snowfall in downtown Conover shows Trinity Church in the background. To the left is the old Phillips 66 station operated by Hal Holler. The First National Bank of Catawba County is next to Conover Cleaners, operated by Marshall Lincoln Travis. It is rumored that card games of chance were enjoyed during the day. Gin anyone? Next to the cleaner's is the first location of Stewart Jewelers.

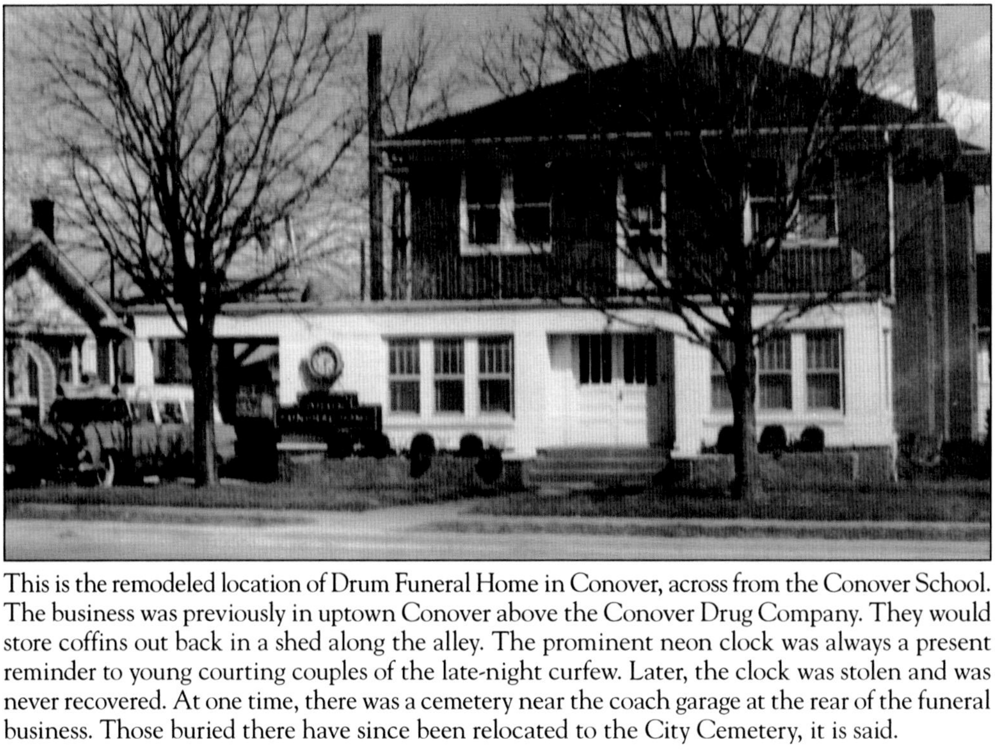

This is the remodeled location of Drum Funeral Home in Conover, across from the Conover School. The business was previously in uptown Conover above the Conover Drug Company. They would store coffins out back in a shed along the alley. The prominent neon clock was always a present reminder to young courting couples of the late-night curfew. Later, the clock was stolen and was never recovered. At one time, there was a cemetery near the coach garage at the rear of the funeral business. Those buried there have since been relocated to the City Cemetery, it is said.

This is the bridal portrait of Sonya (Brady) Massi. She was the daughter of Clifford and Louise Brady. Clifford was the son of C.R. Brady, of Conover. He would later move to Charlotte. Sonya married Julian Massi of that city. Julian and Sonya had four children, Mark, David, and twin daughters Lisa and Cathy. Sonya was a shepherdess to everyone she met.

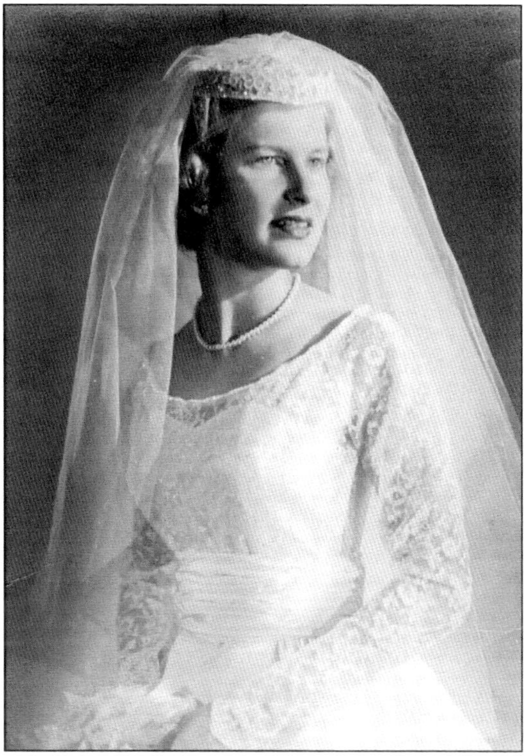

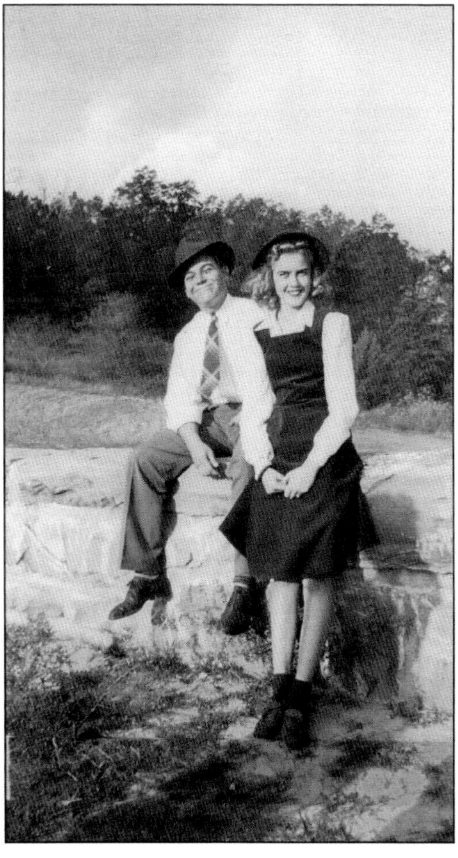

This is Marshall Cline with his sweetheart Helen McRee, of Conover. Although of completely different personalities, Cline was very fond of her and treated her like the lady she was. Helen was the daughter of Conover grocery store owner Robert "Bob" McRee. Helen's brothers were Rudolph (known as "Rudy") and Martin. Cline served in the 5th Marine Division in the Pacific theater on Guadalcanal and Bougainville. After World War II, he became a district judge in Caldwell County.

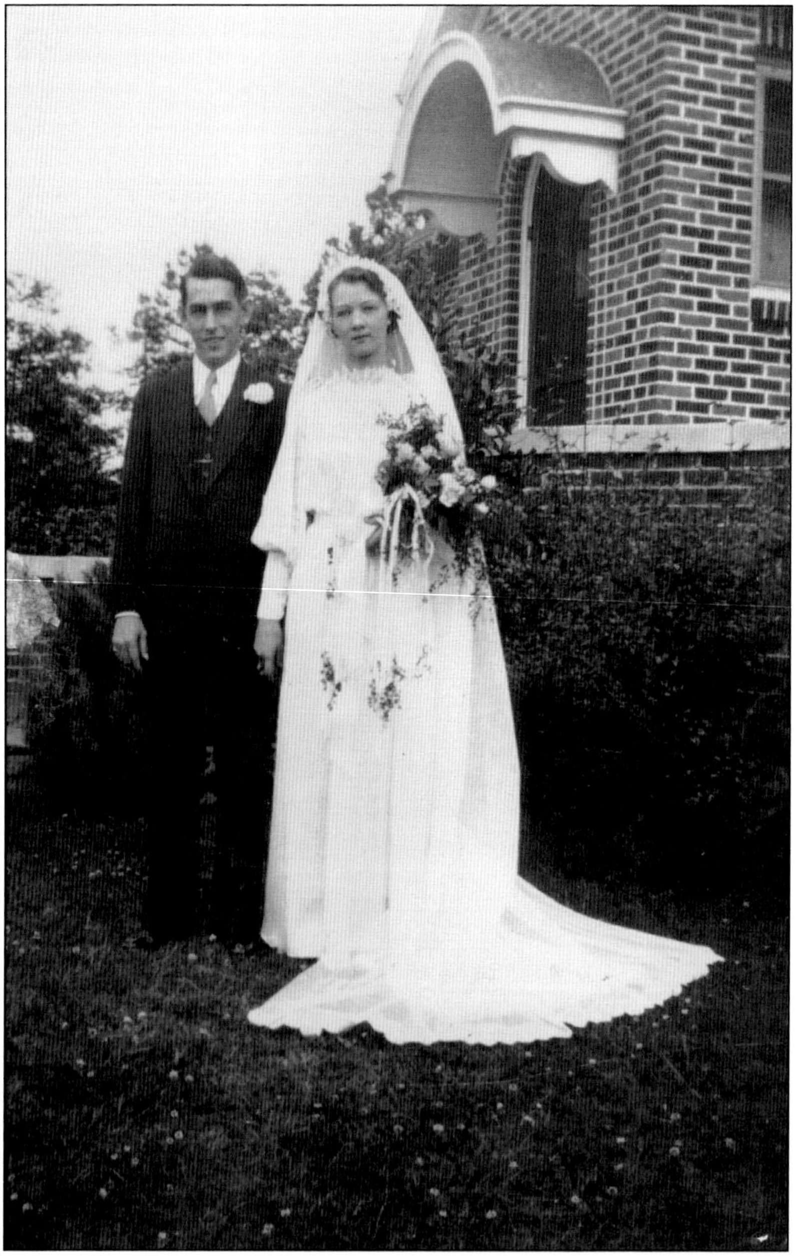

Pictured here on their wedding day in 1934 are the Reverend Richard Franklin Lineberger and his new bride, Ruth Moehlmann, of Conover. Lineberger was born in Mt. Holly, North Carolina, on August 8, 1908. He graduated from Concordia College in Conover, and continued his studies at Concordia Seminary in St. Louis, Missouri. He began his ministry at Zion Lutheran in New Orleans. While ministering in New Orleans, their union was blessed with children Lawrence Richard, Linda Ruth, and Ladell Rose. In 1943, Lineberger accepted the call to Concordia Lutheran Church in Conover. It was under his prayerful guidance and direction that a new edifice was built across from the old church. At the time, the new structure was controversial, but still it would prevail and become the most outstanding church architecture in the nation. He served there with distinction until his untimely death in April 1961.

Shown is Wallace Perry, of Conover. He was employed with the Catawba County Sheriff's Department from December 1978 until August 1998. Perry could often be seen on duty as bailiff at the courthouse in Newton. He was also a license examiner with the North Carolina Department of Motor Vehicles. He was the last manager of the Canova Theater in Conover. Perry served in the US Army in Europe in the 275th Infantry Division, the Trailblazers. Perry became a prisoner of war when his unit was surrounded near the Ardennes forest in Germany. He was imprisoned at Stalag 4B at Muhlberg Sachsen, near Falkensberg, Germany. In January 1945, he was rescued by American and Russian forces.

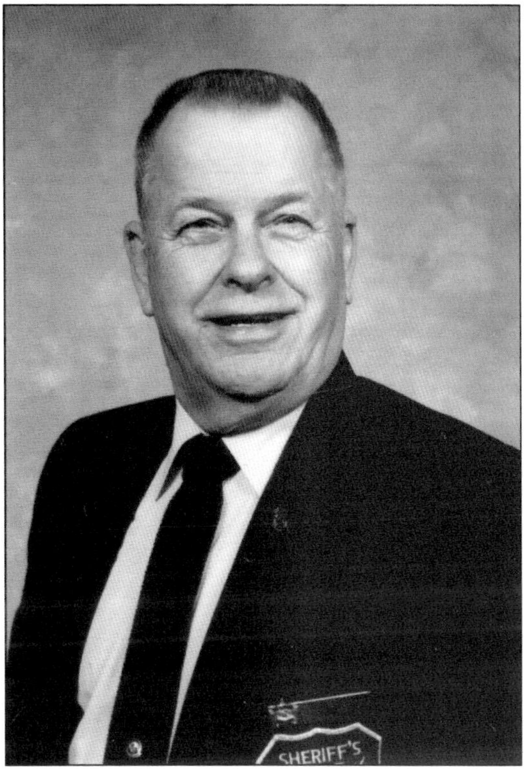

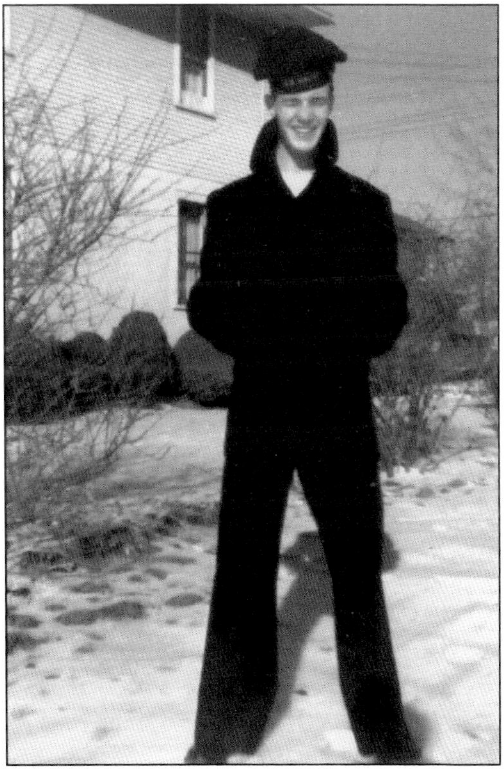

This handsome seaman from Conover is Derick Hartshorn. He served as a US Navy mine warfare specialist and was stationed in the Pacific theater. He is retired from General Electric, where he was a computer specialist at the Conover plant. A 40-year resident of Conover, he is a genealogist and current webmaster of the Conover website and several other local genealogical and historical websites.

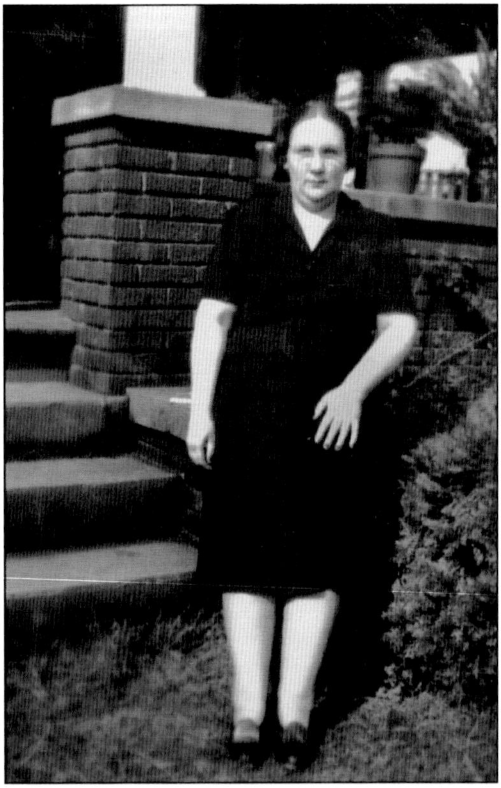

On February 8, 1946, three women were killed and a fourth was critically injured shortly before 1:00 p.m. when a westbound Southern Railway passenger train plowed into the 1937 Chevrolet in which the ladies were riding, returning from a downtown cafe. It happened right outside the office area at the Warlong Glove Company where the other workers were having their lunch break. Those dying in the crash included Littie "Bill" Spencer (pictured) and Floy Gilbert, both from Conover, and Morene Perry, of Claremont. Floy Sipe Presswood, of Conover, was critically injured. Spencer and Gilbert had been employed at the Warlong plant for nearly 20 years.

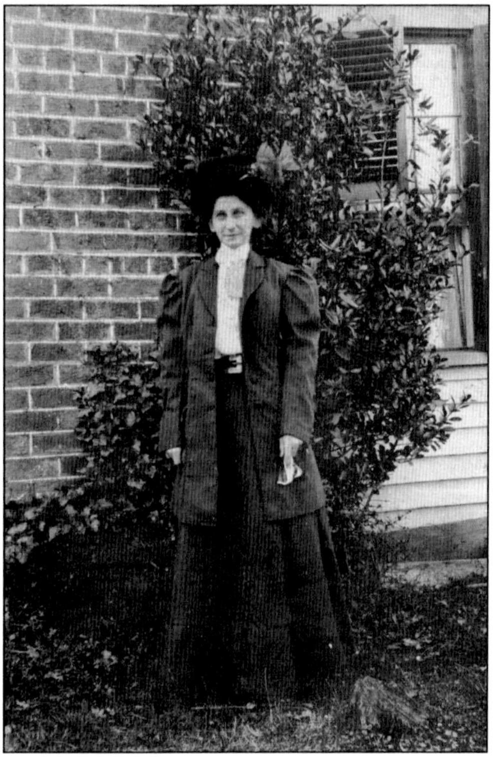

This vintage photograph is of Mildren (Robert) Washburn, of Conover, one of Conover's most prominent residents. She was educated at Concordia College, Catawba College, Claremont College, and Elizabeth College in Charlotte. She always had concern about cultural advantages for the young people of Conover. She was founder of the Etude Music Club of the town. She taught music here for more than 50 years. Washburn served as organist for Beth Eden Lutheran Church and Trinity United Church of Christ. Her brother the late P.O. Carpenter, a Newton merchant, preceded her in death.

Pictured is Bobby Matthews, of Conover. Today, he heads up Matthews Construction Company, one of the most prestigious firms in the Southeast, with offices in Conover and Charlotte. He was born the second child of seven to Robert and Metta Hefner Matthews. At the age of nine, he helped his father build their first home. He held a number of jobs, including usher at the Canova Theater, employee at Warlong Glove, and farming and working at the Frank Hollar farm. Bobby would hone his skills as a bricklayer. In 1950, he married Frankie Moser, and their union produced six children. He gives much credit for his success to Charlie Moser and Gus Palmer. Later, Bobby purchased the then closed Canova Theater building and established his firm there. That would end his lifetime dream of becoming a country-western singer.

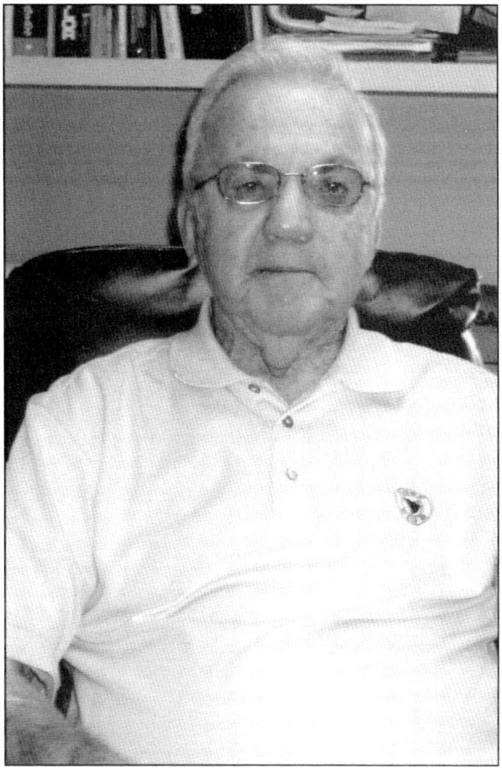

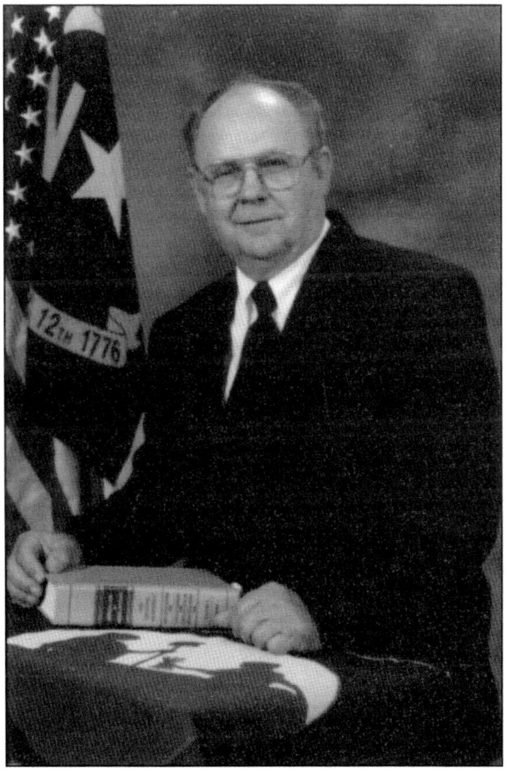

Shown is James "Jimmy" Sigmon, of Conover. Jimmy was employed at the Troop F headquarters in Newton, at the North Carolina State Patrol Maintenance Division garage. He served 22 years with the patrol. He was married to Ann Fairchild, daughter of John Fairchild, a wildlife officer for the state of North Carolina. They were members of Concordia Lutheran Church.

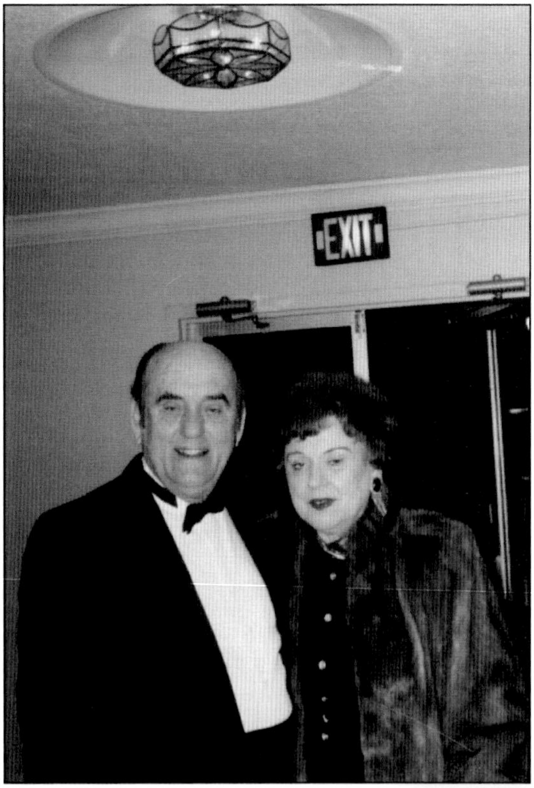

This attractive couple is Jack and Julia Bolick, of Conover. He was once employed at Conover Chair, but most remember him as the postmaster. He was greatly involved in community and civic organizations and held various positions at Trinity United Reformed Church. Bolick served four years with the Air Force, attached to the 485th Bomb Group in Salina, Kansas. He attended radio operator's school and training on the Boeing B-29 aircraft. He was discharged in 1945. In Conover, he worked as a substitute clerk at the post office, and in February 1961, was appointed acting postmaster and received his permanent appointment in July of that year. It was during his tenure that home delivery was implemented for Conover residents. The Bolicks have four children: Tommy, David, Beth, and Mary Ann. Jack was an avid golfer.

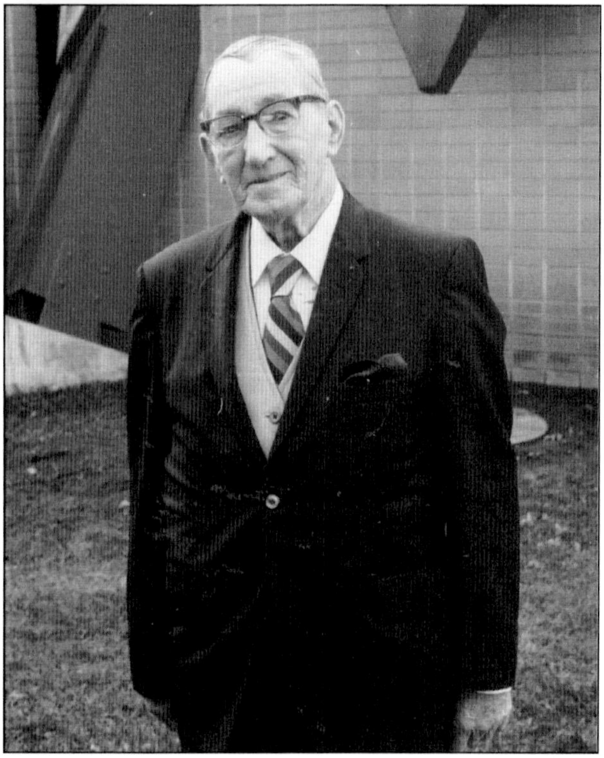

Pictured is Claude Schell, another Conover postmaster. This kind, gentle person had the respect of the entire town. He served in that position for 17 years, having succeeded Clinton Bolick at the post office. Incidentally, it was during the Bolick tenure that airmail was received in Conover. The air delivery was in the field across from the YMCA. Prior to Jack Bolick, there were 15 Conover postmasters from 1873 to 1961.

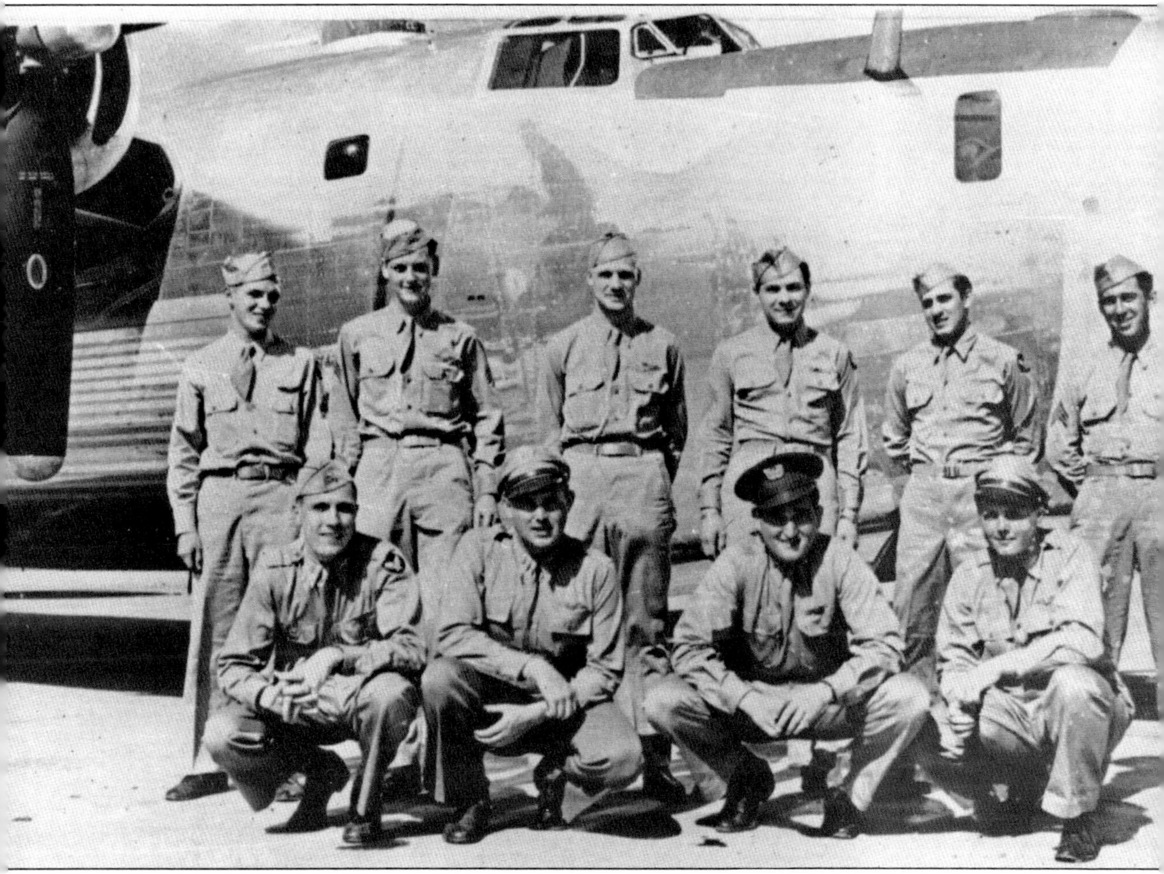

Another Conover hero is Lewis "Pete" Setzer. After graduating from Newton-Conover High School, Setzer attended flight school in Texas and earned his Army Air Corps pilot wings. He was then assigned to the 450th Bomb Group, 720th Squadron, as a command pilot with the Cottontails, based with the 15th Air Force in Manduria, Italy, flying the Boeing B-24 Liberator. On one mission, his aircraft lost two engines over Farrari, Italy, and was forced to ditch. Partisans helped the crew back to their base. The most dreaded flights were the missions over the Ploesti oil fields in Romania. Setzer completed 50 missions in 1944. After the war in Europe, he was recalled in 1951 and assigned to B-29 aircraft during the Korean War, flying 35 missions. Setzer received the Distinguished Flying Cross, Air Medal with 11 clusters, Theater Ribbons for World War II, Korean United Nations Service Medal, and many other theaters of operation awards. He held the rank of major. He served as president of Hickory Printing Group in Conover. He and his wife, Joann, had four children. They were members of Concordia Lutheran Church.

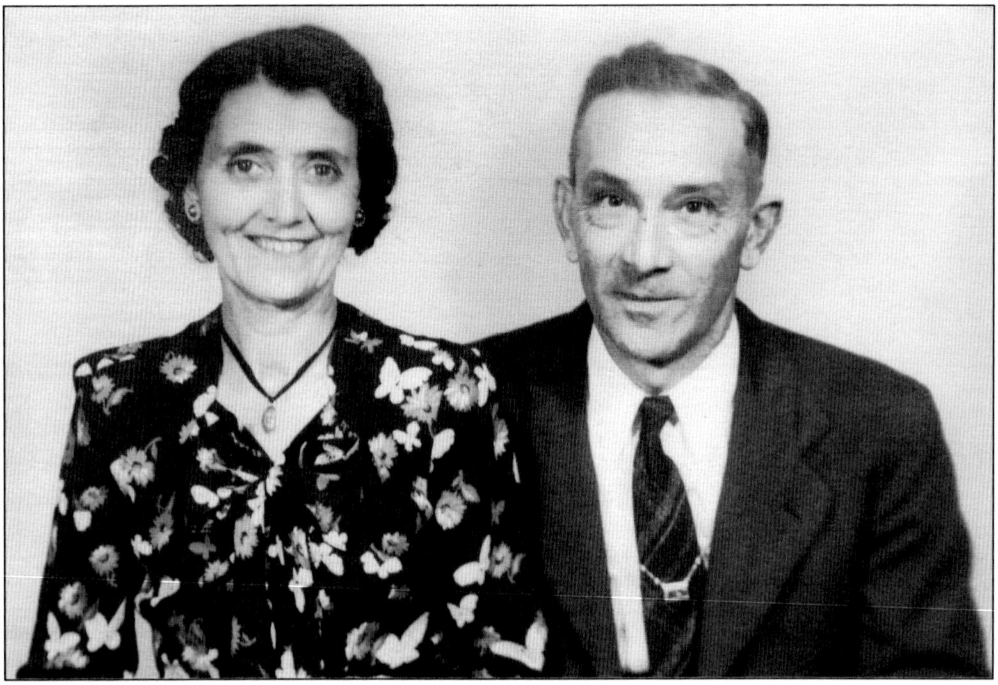

This is Eva and Robert A. Spencer, of Conover. They had 11 children: Rena, Frank, Martha, Myrtle (Winters), Mary (Justice), Marion (Pete), Frances (Winters), Thelma (Smith), Zula (Rockett), Richard "Bud" Spencer, and Hilda (Price). All but three are deceased. Frances, Richard, and Hilda survive.

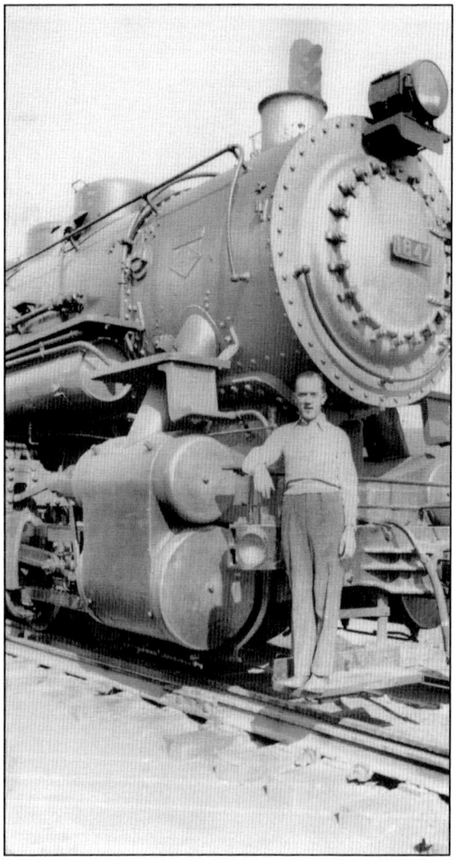

Daring and bold, Frank Spencer is shown standing on the front of the huge Southern Railway Baldwin engine No. 1847 at the Conover Station. During the war years, children of the town could rush to the station and observe trains carrying military trucks, cannons, tanks, and military supplies. On some days, as many as 20 military troop trains would pass through Conover, likely headed for debarkation points along the coast.

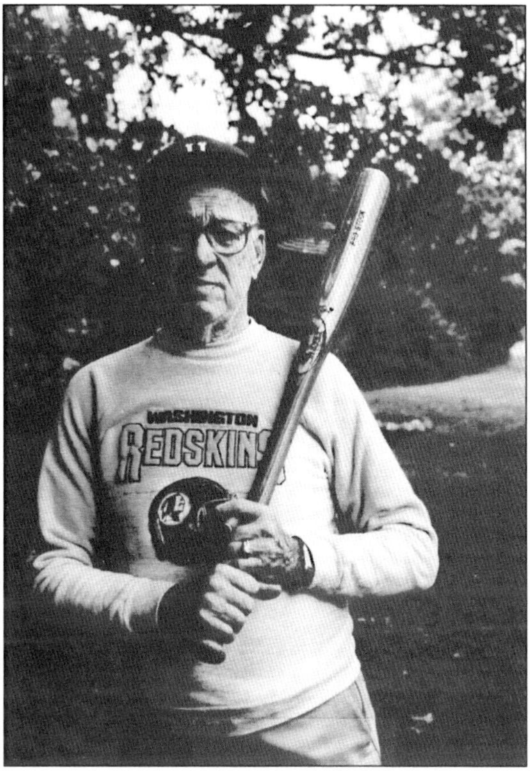

John Alvin Bolick, pictured here, was best known for his love of the game of baseball. He played for the first team in Conover, the Blue Sox. Later, he was on the roster of the Newton Conover Twins in 1937–1939. He was best known as a long-ball hitter. He hit the longest homerun against home team the Shelby Farmers; it measured 499 feet. In one game he hit for the cycle, which is a single, double, triple, and a homerun. His lifetime batting average was .380. In 1950, he was appointed fire chief with the City of Conover Fire Department, a position he held for many years. He was married to Catherine (Cassels) Bolick. Concordia was their church home.

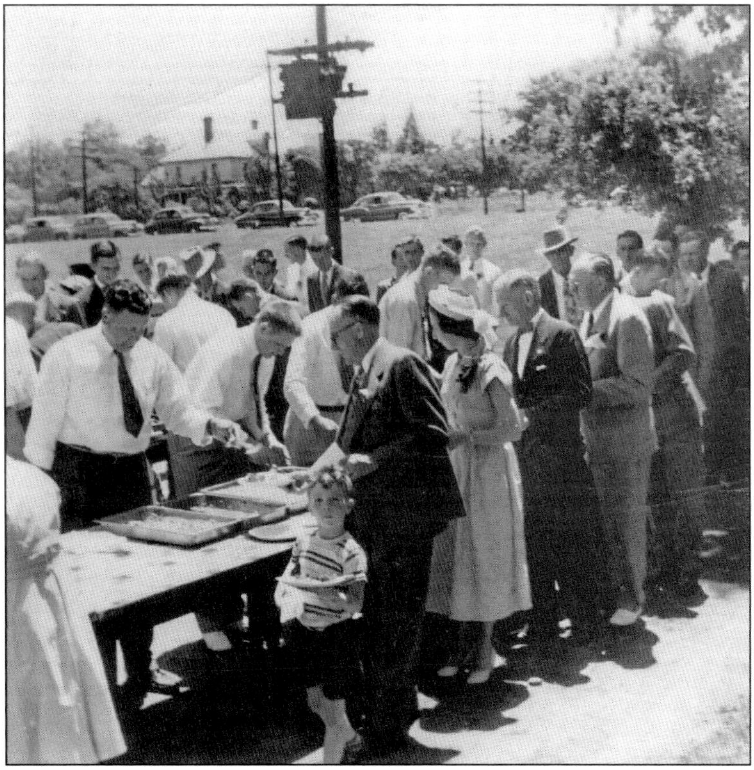

After services, many local churches held a traditional "dinner on the lawn." Here, members of Trinity Church in Conover are preparing to sample the many varieties of food laid upon the tables. The young man in the lower center is a young Kenneth Herman alongside his parents. The large, white house in the background is that of the Grace Hunsucker family.

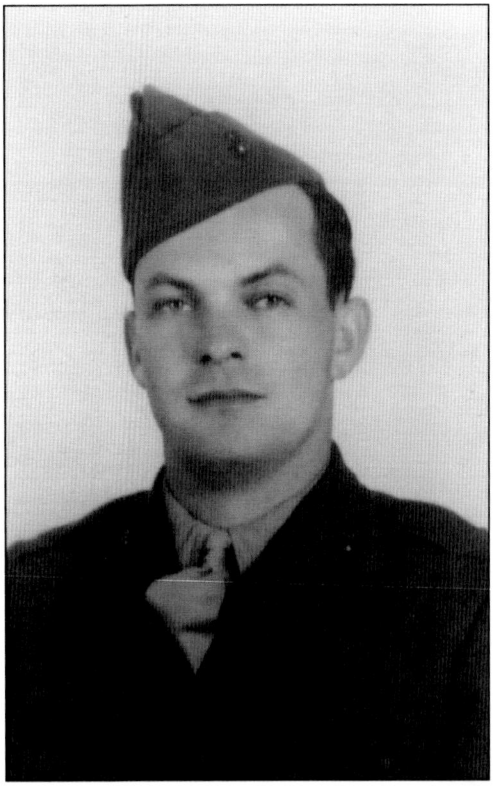

Young Conover veteran Pfc. Oswald G. Lowrance, 5th Marine Division, 28th Regiment, 1st Battalion, Company B, was killed in March 1945. On February 19, Bobo's Bastards (B Company) landed on Iwo Jima near the base of Mt. Suribachi. In combat for the next 14 days, Lowrance was mortally wounded on March 3, 1945, in the taking of Nishi Ridge. Of the 6,775 men who died from the Iwo Jima campaign, nearly half of this number was from the 5th Marine Division.

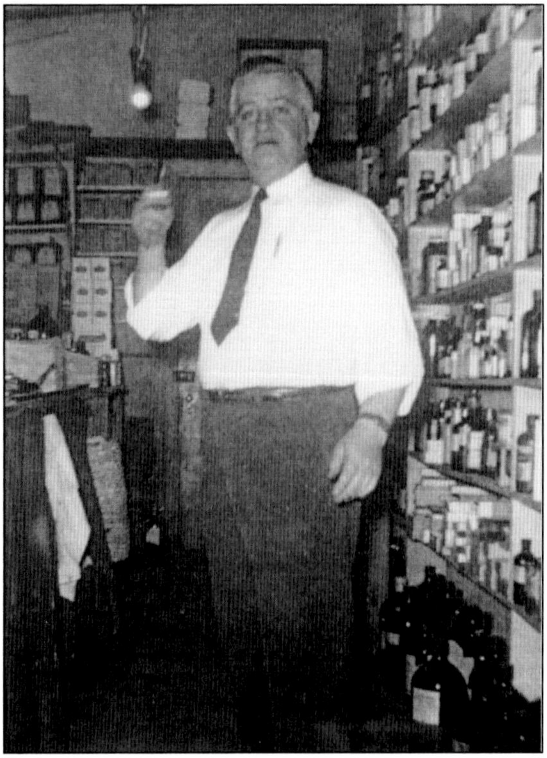

Pictured here is Carl Bowman, a pharmacist better known to all as "Doc." He was the owner of the longstanding Bowman Drug Company. If someone had an ailment, Doc would be consulted. He had a secret formula for athlete's foot. Many soldiers from Conover serving in the Korean War knew of the mixture that was truly a cure. Hundreds of small bottles were shipped from the drugstore overseas to the men and women at no charge.

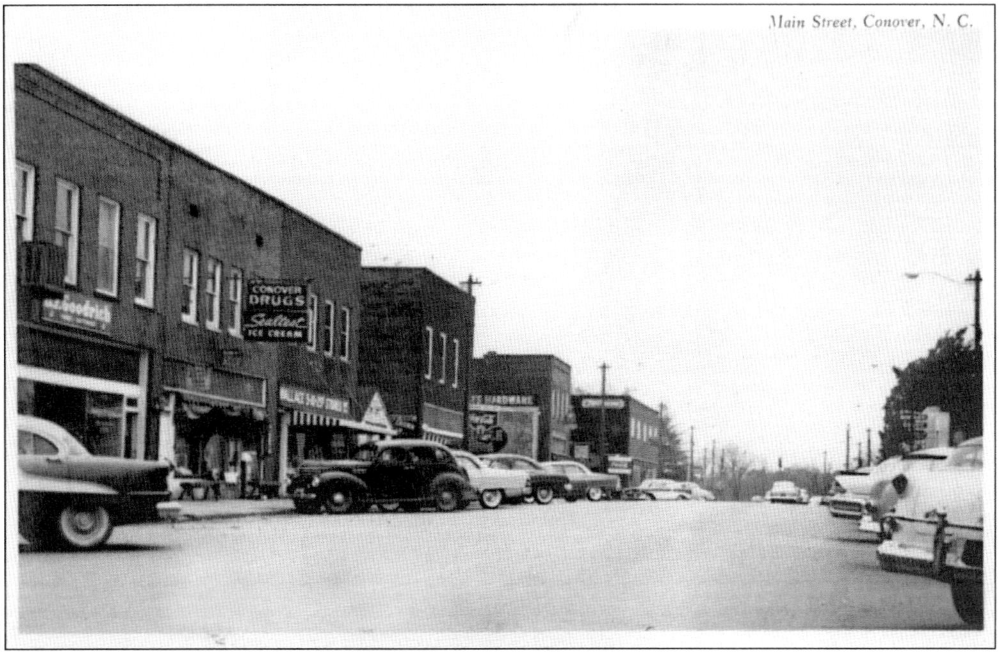

This 1950s postcard shows Conover's Main Street. Not a lot has changed throughout the years, just the names on the brick buildings: from the Goodyear Tire and Bike store of Worth Hunsucker, the Conover Drug, Wallace Five and Dime, the little wooden barbershop of Preston Baker, and the Conover Grocery, owned by Clyde Herman. Clyde kept chickens out back in a coop to sell to customers. Boys would remove them, take them around to the front of the store, and sell them back to Clyde.

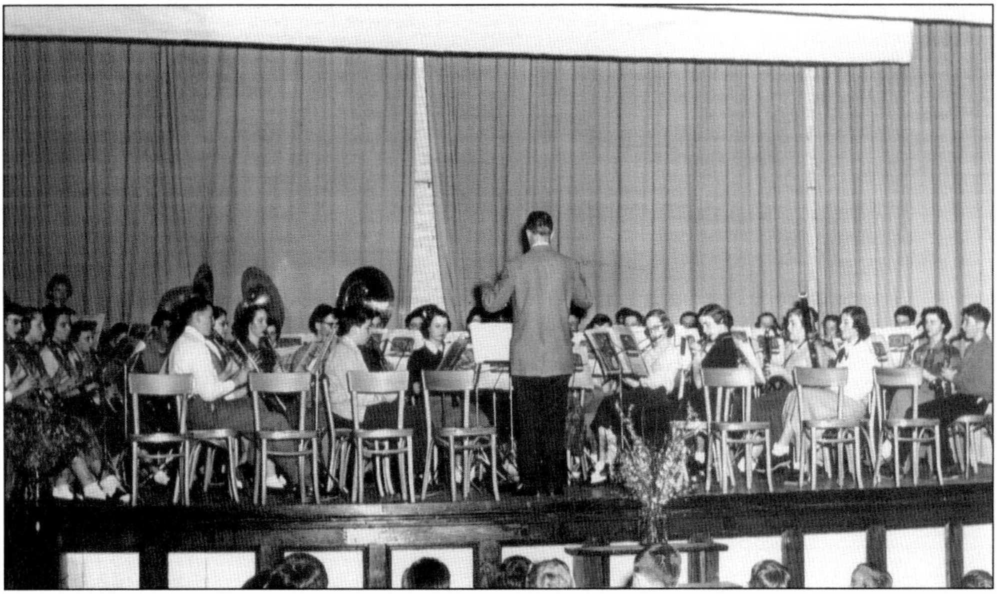

Treating the public and students at the Conover Graded School is the Newton-Conover Senior Concert Band. At that time in the early 1950s, the band conductor and director was former US Marine musician Joshua Tyler. It was during his tenure that the high school band really took shape in forming the championship bands it has today.

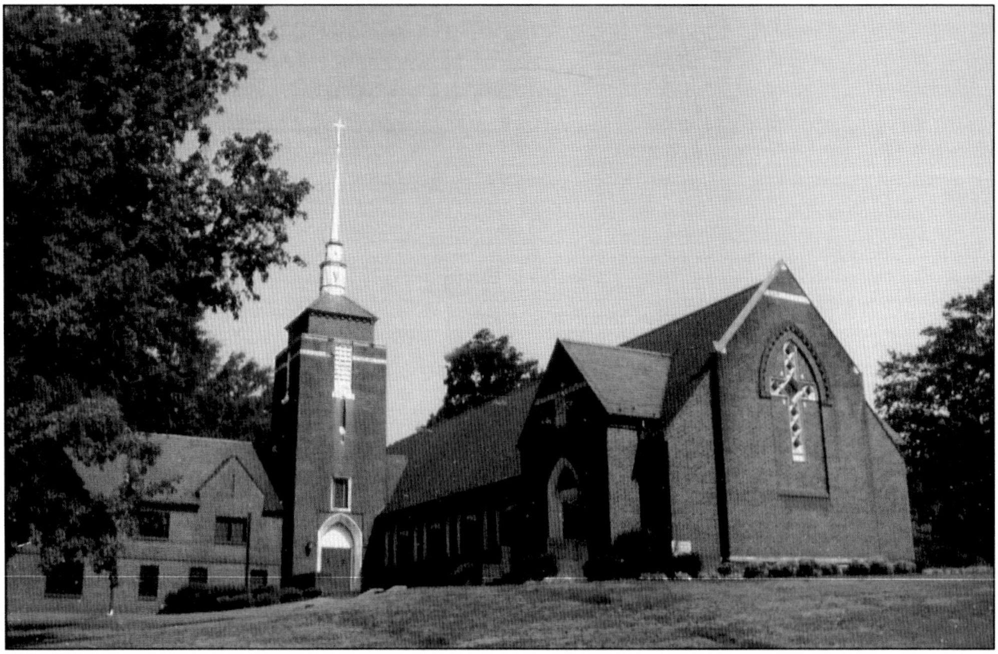

The new Trinity Reformed United Church of Christ stands atop a high ridge in downtown Conover. The first church was a small brick structure built in 1919; the second building, called the Rock Church, was built from locally quarried stone and dedicated in July of 1935. With a new city hall in the planning stages and considering the age of the Rock Church, the congregation decided upon a new building, which was dedicated August 2, 1953. With the generous monetary offering by Adrian L. Shuford Jr., this new and beautiful brick house of worship gives evidence to the ministry of Trinity Church.

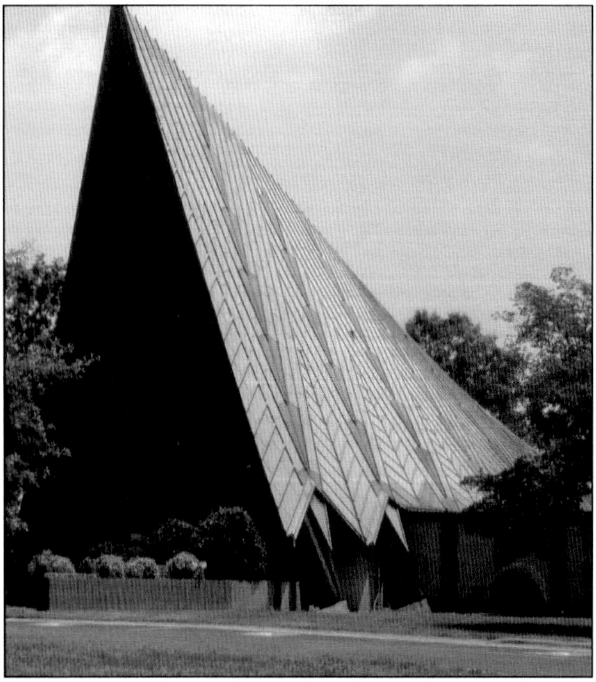

Concordia Lutheran Church in Conover appears in the *Guide to Historic Architecture of Piedmont North Carolina*. Lutherans affiliated with the Tennessee Synod founded Concordia College in 1877 and formed a church by the same name. The old Concordia church building was falling apart at the seams with no air conditioning and aging boilers for steam heat; it was time for a new home. With the guidance of pastor Rev. Richard Lineberger, the building committee and a vote by the congregation approved the plans from A.G. Odell of Charlotte. In 1957, it was dedicated to the "Glory of God." This was a dramatic statement of 20th-century Modernism, which also won the American Institute of Architects award.

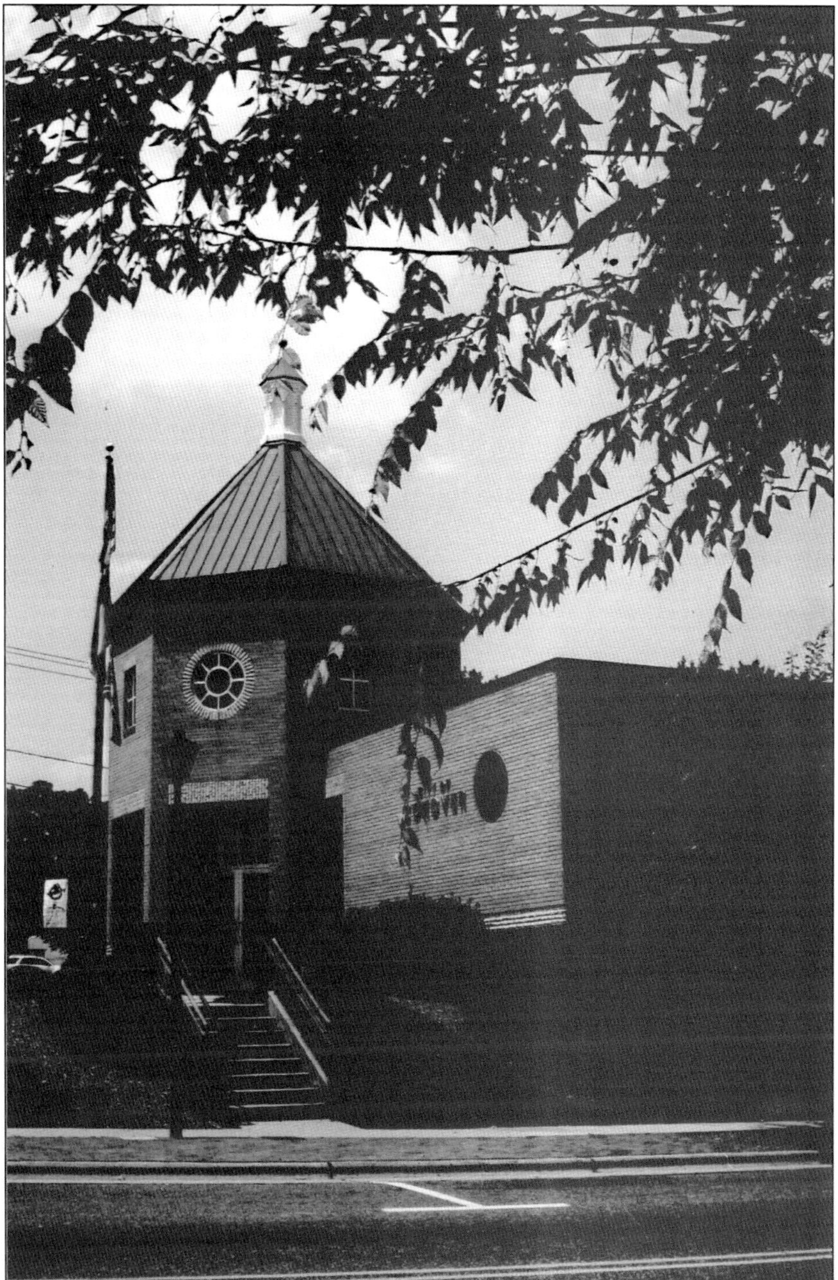

The present city hall in Conover stands as evidence of the town's proud history. Throughout this book, the reader has seen the works and labors begun by the residents who molded the stones that mark our footsteps, from the past, to the present, and into the future. It is through their efforts and with the grace of almighty God that Conover has prospered into the city it is today. With a strong city government and guided principles, Conover continues to always look forward into the future—the Conover way. A person was heard asking, "If people in Newton are called Newtonians, what are the people in Conover called?" The simple answer is, "Blessed."